THE PEOPLE SPEAK!
EXCERPTS FROM LETTERS RECEIVED BY THE AUTHOR:

"For the first time I began to understand the reason behind some of my 18-year-old son's views which had heretofore perplexed and worried me. But, more important, it reinforced my once passionate, long-denied feeling that each human being was important."

—Mrs. Alfred Cosmann,
Great Neck, New York

"Thank you for such a remarkably perceptive and brilliant explanation of the United States my husband and I are trying to understand and feel so frustrated about most of the time. I am now hopeful and eager to contribute more than letter-writing to Nixon and Senators; but to actually take part."

—Mrs. Frederick Anderson,
Pipersville, Pennsylvania

"**GREENING OF AMERICA** is the most truth in one place that I have seen in a long, long time."

—William M. Mack,
Guilford, Connecticut

"As a teacher on her 47th year of teaching young people, I cannot thank you enough . . . I've always had beautiful students but today's are something else! I have a feeling it's truly spectacular I should have lived long enough to know these fine children!"

—Mary Gwen Owen,
Macalester College,
St. Paul, Minnesota

"It has been devastating to feel the mechanics of our lives continuing to strangle us because resistance to ideas—any ideas—is inherent in the system. But you make us see that the 'great leap' is already being taken. And we thank you."

—Audrey Hoyt Johnson,
Ojai, California

"You have defined our situation with a clarity I would not have thought possible, and our relationship to our society in a manner which allows us to entertain alternatives we had long ago discarded as romantic . . . You have confronted the problem so honestly and made your argument so beautifully that I am moved beyond words. I write this letter less for your gratification than my own —a piece of evidence that at thirty-six, five kids, two dogs, things all around, it is possible to begin. This letter commits me somehow."

—Mrs. Edward M. Post,
Louisville, Kentucky

"Right on. You've managed to put into words what we have known for a long time."

—The Folks at Wheeler Ranch

"Your book is so important, I think, that the extent to which it is recognized will be an exact indication of whether or not we will pull through, whether or not the culture will realize that it has no choice but integrity, whether we will have reality or extinction. What you know is what Wallace Stevens knew when he wrote 'The rock cannot be broken. It is the truth.' You have illuminated our world with grace and meaning, and I thank you."

—Francis G. Couvares,
Pittsburgh, Pennsylvania

"You have produced the first statement of the condition here in America that feels true. Please write more and publish **THE GREENING** in paperback form for [some] high school teachers to disseminate."

—Mrs. Peter Stenzel,
Portland, Oregon

"It seems to me that you have traced the history of, and set forth the present depth of our predicament in a way that, as far as I know, has not existed before."

—Robert L. Anthony,
Moylan, Pennsylvania

The Greening of America
Charles A. Reich

A NATIONAL GENERAL COMPANY

THE GREENING OF AMERICA

A Bantam Book / published by arrangement with
Random House, Inc.

PRINTING HISTORY

Random House edition published October 1970

2nd printing	..November 1970	7th printing	...December 1970
3rd printing	..November 1970	8th printing	.....January 1971
4th printing	..December 1970	9th printing	....February 1971
5th printing	..December 1970	10th printing	....February 1971
6th printing	..December 1970	11th printing	....February 1971
	12th printing	........March 1971	

Literary Guild edition published 1970

Book Find/Seven Arts edition published 1970

Professional & Technical Programs Inc. edition published 1970

New Republic edition published 1970

A portion of this book appeared in THE NEW YORKER
in somewhat different form

Bantam edition published June 1971

2nd printing

3rd printing

4th printing

5th printing

6th printing

7th printing

ACKNOWLEDGMENTS

Acknowledgment is gratefully extended to the following for permission to reprint from their works:
Blackwood Music, Inc.: "It's a Beautiful Day," by Bob Mosley. Copyright © 1969 by Blackwood Music, Inc., & South Star Music.
Holt, Rinehart and Winston, Inc.: From Cat's Cradle, *by Kurt Vonnegut.*
Irving Music, Inc.: From "Let's Get Together," by Chet Powers. Copyright © 1963, 1965.
McGraw-Hill Book Company: From Soul on Ice, *by Eldridge Cleaver. Copyright © 1968 by Eldridge Cleaver.*
The Viking Press, Inc.: From "Stoned" in Head Comix, *by Robert Crumb. Copyright © 1967, 1968 by Robert Crumb. All Rights Reserved.*

Published simultaneously in the United States and Canada

Bantam Books are published by Bantam Books, Inc., a National General company. Its trade-mark, consisting of the words "Bantam Books" and the portrayal of a bantam, is registered in the United States Patent Office and in other countries. Marca Registrada. Bantam Books, Inc., 666 Fifth Avenue, New York, N.Y. 10019.

PRINTED IN THE UNITED STATES OF AMERICA

FOR THE STUDENTS AT YALE,
WHO MADE THIS BOOK POSSIBLE,
AND FOR THEIR GENERATION

This is the Revolution:

This land is your land,
this land is my land,
from California
to the New York Island*
— WOODY GUTHRIE

Come on people now
Smile on your brother
Everybody get together
Try to love one another right now
— CHET POWERS,
FOR THE YOUNGBLOODS

There is not any haunt of prophecy,
Nor any old chimera of the grave,
Neither the golden underground, nor isle
Melodious, where spirits gat them home,
Nor visionary south, nor cloudy palm
Remote on heaven's hill, that has endured
As April's green endures; or will endure
— WALLACE STEVENS

CONTENTS

I

THE COMING AMERICAN REVOLUTION

America is dealing death, not only to people in other lands, but to its own people. So say the most thoughtful and passionate of our youth, from California to Connecticut. This realization is not limited to the new generation. Talk to a retired school teacher in Mendocino, a judge in Washington, D.C., a housewife in Belmont, Massachusetts, a dude rancher in the Washington Cascades. We think of ourselves as an incredibly rich country, but we are beginning to realize that we are also a desperately poor country— poor in most of the things that throughout the history of mankind have been cherished as riches.

There is a revolution coming. It will not be like revolutions of the past. It will originate with the individual and with culture, and it will change the political structure only as its final act. It will not require violence to succeed, and it cannot be successfully resisted by violence. It is now spreading with amazing rapidity, and already our laws, institutions and social structure are changing in consequence. It promises a higher reason, a more human community, and a new and liberated individual. Its ultimate creation will be a new and enduring wholeness and beauty—a renewed relationship of man to himself, to other men, to society, to nature, and to the land.

This is the revolution of the new generation. Their protest and rebellion, their culture, clothes, music, drugs, ways of thought, and liberated life-style are not a passing fad or a form of dissent and refusal, nor are they in any sense irrational. The whole emerging pattern, from ideals to campus demonstrations to beads and bell bottoms to the Woodstock Festival, makes sense and is part of a consistent philosophy. It is both necessary and inevitable, and in time it will include not only youth, but all people in America.

The logic and necessity of the new generation—and what they are so furiously opposed to—must be seen against a background of what has gone wrong in America. It must be understood in light of the betrayal and loss of the American dream, the rise of the Corporate State of the 1960's, and the way in which that State dominates, exploits, and ultimately destroys both nature and man. Its rationality must be measured against the insanity of existing "reason" —reason that makes impoverishment, dehumanization, and even war appear to be logical and necessary. Its logic must be read from the fact that Americans have lost control of the machinery of their society, and only new values and a new culture can restore control. Its emotions and spirit can be comprehended only by seeing contemporary America through the eyes of the new generation.

The meaning and the future of the revolution emerge from a perspective on America. The revolution is a movement to bring man's thinking, his society, and his life to terms with the revolution of technology and science that has already taken place. Technology demands of man a new mind—a higher, transcendent reason—if it is to be controlled and guided rather than to become an unthinking monster. It demands a new individual responsibility for values, or it will dictate all values. And it promises a life that is more liberated and more beautiful than any man has known, if man has the courage and the imagination to seize that life.

The transformation that is coming invites us to reexamine our own lives. It confronts us with a personal and individual choice: are we satisfied with how we have lived; how would we live differently? It offers us a recovery of self. It faces us with the fact that this choice cannot be evaded, for as the freedom is already there, so must the responsibility be there.

At the heart of everything is what we shall call a change of consciousness. This means a "new head"— a new way of living—a new man. This is what the new generation has been searching for, and what it has started achieving. Industrialism produced a new man, too—one adapted to the demands of the machine. In contrast, today's emerging consciousness seeks a new knowledge of what it means to be human, in order that the machine, having been built, may now be turned to human ends; in order that man once more can become a creative force, renewing and creating his own life and thus giving life back to his society.

It is essential to place the American crisis and this change within individuals in a philosophic perspective, showing how we got to where we are, and where we are going. Current events are so overwhelming that we only see from day to day, merely responding to each crisis as it comes, seeing only immediate evils, and seeking inadequate solutions such as merely ending the war, or merely changing our domestic priorities. A longer-range view is necessary.

What is the nature of the present American crisis? Most of us see it as a collection of problems, not necessarily related to each other, and, although profoundly troubling, nevertheless within the reach of reason and reform. But if we list these problems, not according to topic, but as elements of larger issues concerning the structure of our society itself, we can see that the present crisis is an organic one, that it arises out of the basic premises by which we live and that no mere reform can touch it.

1. Disorder, corruption, hypocrisy, war. The front pages of newspapers tell of the disintegration of the social fabric, and the resulting atmosphere of anxiety and terror in which we all live. Lawlessness is most often associated with crime and riots, but there is lawlessness and corruption in all the major institu-

4

tions of our society—matched by an indifference to responsibility and consequences, and a pervasive hypocrisy that refuses to acknowledge the facts that are everywhere visible. Both lawlessness and evasion found expression in the Vietnam War, with its unprincipled destruction of everything human, and its random, indifferent, technological cruelty.

2. *Poverty, distorted priorities, and law-making by private power.* America presents a picture of drastic poverty amid affluence, an extremity of contrast unknown in other industrial nations. Likewise there is a superabundance of some goods, services, and activities such as defense manufacture, while other needs, such as education and medical care, are at a starvation level for many. These closely related kinds of inequality are not the accidents of a free economy, they are intentionally and rigidly built into the laws of our society by those with powerful influence; an example is the tax structure which subsidizes private wealth and production of luxuries and weapons at the direct expense of impoverished people and impoverished services. The nation has a planned economy, and the planning is done by the exercise of private power without concern for the general good.

3. *Uncontrolled technology and the destruction of environment.* Technology and production can be great benefactors of man, but they are mindless instruments; if undirected they roll along with a momentum of their own. In our country they pulverize everything in their path: the landscape, the natural environment, history and tradition, the amenities and civilities, the privacy and spaciousness of life, beauty,

and the fragile, slow-growing social structures which bind us together. Organization and bureaucracy, which are applications of technology to social institutions, increasingly dictate how we shall live our lives, with the logic of organization taking precedence over any other values.

4. Decline of democracy and liberty; powerlessness. The Constitution and Bill of Rights have been weakened, imperceptibly but steadily. The nation has gradually become a rigid managerial hierarchy, with a small elite and a great mass of the disenfranchised. Democracy has rapidly lost ground as power is increasingly captured by giant managerial institutions and corporations, and decisions are made by experts, specialists, and professionals safely insulated from the feelings of the people. Most governmental power has shifted from Congress to administrative agencies, and corporate power is free to ignore both stockholders and consumers. As regulation and administration have grown, liberty has been eroded and bureaucratic discretion has taken the place of the rule of law. Today both dissent and efforts at change are dealt with by repression. The pervasiveness of police, security men, the military, and compulsory military service show the changed character of American liberty.

5. The artificiality of work and culture. Work and living have become more and more pointless and empty. There is no lack of meaningful projects that cry out to be done, but our working days are used up in work that lacks meaning: making useless or harmful products, or servicing the bureaucratic structures. For most Americans, work is mindless, exhausting, boring, servile, and hateful, something to be endured while "life" is confined to "time off." At the same time our culture has been reduced to the grossly commercial; all cultural values are for sale, and those that fail to make a profit are not preserved. Our life activities have become plastic, vicarious, and false to our genuine needs, activities fabricated by others and forced upon us.

6. *Absence of community.* America is one vast, terrifying anti-community. The great organizations to which most people give their working day, and the apartments and suburbs to which they return at night, are equally places of loneliness and alienation. Modern living has obliterated place, locality, and neighborhood, and given us the anonymous separateness of our existence. The family, the most basic social system, has been ruthlessly stripped to its functional essentials. Friendship has been coated over with a layer of impenetrable artificiality as men strive to live roles designed for them. Protocol, competition, hostility, and fear have replaced the warmth of the circle of affection which might sustain man against a hostile universe.

7. *Loss of self.* Of all of the forms of impoverishment that can be seen or felt in America, loss of self, or death in life, is surely the most devastating. It is, even more than the draft and the Vietnam War, the source of discontent and rage in the new generation. Beginning with school, if not before, an individual is systematically stripped of his imagination, his creativity, his heritage, his dreams, and his

personal uniqueness, in order to style him into a productive unit for a mass, technological society. Instinct, feeling, and spontaneity are repressed by overwhelming forces. As the individual is drawn into the meritocracy, his working life is split from his home life, and both suffer from a lack of wholeness. Eventually, people virtually become their professions, roles, or occupations, and are thenceforth strangers to themselves. Blacks long ago felt their deprivation of identity and potential for life. But white "soul" and blues are just beginning. Only a segment of youth is articulately aware that they too suffer an enforced loss of self—they too are losing the lives that could be theirs.

What has caused the American system to go wrong in such an organic way? The first crucial fact is the existence of a universal sense of powerlessness. We seem to be living in a society that no one created and that no one wants. The feeling of powerlessness extends even to the inhabitants of executive offices. Yet, paradoxically, it is also a fact that we have available to us the means to begin coping with virtually all of the problems that beset us. Most people would initially deny this, but reflection shows how true it is. We know what causes crime and social disorder, and what can be done to eliminate those causes. We know the steps that can be taken to create greater economic equality. We are in possession of techniques to fashion and preserve more livable cities and environments. Our problems are vast, but so is our store of techniques; it is simply not being put to use.

Urban riots offer a well-documented case in point

for the late 1960's. They were predictable and they were predicted. Their causes and the appropriate remedies (which include education, housing, and jobs) have been known and described for many years by students of social problems. After the riots took place, a presidential commission reviewed the events, and their findings gave wide publicity to the same knowledge; the commission's recommendations were not acted upon, just as the preexisting knowledge had not been acted upon. Response was either nonexistent, absurdly inadequate, or childishly irrational (such as the proposal to deprive looters of jobs with public agencies).

The American crisis, then, seems clearly to be related to an inability to act. But what is the cause of this paralysis? Why, in the face of every warning, have we been unable to act? Why have we not used our resources more wisely and justly? We tell ourselves that social failure comes down to an individual moral failure: we must have the will to act; we must first find concern and compassion in our hearts. The theme is deep in America, from Hawthorne to E. B. White, from the Puritans to Richard Nixon, from *Time* to *The New York Times*. But this diagnosis is not good enough. It is contradicted by the *experience* of powerlessness that is encountered by so many people today. In 1968 a majority of the people certainly wanted peace, but they could not turn their individual wills into action by society. It is not that we do not will action, but that we are unable to act, unable to put existing knowledge to use. Is something wrong with the machinery of society? It apparently no longer works, or we no longer know how to make it work.

What is the machinery that we rely upon to turn our wishes into realities? In the private sphere, the market system. In the public sphere, the public version of the market system: voter democracy, or democratic pluralism. In both spheres, a system of administration and law, resting ultimately on the Constitution. Could it be that the American crisis results from a structure that is obsolete? All of the other machinery we use becomes obsolete in a short time. A social institution, which is, after all, only another type of machinery, is not necessarily immune from the same laws of obsolescence. The ideals or principles of a society might remain valid, but the means for applying the principles could lose their effectiveness.

If we seek to explain the American crisis in terms of obsolete structure, we might find an illustration in the ideal and the machinery of free speech. The ideal or principle is that every opinion must be expressed freely in order that truth be arrived at. But the machinery for carrying out this ideal was designed for a very different society than ours, a society of small villages, town meetings, and face-to-face discussions. The First Amendment furnishes no workable means for the public to be adequately informed about complex issues. News is cut down into a commodity by the mass media, a staccato piece of show business, and no one who only watches television and reads a typical newspaper could possibly know enough to be an intelligent voter. The vital decisions of the private sector of the economy receive even less adequate coverage and reporting. Moreover, the media systematically deny any fundamentally different or dissenting point of view a chance to be heard at all—it is simply kept off the air and out of the newspapers. The opinion that does get on television is commercially sponsored and thus heavily subsidized by government tax policies; the opinion that is not allowed is sometimes heavily penalized by the same tax laws (thus: the Georgia-Pacific Lumber Company's advertising is tax deductible; conservation advertising may not be). In short, our machinery for free speech is hopelessly ineffectual in the light of the way society is organized today, and this illustrates the plight of most of our democratic machinery which has not adapted to changing realities.

To explain the American crisis only in the above terms is, however, far from adequate. For one thing, it fails to take account of the whole Marxist analysis of capitalism. Those who analyze society in terms of class interests point out that there are powerful and privileged groups that profit greatly by the status quo. This power elite, and the monopolistic corporations it represents, has long exploited both people and environment. It profits from poverty, inequality, and war; it has a well-founded fear of democracy, liberty, and communal solidarity. The Marxists would argue that our government machinery is not naïvely obsolete; it has been captured by class interests. The same free speech illustration we used above would also illustrate a Marxist analysis: the media only disseminate the opinions that serve the interests of monopoly capital.

The Marxist analysis of the American crisis seems convincing. But is it a satisfactory explanation? The difficulty is that in focusing so strongly on economic interest, it does not take into account the vital factors of bureaucracy, organization, and technology which so dominate America today. These factors have a powerful momentum of their own that may not be inconsistent with class interests, but may well be indifferent to them. Thus we may be in the grip, not of capitalist exploiters, but of mindless, impersonal forces that pursue their own, non-human logic. A great deal of evidence supports this view.

Can the American crisis be defined, then, in terms of obsolete structure, monopoly capitalism, mindless technology, or perhaps some combination of the three? The question that we started with still remains: why are we unable to do anything to solve our problems? Government machinery can be overhauled; monopoly capitalism may be subjected to social regulation, as it has been in not only the communist countries but in the moderate-socialist countries; and technology is, after all, only a tool. There is something even deeper behind the crisis of structure and the crisis of inaction.

Whenever any attempt is made to begin confronting America's problems, we encounter a profound lack of understanding. This lack of understanding is not merely a phenomenon of the masses, for it extends to the powerful, the well educated, and the elite; it is not simply a lack of knowledge, for it includes many people who possess more than enough information. Its basis is a pervasive unreality. Our picture of our economy, of how we are governed, of how our culture is made, of how we may be threatened at home or abroad, is fantastically out of keeping with contemporary realities. Indeed, the central fact about America in 1970 is the discrepancy between the realities of our society and our beliefs about them. The gap is even greater in terms of our failure to understand the possibilities and potential of American life.

Unreality is the true source of powerlessness. What we do not understand, we cannot control. And when we cannot comprehend the major forces, structures, and values that pervade our existence, they must inevitably come to dominate us. Thus a true definition of the American crisis would say this: we no longer understand the system under which we live, hence the structure has become obsolete and we have become powerless; in turn, the system has been permitted to assume unchallenged power to dominate our lives, and now rumbles along, unguided and therefore indifferent to human ends.

What is this "understanding" that holds such a key place in our contemporary situation? Clearly the word "understanding" is inadequate, for we are talking about something much broader and deeper than "understanding" usually connotes. To describe what we are talking about, we propose to use the term "consciousness." It is a term that already has several meanings, including an important one in Marx, a medical one, a psychoanalytic one, a literary or artistic one, and one given us by users of hallucinogenic drugs. Our use of the term "consciousness" will not be exactly like any of these, but it gains meaning from all of them, and is consistent with all of them.

Consciousness, as we are using the term, is not a set of opinions, information, or values, but a total configuration in any given individual, which makes up his whole perception of reality, his whole world view. It is a common observation that once one has ascertained a man's beliefs on one subject, one is likely to be able to predict a whole range of views and reactions. Ask a stranger on a bus or airplane about psychiatry or redwoods or police or taxes or morals or war, and you can guess with fair accuracy his views on all the rest of these topics and many others besides, even though they are seemingly unrelated. If he thinks wilderness areas should be "developed" he is quite likely to favor punitive treatment for campus disruptions. If he is enthusiastic about hunting wild animals, he probably believes that the American economic system rests on individual business activity, and has an aversion to people with long hair.

It is apparent that the particular views we have mentioned really are related, and that an individual's opinions, understanding, and values are all part of some invisible whole. It is also apparent that consciousness is in substantial degree (but not necessarily entirely) socially determined. One evidence of this is the fact that many people have consciousnesses that are roughly similar, especially members of the same generation with the same social backgrounds. Also, when one hears a person's views and opinions, one can often tell something about his background, experience, and social role. The unity of consciousness in any individual is also revealed by the way in which it resists change, even in the smallest detail, and maintains a remarkable cohesion. Quite evidently the individual cannot allow any part of his consciousness to be challenged without feeling that the whole configuration is threatened. Thus a person who believes in "free enterprise" as part of his total perception of reality may resist, despite an overwhelming showing, the conclusion that "free enterprise" no longer serves to produce the same social consequences that it used to. Such a conclusion might undermine all of the assumptions under which this person has lived. Similarly, the violent reaction of some older people to long hair on boys shows that the adults feel a threat to the whole reality that they have constructed and lived by. An argument between people who are on different levels of consciousness often goes nowhere; there is no common ground on which they can meet.

Included within the idea of consciousness is a person's background, education, politics, insight, values, emotions, and philosophy, but consciousness is more than these or even the sum of them. It is the whole man; his "head"; his way of life. It is that by which he creates his own life and thus creates the society in which he lives.

As a mass phenomenon, consciousness is formed by the underlying economic and social conditions. There was a consciousness that went with peasant life in the Middle Ages, and a consciousness that went with small town, preindustrial life in America. Culture and government interact with consciousness; they are its products but they also help to form it. While consciousness is the creator of any social system, it can lag behind a system, once created, and even be manipulated by that system. Lag and manipulation are the factors that produce a consciousness characterized by unreality. If we believe in free enterprise, but the nation has become an interlocking corporate system, we are living in unreality as the victims of lag, and we are powerless to cope with the existing corporate system.

To show how this has worked out in America, and

to show the true meaning of the new generation, we have attempted to classify three general types of consciousness. These three types predominate in America today. One was formed in the nineteenth century, the second in the first half of this century, the third is just emerging. Consciousness I is the traditional outlook of the American farmer, small businessman, and worker who is trying to get ahead. Consciousness II represents the values of an organizational society. Consciousness III is the new generation. The three categories are, of course, highly impressionistic and arbitrary; they make no pretense to be scientific. And, since each type of consciousness is a construct, we would not expect any real individual to exhibit in symmetrical perfection all the characteristics of one type of consciousness.

The concept of consciousness gives us the elements from which we can fashion an argument about what has happened and what is happening to America. For the chaos we have just described is not chaos at all, but part of a coherent pattern of history, values, and thought. In the paragraphs that follow, we set forth the logic that emerges from behind the crisis of our contemporary life.

The great question of these times is how to live in and with a technological society; what mind and what way of life can preserve man's humanity and his very existence against the domination of the forces he has created. This question is at the root of the American crisis, beneath all the immediate issues of lawlessness, poverty, meaninglessness, and war. It is this question to which America's new generation is beginning to discover an answer, an answer based on a renewal of life that carries the hope of restoring us to our sources and ourselves.

At the opening of the industrial era, Western society underwent a major change of values in which scientific technique, materialism, and the market system became ascendant over other, more humanistic values. Although the contradiction was not recognized at the time, these industrial values were inconsistent with the democratic and spiritual ideas of the new American nation, and they soon began to undermine these American ideals.

Every stage of human civilization is accompanied by, and also influenced by, a consciousness. When civilization changes slowly, the existing consciousness is likely to be in substantial accord with underlying material realities. But industrialism brought sudden uprooting and a rapidly accelerating rate of change. Consciousness then began to lag increasingly far behind reality, or to lose touch with a portion of reality altogether. Today a large segment of the American people still have a consciousness which was appropriate to the nineteenth-century society of small towns, face-to-face relationships, and individual economic enterprise. Another large segment of the people have a consciousness formed by organized technological and corporate society, but far removed from the realities of human needs.

In the second half of the twentieth century, this combination of an anachronistic consciousness characterized by myth, and an inhuman consciousness dominated by the machine-rationality of the Corporate State, have, between them, proved utterly unable to manage, guide, or control the immense apparatus of technology and organization that America has built. In consequence, this apparatus of power has become a mindless juggernaut, destroying the environment, obliterating human values, and assuming domination over the lives and minds of its subjects. To the injustices and exploitation of the nineteenth century, the Corporate State has added depersonalization, meaninglessness, and repression, until it has threatened to destroy all meaning and all life.

Faced with this threat to their very existence, the inhabitants of America have begun, as a matter of urgent biological necessity, to develop a new consciousness appropriate to today's realities and therefore capable of mastering the apparatus of power and bringing it under human control. This new consciousness is based on the present state of technology, and could not have arisen without it. And it represents a higher, transcendent form of reason; no lesser consciousness could permit us to exist, given the present state of our technology.

This transcendent reason has made its first appearance among the youth of America. It is the product of the contradictions, failures, and exigencies of the Corporate State itself, not of any force external to the State. It is now in the process of rapidly spreading to wider and wider segments of youth, and by degrees to older people, as they experience the recovery of self that marks conversion to a different consciousness. The new consciousness is also in the process of revolutionizing the structure of our society. It does not accomplish this by direct political means, but by changing culture and the quality of individual lives, which in turn change politics and, ultimately, structure.

When the new consciousness has achieved its revolution and rescued us from destruction, it must go about the task of learning how to live in a new way. This new way of life presupposes all that modern science can offer. It tells us how to make technology and science work for, and not against, the interests of man. The new way of life proposes a concept of work in which quality, dedication, and excellence are preserved, but work is nonalienated, is the free choice of each person, is integrated into a full and satisfying life, and expresses and affirms each individual being. The new way of life makes both possible and necessary a culture that is nonartificial and nonalienated, a form of community in which love, respect, and a mutual search for wisdom replace the competition and separation of the past, and a liberation of each individual in which he is enabled to grow toward the highest possibilities of the human spirit.

The task of learning how to live in this way represents the chief philosophic undertaking for man after he saves himself from his present danger. It requires man to create a reality—a fiction based on what can offer men the best hope of a life that is both satisfying and beautiful. The process of that creation, which has already been started by our youth in this moment of utmost sterility, darkest night, and extremest peril, is what we have undertaken to describe in this book.

II

CONSCIOUSNESS I:
LOSS OF REALITY

To the American people of 1789, their nation promised a new way of life: each individual a free man; each having the right to seek his own happiness; a republican form of government in which the people would be sovereign; and no arbitrary power over people's lives. Less than two hundred years later, almost every aspect of the dream has been lost. In this chapter we shall be concerned with the forces that destroyed the American dream and with the consciousness that allowed this to happen.

Every form of consciousness is a reaction to a way of life that existed before, and an adaptation to new realities. In the case of what we call Consciousness I, there was a liberation from the constraints of class status and the settled village life that still existed in the old world. Consciousness I had its moment of exhilaration. Facing a new and vast land, a new freedom, and seemingly limitless riches, its reality centered on the truth of individual effort. America would prosper if people proved energetic and hard working. The crucial thing was to release the individual energy so long held back by rigid social customs and hierarchical forms. Each newly sovereign individual could be the source of his own achievement and fulfillment. One worked for oneself, not for society. But enough individual hard work made the wheels turn. Consciousness I focused on self, but it saw self in harsh and narrow terms, accepting much self-repression as the essential concomitant of effort, and allowing self to be cut off from the larger community of man, and from nature (defined as an enemy) as well. This uniquely American consciousness expressed the realities of the new nation.

To the people who came here, America represented a new beginning. They had been granted freedom from the past—a second chance. They believed that the earth belongs to the living, and that they need not be bound by traditions, customs, or authority from other lands. America would be, for them, a new community. R. W. B. Lewis, in *The American Adam* (1955), described them thus, emphasizing, above all, the admired quality of innocence. They had an idealistic view of what man could be in the new community. The American dream was not, at least at the beginning, a rags-to-riches type of narrow materialism. At its most exalted, in Whitman's words, it was a spiritual and humanistic vision of man's possibilities:

> Each of us inevitable,
> Each of us limitless—each of us with
> his or her right upon the earth,
> Each of us allow'd the eternal purports
> of the earth.
>
> —"SALUT AU MONDE!"

> Divine am I inside and out, and I
> make holy whatever I touch or
> am touch'd from . . .
>
> I dote on myself, there is a lot of
> me and all so luscious,
> Each moment and whatever happens
> thrills me with joy . . .
>
> —"SONG OF MYSELF"

Whitman could be speaking for today's youth. But he was also summing up one side of the original American dream—the dream shared by the colonists and the immigrants, by Jefferson, Emerson, the Puritan preachers and the western cowboy—a dream premised on human dignity, a dignity that made each man an equal being in a spiritual sense, and envisioned a community based upon individual dignity.

This broad humanism, in distinction to materialism, is revealed in the literature of the western frontier. Here was a search for adventure and challenge, for man-in-nature, for the nonspecialized individual able to do many different kinds of work. It was a search for a kind of human companionship built out of sharing. It had a strong spiritual element, as the Mormon quest shows. As Pierre Berton unforgettably relates in *The Klondike Fever* (1958), even where the object seemed to be material—gold—the real finding was an expansion of man's nature which was remembered long after gold had become a dim memory.

What sort of man was the hero of this new land? R. W. B. Lewis tells us that the hero was not worldly, cunning, overly learned, or intellectual. His triumph would be due to the ordinary virtues—plainness, character, honesty, hard work. The innocent was the pioneer, the settler, the westerner, the boy who makes good. He was a moral being, and ultimately it would be his goodness, not his knowingness, that would triumph. Emerson, in his essays on self-reliance and on politics, put his emphasis not on the forms of government but on individual character—spiritual and moral—as the basic source of the national being. The belief that the character of the people is what ultimately matters retains its strength to the present day. But innocence has its great drawbacks, as America was eventually to discover. When it encounters the more worldly, it risks disaster. Thus in American literature, from Melville's *Billy Budd* to James' *The Portrait of a Lady*, the catastrophe of innocence is a major theme. And this theme, in a symbolic way, accurately forecast what would happen in nineteenth-century America.

There was another side to the American character —the harsh side of self-interest, competitiveness, suspicion of others. Each individual would go it alone, refusing to trust his neighbors, seeing another man's advantage as his loss, seeing the world as a rat race with no rewards to losers. Underlying this attitude was the assumption that "human nature" is fundamentally bad, and that a struggle against his fellow men is man's natural condition. "There'll always be aggression and a struggle for power, and there'll always be a pecking order," says Consciousness I. There is a deep isolation and suspicion of others in Consciousness I and more faith in winning than in love. The belief in self-interest led to the corruption of American life and government by venality, dishonesty, the sale of offices, favors and votes, all under the theory that each man has a right to pursue his opportunities wherever he finds them, that "the game" is winning and getting rich and powerful, and nothing else, and that no higher community exists beyond each individual's selfish appraisal of his interests.

But it was not merely corruption that undermined the America of Consciousness I. Consciousness I proved unable to change with the changing realities of America. Today it still sees America as if it were a world of small towns and simple virtues. Invention and machinery and production are the equivalent of progress; material success is the road to happiness; nature is beautiful but must be conquered and put to use. Competition is the law of nature and man; life is a harsh pursuit of individual self-interest. Consciousness I believes that the American dream is still possible, and that success is determined by character, morality, hard work, and self-denial. It does not accept the fact that organizations predominate over individuals in American life, or that social problems are due to something other than bad character, or that the possibility of individual success, based on ability and enterprise, is largely out of date. Consciousness I still thinks that the least government governs best. It votes for a candidate who seems to possess personal moral virtues and who promises a return to earlier conditions of life, law and order, rectitude, and lower taxes. It believes that the present American crisis requires reducing government programs and expenditures, greater reliance on private business, forcing people now on welfare to go to work, taking stern measures to put down subversion at home and threats from abroad, and, above all, a general moral reawakening in the people. Today Consciousness I includes a great variety of Americans: farmers, owners of small businesses, immigrants who retain their sense of nationality, AMA-type doctors, many members of Congress, gangsters, Republicans, and "just plain folks." In the second half of the twentieth century the beliefs of Consciousness I are drastically at variance with reality. But they are held in a stubborn, belligerent, opinionated way against all contrary evidence. The great problem concerning Consciousness I is this: it is understandable how Consciousness I led to corruption, inequality, and self-interest. But how did it lose contact with reality? How did it lose the ability to comprehend, or to govern?

American history, as it is usually taught, makes today's reality of failure and crisis a mystery and a paradox. After two hundred years of brilliant, unmatched progress, how can it be possible that we are beset by vast problems and desperate impoverishment? After watching the steady improvement of all our institutions, the development and preservation of our Constitution, and the limitless expansion of individual opportunity, why do our institutions, our personal lives, the whole character of America suddenly seem changed beyond recognition? And if Americans had always been the most independent and self-reliant people, the most jealous of their liberties, how have they permitted themselves to be reduced to the impotent "little man" of today, dominated by public and private power?

If history is told this way, it is no wonder so many people are led to blame "communists" or minority groups, youth, foreign influences, or radicals, for all that has gone wrong. Our history seems to preclude any other explanation; only some malign outside influence could have poisoned the nation's growth; anger and bitterness are understandable. But if these explanations cannot be credited, then something must be wrong with our history. Something must have been omitted, ignored, or falsified.

What was it in our history that Consciousness I failed or refused to see? Where was it that the American dream began to be eroded? Where did democratic values run into trouble, where and to whom did the little man begin to lose his power and his independence? What caused the transformation of America? What were the new realities that went unacknowledged so long that Consciousness I was left as the repository and supporter of myth?

Soon after Americans began their experiment in a new community, the assumptions upon which the nation was based were threatened by the rise of two powerful forces, worldwide in influence: the competitive market economy and scientific technique. The forces came as benefactors (as in large part they were), offering men in all countries the possibility of liberation from static toil. The market system transforms all men into competitors in order to get them to be more aggressively productive; it does this by defining man's labor, his environment, and his culture as commodities which can be valued in money and exchanged for money, and by permitting "successful" competitors to accumulate "profit" and "surplus" in return for the exploitation of labor and resources. Scientific technique is a philosophy concerned with the basic values of life; it asserts that all activities should be carried on in that manner which is scientifically or technically "best" and "most efficient." It is technique which dictates specialization of labor, the use of machinery, systems of organization, and mass production. These forces threatened the most fundamental aspects of the American dream: the physical-human environment that made possible the pursuit of happiness, and the form of government that rejected arbitrary power.

Prior to the coming of the industrial revolution, most people were born, lived, worked, and died in the same place, among people they knew and saw every day. There was no separation between work and living. Ties to the community were strong and seldom severed; each man lived within a circle which did not depend upon his own action, began before him, and lasted beyond him. Food and shelter were communal enterprises; no one grew fat or starved alone. The scale of everything was smaller: tools, houses, land, villages. There were no large, impersonal institutions—apartment houses, factories, or hospitals. Scale and activity were influenced by nature (for example, time was measured by the daily sun and the seasons). Laws were administered by visible local people. Most important of all, man's economic activity was rooted in, and subordinate to, his social system. That is, there were no purely economic or scientific "laws." Customs or religion—communal traditions, in short—were the regulators of life. Play, art, ritual, ceremony, and the spiritual were not separated from the other aspects of life; they were an integral part of the whole. Activity of all kinds was rooted in folk and religious culture which developed "irrationally" and without conscious design, in response to human needs. This world, both in Europe and in frontier America, was destroyed in the making of our modern world.

The impact of technology, market, and capitalism is written on our landscape, our culture, our faces. Perhaps the landscape shows it most vividly. In all societies prior to the modern, no matter how diverse in other ways, there existed an essential harmony between the people and the land, a harmony in which nature was not violently altered or violated. Modern society makes war on nature. A competitive market uses nature as a commodity to be exploited—turned into profit. Technology sees nature as an element to be conquered, regulated, controlled. In England the two forces brought about the destruction of the countryside, the raising of hideous and unhealthy slums and mill towns. When the forces seized the once beautiful eastern states of America, they left forests denuded; rivers, harbors, and seacoasts polluted; the cities sterile; the land ripped by highways, high tension wires, and suburban swaths. They left little of the country unblighted, not even the miraculous and seemingly limitless beauty of California where today the devastation seems most wanton and cruel of all.

What happened to the land also happened, in Europe and America, to the basic social fabric. The village community was broken as men were forced to seek jobs in factories or cities. Family ties shattered for the same reason. The separated apartment replaced the village and the family home. The bonds of affection and concern between men were broken by the harsh imperatives of competition. As pecuniary relationships replaced ties of tradition, custom, religion, and respect, men obeyed authority only when forced to by economic necessity or penal laws, and in consequence modern crime became the obverse face of society. Man was uprooted from his supporting physical and social environment and, like a polar bear in a city zoo, he would from then on suffer an alienated existence.

The most profound impact of the commodity system and technology was on man's own individual being. The visible ravaging of the land and the social fabric was matched by an invisible ravaging of man within. Man was not merely alienated from environment and society, he was alienated from his own functions and needs. His principal activity—work—ceased to be self-expression. He felt little of the normal satisfactions of work; he was a mere cog in production; his tasks no longer expressed his abilities. Man's most basic activity was dominated by the most impersonal of masters—money. Man became alienated from himself as money, not inner needs, called the tune. Man began to defer or abandon his real needs, and increasingly his wants became subject to outside manipulation. Losing both his work-essence and his need-essence, man was no longer a unique individual but an extension of the production-consumption system.

Why did the forces of industrialism, designed to be beneficent, have such devastating, unforeseen effects? In preindustrial societies, change takes place very gradually, subject at all times to a humanistic cultural and social system. In contrast, when rapid and drastic changes are made to accomplish specific scientific or rational objectives, the unconscious, invisible, and non-material human values are likely to be neglected. Gradual change allows the cultural tradition to carry along a more balanced set of values. Industrialism was not only violently rapid, it was singleminded, and had little concern for what happened to other values; it complacently assumed that "the market" would take care of these. In short, the changes introduced by technology and the market inevitably caused devastation to the natural and the human environment because no measures were taken to preserve a continued organic balance of values. Industrialism, in Karl Polanyi's phrase, placed man under the rule of laws that were not human.

The second effect of industrialism was on the American political and economic system. It is worth recalling the nation's constitutional scheme. The central idea was individual sovereignty. The framers of the Constitution were men who deeply feared power, believed that any and all power corrupts, and rejected the idea of any form of power over individual lives. They laid their strictures against all the types of power they knew about or had experienced. The plan was to divide power, limit it, and subject its use to many sorts of safeguards. All power was limited to that specifically granted. Thus the framers showed their conviction that power of any sort was the chief evil that could beset any people. Democracy was also a part of the plan, and with it the concept that the people were the ultimate and only sovereigns. This scheme of government went along with an economic system which attempted to embody the American dream. It sought to make it possible for every American citizen to achieve personal economic independence, ownership of his own land and home, and an opportunity to define and engage in work of his own choosing. Within this plan there was, of course, room for some people to become rich, some to remain rich, and others to remain or become poor. But this was thought necessary for the over-all objective of personal independence. The frontier lay open; opportunity was to be found on all sides; no laws restricted freedom of movement; there was virtually unlimited freedom to define "the pursuit of happiness" in any manner that might seem fulfilling to the individual concerned.

It was not so for long. The forces of the market and technique were oblivious to the individual pursuit of happiness. Consider the factory system, in which technique dictated the organization and specialization of labor, and where the market forced long hours, low wages, and a precarious security. The early miseries of factories have often been recounted; what needs to be seen here is the contrast between the factory system and the ideals concerning independence, for the factory worker was subject to overwhelming power over his life. He was rigidly disciplined. His hours, his conduct, his meals, his clothes, ultimately his friendships and thoughts were all controlled. Cities developed to house factory workers, and the cities demanded a limitation of freedom in living arrangements almost as great as that of the factory itself. Of course, no one "needed" to work in a factory or live in a city. But gradually, as the decades passed, the alternatives narrowed. Not everyone could any longer be a pioneer, settler, farmer, or individual craftsman.

For employees, whether of a factory, a business

concern, or a large-scale farm, sovereign independence largely ceased to exist in practice. The power exercised over their lives was not constitutionally limited, or divided, or subject to checks and balances; no bill of rights or court protected them. No democracy existed for the employee; he was not consulted about any decision, however vital to his own life. Nor was there, for the vast majority, any hope of success; their hopes were limited to the chance to find a place within a powerful structure, and although a few did rise, the dream was realized only for those few. What was supposed to be a chance for all was now statistically impossible for most. Even more drastic, perhaps, was the loss of the pursuit of self-fulfillment. For the employee could no longer define his own quest. The kind of work he did, the manner in which he did his work, his opportunities for expression, leisure, and play were all subject to external power.

The discipline to which the worker fell subject was a harsh one. He worked long hours which absorbed nearly all of his time and energy. He was cut off from fresh air, nature, and beauty, and confined to a machine-interior. His housing was little more than an extension of the factory itself, barracks jammed together without amenities of any kind. His movements were closely regulated on the job, and what was "free" became a conventionalized movement to and from the factory, plus the motions of eating, sleeping, procreating at home. The worker was deprived of his role as a father, and this function turned over to wives and to public schools. Independence was replaced by a grumbling servility; the worker must submit to the authority of the bosses; all sense of power and potency passed out of his hands. His mind was not wanted, nor his judgment, nor his imagination. His sense of design, of rhythm, of music, of craftsmanship was rejected. Boldness, courage, leadership, fun, play, kindness, affection, had no place in the discipline of the factory or the office. The authority of the industrial rulers was different from the rule of the southern slave owners, but in some ways it required an equally great submission, an equally great loss of human possibility. We have often spoken of the industrial worker as a wage slave. But this imposes a narrowly economic view on his condition. His mind, his spirit, his personality, his human functions were chained as well, and, like the sad, yearning, awkward, and speechless monster created by technology in the film version of *Frankenstein*, he was irrevocably cut off from the circle of humanity.

Growth of power over individuals was matched by the growth of power on a vaster stage. After the Civil War the country entered a period of business mergers, consolidations, and monopolies. This resulted in a gradual destruction of the free market, and the assumption of corporate power to plan the economy, allocate resources, divide areas of business activity, fix prices, limit entry of new businesses, and (although this was still far off) control the buyers themselves. A small group in steel and railroads, another group in oil, another in finance, became rulers of nation-states, controlling economic forces, in some ways as tightly as any socialist country has attempted to do.

The power that now was assumed, from regulation of the factory worker to regulation of the market, was power that had not previously existed in anyone's hands in America, if anywhere in the world. Thus it was not a seizure from someone else, but the subjugation of a previously free people and a previously free economy. It was, in the most literal and true sense, a conquest of the American nation. The new lords arrayed themselves in the trappings of royalty. Monarchical homes were built, with furnishings suited for, and sometimes actually purchased from, the European aristocracy. The library-offices of J. P. Morgan and Henry Clay Frick, both still preserved in New York, resemble nothing so much as two imperial throne rooms. And the American language quickly recognized the realities of the loss of democracy; there were copper "kings" and railroad "barons," an American aristocracy. The American people, who fled the monarchies of Europe, had only a few decades of freedom before they were conquered by a set of autocrats wielding, if anything, greater power than the old.

But these were not merely the triumphs of certain successful individuals over their fellow men. From a longer perspective we can see that the seizure was also a triumph of impersonal forces—the forces of organization, efficiency, technology, planning; the forces of modern rationalism and scientific management. John D. Rockefeller was as impersonal as a mathematical formula—he was the embodiment of technique, efficiency, and, above all, of economic planning. He was the apostle of collectivism, ending individualism in the oil industry and replacing it with a centralized, planned, collective enterprise. Of course he and others were also rapacious, ambitious, ruthless; but these qualities—and even more so the individual buccaneering and piracy that characterized the great age of robber barons—obscured the longer-range thrust of the times. The cold and calm Rockefeller, a true business scientist, expresses what was happening far better than some frontiersman-turned-millionaire who kept his vitality and his largely irrational ways.

The true ethic that transformed America was not the ethic of piracy and rapacity standing by itself, but that of power joined to repression and order. Organization and efficiency repressed unruly, undisciplined life. It substituted the clean, spare, inhuman direction of affairs for the random, spontaneous burgeoning of life that seemed so typical of frontier America. It is worth recording who were the real socialists, collectivizers, subversives in America—who were the enemies of the American way, the spoilers, the uprooters of tradition, the killers of the American dream. They did not have beards and bombs, foreign accents and manifestoes. They were, these enemies of the original American ideal, the great names: Vanderbilt, Carnegie, Harriman, Ford. The forces of market exploitation and technology, active through them, cut down democracy, independence, and the pursuit of happiness, and fostered instead a new managerial order, a hierarchy of power and privilege that replaced communal values with antisocial "success" and with inhuman science.

Looking back, it can be seen that the forces loosed on the world at the beginning of the modern era had the potential to create all the kinds of troubles which beset us today: lawlessness and disorder, because the basis for social order was destroyed; destruction of environment and culture by exploitation; threats to democracy and liberty, because man was subject to the impersonal lordship of an economic and technological system; loss of values as all values became subject to manipulation. If Americans were to preserve their dream of a republican form of government and individual economic sovereignty, as well as the environment of their lives, they would have needed to understand the forces that were threatening them, and to take action to assure that these forces worked for, not against, the American dream.

Consciousness I was unwilling or unable to comprehend the transformation of America. Innocence and optimism have one basic failing: they have no fundamental depth. It is this shallowness that drove Henry James into exile, and which he described so marvelously in his notes on his return visit, published as *The American Scene*. To James, the American lacked a culture, lacked a past, possessed no social order. James found Americans obsessed by the need to move-move-move. They tore down buildings before the building could acquire meaning and tradition; they allowed commerce and engineering to dominate principles of architecture and city planning; they were uprooted from everything. In consequence they prevented anything interior or private from forming, anything traditional from being carried along, and all of this change made individuality increasingly impossible to maintain. The momentum of change swept the people along so rapidly, with so little chance to become individually self-conscious, that people were cut off from their own history. Without a sense of self and history, Americans had no chance to know what they wanted, and no way of knowing how to get it if they did know. James saw coming to America what he called the Hotel Spirit.

By this he meant that life would be like living in a grand hotel—luxurious, in a material sense, but all individuality sacrificed, and all choices abandoned to the hotel management. In James' sense of the word, people in America lacked consciousness—that precious ability to *see* for which James himself was willing to sacrifice everything. Had James used more modern terms, he might have added that Americans were a people who had lost their identity. Their past traditions had vanished into the melting pot, their present was in flux, and no repose or reflection existed to permit the formulation of a concept of self.

Innocence, self-interest, and shallowness combined in Consciousness I to produce a massive flight from responsibility and from awareness. There is a quality of willful ignorance in American life—ignorance of existing injustices, such as the treatment of the black minority, ignorance of the causes of social problems, ignorance of the world. Americans demanded the superficial "normalcy" of the Twenties or the Fifties; they were willing to see the news about their government come to them in the form of tabloid or television entertainment; they tolerated ignorance and incompetence in high office; and when something went wrong, it was childishly blamed on "them." Politics early became the realm of untruth, and it has stayed that way ever since. That politician was elected who painted the most untrue picture of America, who took us farthest from the changes that were actually taking place in America. If the American Eden was being challenged by inhuman industrial forces that were capable of destroying it, many Americans preferred denying the truth to fighting back—and still do.

Although many writers saw these aspects of the American character, few realized what we are now able to see—how disastrous the shortcomings of Consciousness I would prove to be. Not only would Americans have no understanding of the dangers of industrialism, they would possess no set of values to oppose those of industrialism; no culture, tradition, social order, or inner knowledge of self by which to guide industrial values and choose among them. Moreover, Americans could not rise to a level of community responsibility in the face of the dangers of industrialism. Divided up into individual units defined by self-interest, they had no way of thinking for the common good, or thinking ahead, and the anti-intellectual and sometimes childish tendency of Americans not to think at all allowed them to rest easy in this posture.

Consciousness I has been, and continues to be, utterly unable to come to terms with the realities of private power created by industrialism. Although opposition to power is part of the essential American idea, Americans have watched corporations acquire power to plan the economy, to decide what is to be produced, to fix prices, to regulate essential services, including the distribution of news and information (so vital to the working of a democracy), and to regulate the lives of workers, without taking effectual steps to cope with any of it. Antitrust, collective bargaining, and utility regulation were some of the measures eventually taken, but, as we shall see in the next chapter, they were not effective. Consciousness I could not grasp, or could not accept, the reality that the individual was no longer competing against the success of other individuals, but against a system.

It could not understand that "private property" in the hands of a corporation was a synonym for quasi-governmental power, far different from the property of an individual. It could not understand the crucial point that collective action against corporate power would not have been a step toward collectivization, but an effort to preserve democracy in a society that had already been collectivized.

Consciousness I also failed to recognize that private production was not paying its costs. For example, a manufacturer would dump its wastes into a stream but pay nothing on account of the pollution, leaving the public to share in the costs but not in the profits. The manufacturer fought against having to pay for accidental injuries to workers, although these were statistically predictable, leaving the costs to be borne, sometimes for a whole lifetime, by the unfortunate individual and his family. Unemployment, old-age insecurity, and inadequate education for an advancing technology were part of the price of manufacture, and should have been rectified through taxation. But the relationship between the corporation and society was not recognized.

Most characteristic of all, Consciousness I insisted on seeing the ills of industrialism not for what they were, but as moral problems. If a given number of automobiles are crowded onto a highway, there will be a predictable number of accidents. The moral approach tries to deal with this as a question of individual driver responsibility. It stresses safe driving and criminal penalties. Yet reduction of the accident rate is demonstrably a problem in engineering. Similarly, urban crime is seen as a moral and law enforcement problem, although crime is a product of identifiable environmental factors. The moralistic approach to public welfare is similar. Over and over again, Consciousness I sought scapegoats rather than face the forces of industrialism directly.

If the people would not dominate the forces that were changing their country, then those forces would dominate the people. Consciousness I, losing its own roots but holding tight to its myths, was ready game for manipulation by the organized forces of society. These Americans could be sold a colonial war in the name of national honor. They could be sold hundreds of billions of dollars' worth of military technology in the name of American independence. They could be sold governmental irresponsibility in the name of the old American virtue of thrift. They could be sold an ignorant and incapable leader because he looked like the embodiment of American virtues. Worst of all, perhaps, they could be sold artificial pleasures and artificial dreams to replace the high human and spiritual adventure that had once been America.

In northwest Seattle, there is an immensely popular "old-fashioned" ice cream parlor. It is modern, spotless, and gleaming, bursting with comfortable-looking people on a warm summer evening. The parlor is dedicated to nostalgia, from the old-time decor to the striped candy, the ragtime music, the costumes of the smiling young waiters, the Gibson-girl menu with its gold-rush type, and the open-handed hospitality of the Old West. It serves sandwiches, hamburgers, and kiddie "samiches," but its specialty is ice cream concoctions, all of them with special names, including several so vast and elaborate that they cost several dollars and arrive with so much fanfare that all other activities stop as the waiters join in a procession as guards of honor. Nobody seems to care that the sandwiches and even the ice cream dishes have a curious blandness, so that everything tastes rather alike and it is hard to remember what one has eaten. Nothing mars the insistent, bright, wholesome good humor that presses on every side. Yet somehow there is pathos as well. For these patrons are the descendants of pioneers, of people who knew the frontiers, of men who dared the hardships of Chilkoot Pass to seek gold in the Klondike. That is their heritage, but now they only sit amid a sterile model of the past, spooning ice cream while piped-in ragtime tinkles unheard.

III

THE FAILURE OF REFORM

We have described the major forces that transformed America, and the consciousness that determined the nation's inability to respond. Now we turn to a third element in the development of the contemporary American state: efforts at reform, their failure, and the growth of power that resulted. Although we will mention some reforms of the populist and Progressive-Wilsonian eras, the New Deal will be the chief focus.

Since we left our account of the main forces of industrialism at some point in the nineteenth century, we should take note of how they continued during the period of reform. The primary trends we have discussed—erosion of the physical and social environment, and the growth of "private" power over the economy and over individual lives—continued at an accelerating rate, and their impact became vastly greater. The competitive market, however, was gradually replaced by something more consolidated and regulated, and both the labor market and the product market were enveloped in controls, most of them "private."

Karl Polanyi, in *The Great Transformation,* shows that the forces of industrialism inevitably bring about an attempt by society to preserve its threatened values; he calls such efforts "self-protection of society." Most reform legislation in England, on the European continent, and in the United States falls in this general category. That is, the legislation tries to protect the society from the harshest effects of industrialism by such means as minimum wages for workers, prohibition of child labor, and industrial safety laws.

Beginning in the early part of the twentieth century, America became deeply divided between those people who held fast to Consciousness I and those who began to seek governmental and social reform and, beyond that, a new way of life based on the realities of the twentieth century. Perhaps the reformers never achieved a majority. But they did gain enough power to change the structure of our institutions, and to begin the creation of a new consciousness. These changes were commenced with great hope and idealism. Ultimately, however, they failed to produce what their originators wanted. They produced not a reformed democracy, but an even greater domination by industrialism.

A discussion of American efforts at reform and social control must start with the various diagnoses that were made of the ills of society, which supply at least some of the assumptions under which the reforms proceeded. In literature, we can find one diagnosis in such books as Edward Bellamy's *Looking Backward*, Upton Sinclair's *The Jungle*, Stephen Crane's *Maggie: A Girl of the Streets*, Gold's *Jews Without Money*, John Steinbeck's *Grapes of Wrath*. The presumed causes of America's troubles can be summed up simply: the evils of unlimited competition, and abuses by those with economic power. Bellamy vividly described the first when he likened American society to a great coach in which a privileged few were riding in comfort but others were outside, desperately clinging or pushing, driven by the lash of hunger. He pictured the bitter antagonism between people, caused by competition for jobs and the evils of gross inequality and social injustice. Sinclair effectively showed the second half of the picture in his description of the meat-packing industry. He pictured corporate giants turning out unhealthy, adulterated meat products that were a menace to the public, and at the same time ruthlessly oppressing their employees, who lived in perpetual fear, insecurity, and misery. Abuses of the system, the consequences of greed, irresponsibility, and extreme individualism, were the primary target of the reformers. Even Ida Tarbell's far more structurally oriented study, *A History of the Standard Oil Company*, treated Rockefeller as a destroyer of what she considered the basically valid competitive market. And Jacob Riis, who showed that the city slums were already an "urban problem" many decades ago, treated slums as an evil that could be corrected by vigorous action. The fight against abuses would be the major theme of reform.

This American analysis was much less sophisticated and thoughtful than the analysis of industrialism that was being made at the same period, and much earlier, in Europe. Charles Dickens' *Hard Times, Bleak House*, and *Little Dorrit* strike far deeper: depersonalization, the profound separation and loneliness of people and groups, sterile materialism, the absurdity and cruelty of large organizations and institutions, the entire world becoming a prison for the human spirit. Kafka, Dostoevsky, and many Victorians saw it too; Dickens, Ruskin, and others also stressed the destruction of the landscape and man's environment. Although the physical conditions of work improved, Marx's insight was increasingly confirmed: work was becoming meaningless and alienating to the worker. It remained for the German Expressionist painters and moviemakers, beginning in the early 1900's, to attempt to show what was happening to the human soul: in terrifying distortions they portrayed the emergence of something far more fearsome than mere abuses of a basically sound system. The threatening cinema figures of Dr. Caligari and Dr. Mabuse, set against surrealist cities, suggested the darkness of science and technology.

American literature was not lacking in hints of these deeper ills. They can be found in Melville, particularly *Bartleby the Scrivener*, in Howells' *The Rise of Silas Lapham*, in Warren's *All the King's Men*, in Miller's *Death of a Salesman*, in the stories of Fitzgerald and Lardner. Interestingly enough, in retrospect we can see that the most profound insights into

American society were in the popular art of the Thirties, the gangster films and the detective novels. These were grim and despairing portrayals of dehumanization, violence, and the bleakness of the American city. The remarkable novels of Raymond Chandler, James M. Cain, and Dashiell Hammett come closer to the truth than almost anything else in literature or social science. And on the screen or in the newspapers, the gangster era gave America a grotesque portrait of itself, with the whole economic and social system cruelly displayed for those who would and could see it.

But these deeper artistic perceptions never became political perceptions. Reform began with highly specific efforts: laws regulating unhealthy practices in the meat industry, prohibition of monopolies and piratical methods of competition, laws against railroad favoritism, provision of maximum hours for workers in certain employments, regulation of dishonest advertising. The basic theme was simple: economic power, where it has been too severely abused, must be subjected to "the public interest." This meant that government would keep an eye on the *consequences* of the economic system; when these got too bad, it would apply regulation (although self-regulation was always preferred). It was a moralistic system, dealing with crime but not its causes; in this sense it was typically American. Franklin D. Roosevelt stated this moralistic approach, and also the "public interest" philosophy that was later to dominate, in his 1933 and 1937 inaugurals. In 1933, after describing the chaos of the depression, he said:

Primarily this is because rulers of the exchange of mankind's goods have failed, through their own stubbornness and incompetence . . .

They know only the rules of a generation of self-seekers . . .

. . . there must be an end to a conduct in banking and in business which too often has given to a sacred trust the likeness of a callous and selfish wrongdoing . . .

. . . we now realize as we have never realized before our interdependence on each other; that we can not merely take but we must give as well; that if we are to go forward, we must move as a trained and loyal army willing to sacrifice for the good of a common discipline, because without such discipline no progress is made, no leadership becomes effective. We are, I know, ready and willing to submit our lives and property to such discipline, because it makes possible a leadership which aims at a larger good.

In his second inaugural address, FDR summed up the themes of his program:

. . . we must find practical controls over blind economic forces and blindly selfish men . . .

We refused to leave the problems of our common welfare to be solved by the winds of chance and the hurricanes of disaster. . . .

. . . we have begun to bring private autocratic powers into their proper subordination to the public's government . . .

We have always known that heedless self-interest was bad morals; we know now that it is bad economics. . . . in the long run economic morality pays . . .

This new understanding undermines the old admiration of worldly success as such. We are beginning to abandon our tolerance of the abuse of power by those who betray for profit the elementary decencies of life.

It was a diagnosis of selfish men, people left out of the system, the American dream somehow misused.

The New Deal brought together representatives of the major attitudes in the American reform movement, including those committed to the populist-Progressive-Wilson programs and those with far more advanced ideas. Speaking generally, there was a group which wanted to regulate the abuses of capitalism, one which wanted to redistribute power in society, particularly by giving recognition to the labor movement, and another (the most radical) which wanted a substantial amount of government economic planning and redistribution of wealth.

The ideologically mixed and highly pragmatic New Deal program that emerged contained four main aspects.

1. Regulatory. The New Deal tried to protect the system against abuse by creating such devices as the NRA (fair competition), the SEC (honesty and prudence in the securities market), and the Robinson-Patman Act (destructive pricing).

2. Balancing of power. Organized labor was given an opportunity to become a counterpower to business, and other major groups were encouraged in an effort to substitute pluralism for sheer business power.

3. Security and welfare. A floor was placed under the competitive labor market, through unemployment compensation, welfare, and social security, to provide a minimum "freedom from want" to the losers in the competitive struggle.

4. Radical programs. A beginning was made toward affirmative social-economic activity by government such as TVA, public housing programs, public works, and federal subsidies.

Beyond these particular programs the New Deal consisted of an attempt to further certain general values. It believed in the rational use of the nation's resources through organization, cooperation, planning, and regulation: ultimately it believed in reason. It believed in the maximum utilization of technology and science. It believed in a meritocracy of equal opportunity and ability, unencumbered by irrational forms of prejudice and discrimination. It believed that private business should be carried on privately, if possible, but ultimately must be subject to the public good. It believed the best route to reform to be through a strong affirmative government manned by the best educated, most intelligent, most expert men who could be found, devising and carrying out programs in the best interests of the people.

What the New Deal did was to create, in furtherance of these objectives, and to carry out its reforms, a new public state, matching in size and power the private Corporate State. For each piece of regulatory legislation a large, specialized government agency was established, and at the same time the regular executive departments of the government were greatly expanded. This physical growth was accompanied by a growth in power. The Supreme Court gave the government sweeping new constitutional authority—virtually a free hand, in place of the original constitutional idea of expressly limited powers. The dominating concept was that all private activity, individual or corporate, was subject to restriction, licensing, or regulation "in the public interest," meaning, for reasons based on the good of the whole nation. The public state was managerial and administrative in nature; its values were rationality, order, and organization. It saw no evil in technology or power as such, so long as they were in "the public interest." In a sense the public state was government in the shape of technology.

What were the successes and failures of the New Deal and the reforms that preceded it? The question has implications far beyond the New Deal itself: it goes to the ability of an industrial nation to substitute rational management for the unregulated development of industrialism; it is a test of whether self-protection of society is possible, whether an administered state is possible, and whether the New Deal–liberal theory of government balanced against the private sector makes sense. The evidence is of course open to question in many respects, but it is in the nature of the problem of an administered state that laboratory experiments are impossible.

The first thing we might observe is the phenomenon of tremendous lag in American governmental actions. The reforms of the New Deal were mostly responses to ills that had been diagnosed many decades earlier. The Social Security Act, one of the most important and most characteristic New Deal reforms, looked back fifty years to Edward Bellamy's vision of the coach driven by hunger. But as a solution the Social Security Act was far less comprehensive than what Bellamy himself said was needed. Similarly the New Deal welfare program was far less than Bellamy's proposal that each man receive support from society on one basis alone: "because he is a man."

It is only today, more than eighty years after Bellamy, that such a proposal is beginning to be sought (over much opposition) on the political scene. Thus, most of the New Deal came too late—far, far, too late. By 1933 the problems were so different that the programs of Bellamy's era, if enacted, might either fail altogether or even do more harm than good.

Lag is quite plainly an inherent problem in any attempt at social management. There is creaky political machinery to be set in motion, stubborn and powerful vested interests to be overcome. Somebody profits from child labor, from lack of safety in mines. Meanwhile, society keeps on changing. Can government ever be flexible and swift-acting enough to deal with social problems at the same time that they occur? Can it ever act with scientific precision when it must act through the political system? The New Deal, fumbling belatedly with the problems of fifty years earlier, casts some doubt. The New Deal did succeed in coping with the Depression emergency, which might have brought down the whole system, but the system's problems were preserved along with it.

Far greater doubt about reform arises not from lag, but from the shallowness of the New Deal's accomplishments and its failure to follow through. Such radical efforts as redistribution of income, greater public ownership and planning, and programs aimed at improving the quality of life were soon abandoned. The evils that had crept into the American political system—urban disenfranchisement, disenfranchisement of blacks, gerrymandering, bosses and undemocratic political conventions, oligarchical control of Congress, and newspaper domination of the channels of public opinion—were all left to grow worse. The black was allowed to remain in his outcast status. The tendency of American culture to crass and garish materialism was not checked. It is true that the period of reform was brief and shortly interrupted by international events; Dr. New Deal became Dr. Win-the-War. But it is clear that the New Deal never touched the deeper problems of American life, which continued to grow worse all through the 1930's.

A crucial test of the New Deal is how it dealt with the fundamental problems of industrialism. With respect to power, it is apparent that the reforms did not roll back private power. Instead, they sought to require that private power now be exercised according to standards set by the legislatures as well as standards set by the corporations. The legislative standards were those of "reasonableness": only reasonable prices, or reasonable restraints of trade. But technology and corporate power, over the long run, do not have to be *un*reasonable to do their work. Unreasonableness was the hallmark of the early buccaneers. In the long run, technology had to be reasonable, and thus curbs on human unreason were in aid of the long-run assumption of power by more efficient organizations. Neither the New Deal reforms nor the earlier Progressive reforms restored any power to individuals, or limited the power that could be applied against individuals. Originally, individuals lost power to private organizations. What the reforms did, so far as individuals were concerned, was to take some of that lost power and turn it over to "public" organizations—government, labor unions, farmers' groups. Nothing came back to the people. If anything, the public organizations gained greater power over individuals than the private organizations had held previously. And the private power remained, in addition. It was regulated, but, subject to regulation, it still was there. What the reform assumed was that *its* power would be "good" for individuals, whereas the previous power had been "bad."

The New Deal furthered the creation of a hierarchical, elitist society whose principles contrasted with those of democracy and equality. Public and private government were seen as the province of the "best" and "ablest" and "most expert" or "professional" men, the most knowledgeable, the best educated, the specialists, and above all, the lawyers, who were thought of as the "social engineers" or "policy scientists" who manned the centers of administration. In government and in business, planning and "rational allocation of resources" became key ideas, placing controls on the consumer market. Legislative and judicial "interference" with administration was deplored, and the power of elected representatives and stockholders reduced. It was a transfer of power from the man in the street to the man from the *Harvard Law Review*—a transfer that had been taking place gradually for a long time, but now was accelerated, leaving the little man, the ordinary American, more a subject for the plans of others than an actual participant in his own destiny.

On the broader questions of technology and the effects of power, "good" as well as "bad," the New Deal was limited by its diagnosis. None of the great modern problems, such as loss of meaning, loss of community and self, dehumanization of environment, were in any way approached, except to encourage the trends toward making them worse. Assuming that American problems were due to abuse of the system, the New Deal did not question the system itself, nor respond to the darker side of the art of the 1930's. It believed that economic progress and quantitative advance could only be good; most of its rhetoric is about *more* of everything. A planned, rational America was the ideal, where technology would take the lead in creating a better life. But when the reform period of the New Deal was already over, John Dewey asked:

> What gain has been made in the matter of establishing conditions that give the mass of workers not only what is called "security" but also constructive interest in the work they do? What gain has been made in giving individuals, the great mass of individuals, an opportunity to find themselves and then to educate themselves for what they can best do in work which is socially useful and such as to give free play in development of themselves? . . . It is a matter of the state of existing occupations, of the whole set-up of productive work, of the structure of the industrial system . . . *

The New Deal and the earlier reformers did not, of course, set this task for themselves, but we may nevertheless observe that America's periods of reform, in spite of appearances, were in large measure periods of avoidance and inaction.

One accomplishment of the New Deal dwarfed all others: the creation of the public state. But this accomplishment must be assessed, not only in terms of how well it dealt with existing problems, but also in terms of what new problems it created, for any

---

* John Dewey, "The Economic Basis of the New Society" in *Intelligence and the Modern World*, New York: Random House, 1939. Reprinted with the permission of Joseph Ratner.

giant structure, never before known in America, was certain to have its own problems to add to those already in existence. The New Deal naturally gave little thought to the dangers of what it was so enthusiastically building, but we may at least raise some of the questions it failed to raise. What would be the long-range impact of the new public state on the working of the democratic process? How would democracy survive the rule of the expert? What would be the influence of regulation and licensing on personal liberty? How would administrative discretion and bureaucratic authority affect the rule of law? What would be the status of individuals in the new organizations, such as labor unions and the social security–welfare system? And how vulnerable was the structure to capture by special interests? Would the regulated become the regulators and use government machinery to help create restraints of trade? Would the new positive government become a grab bag for those seeking economic favors and special privileges?

Our retrospective of the New Deal may seem unduly harsh and unsympathetic, ignoring its many accomplishments, and blaming it for many problems which it never even undertook to solve. But our objective is not to make a just evaluation of the New Deal, but to discuss the role of reform in the making of the contemporary Corporate State. Our objective is also to see what might have been wrong with the underlying theory of reform. On that question, at least, we can offer some sympathy to the New Deal, for it is now clear how incredibly difficult it was and is to attempt to apply rational control and social self-protection to the chaotic forces of industrialism. There is the difficulty of diagnosis, the difficulty of getting prompt action once the diagnosis is made, the still greater difficulty of following through, the impossibility of conducting experiments, and the danger that solutions may give rise to problems of their own, perhaps even greater than the problems which called them forth. The New Deal was our first great attempt at social control; and if in large measure it failed, we can still put it down as a noble experiment, an improvement on the American habit of unreality.

But have we, up to now, offered an adequate explanation for the failures of the New Deal and for the dangerous structure it built? We have neglected the question of consciousness. What role did it play?

Every step the New Deal took encountered the massive, bitter opposition of Consciousness I people. They found their world changing beyond recognition, and instead of blaming the primary forces behind that change, they blamed the efforts at solving the problems. They totally lacked the sophistication necessary to see that a measure such as the Wagner Act might be redressing an existing oppression rather than creating oppression. The businessmen who were the most vocal in their opposition had a pathological hatred of the New Deal, a hatred so intense and personal as to defy analysis. Why this hatred, when the New Deal, in retrospect, seems to have saved the capitalist system? Perhaps because the New Deal intruded irrevocably upon their make-believe, problem-free world in which the pursuit of business gain and self-interest was imagined to be automatically beneficial to all of mankind, requiring of them no additional responsibility whatever. In any event, there was a large and politically powerful number of Americans who never accepted the New Deal even when it benefited them, and used their power whenever they could to cut it back.

What about the major supporters of the New Deal, most notably organized labor, city dwellers, and portions of the South? These are the groups whose support was gained through the catastrophe of the Great Depression. But how committed were they to the New Deal program as a whole? Looking back, we can see that each was committed only to its own interest, for which it then needed the help of government. The workers needed the Labor Board; the cities needed relief, housing, social security; the South needed the TVA, rural electrification, and farm subsidies. But none of these groups had abandoned an older picture of America save in the one particular that concerned them. Thus we have the spectacle, still to be seen today, of the western rancher who accepts federal aid for his cattle operations and federal aid for his grazing requirements, but bitterly opposes all social programs that do not concern him, and the philosophy that lies behind them. And those political allies of the New Deal, the blue-collar worker, the ethnic groups, the urban poor, were all waiting in line for their chance at the American dream, not for an assigned place in a new managerial state. When they got what they wanted and the Depression was a thing of the past, their enthusiasm for reform waned.

Nor was there any genuine radical consciousness to be found in America. The Communist Party was so tiny, so impotent, so burdened with irrelevant ideology, that it was without significance; nor did any minority, racial, or student group supply a base for radicalism. The New Deal really consisted of an alliance of interest groups, presided over by a narrow ridge of liberal intellectuals who were the main source of New Deal thinking, the only members of the whole alliance who had any general ideas about America.

Though the liberals were the mainstay of the New Deal, they were not only numerically weak, they were also weak in determination and consciousness. Soon after the New Deal got under way, there was a counterattack by the Right aimed at the New Deal's most outspoken members; the House Un-American Activities Committee and other Red hunters succeeded in hounding from the government many of those with the most energy and creative ideas. For the others, moderation was in order, plus a discreet move into lucrative private life. These liberals were bright and aggressive; the system as it stood promised them rich rewards, and they showed little inclination to take personal risks in order to press for more drastic reforms when, for them at least, the promised land was at hand. The war, by putting other issues to the fore, relieved them of any lingering sense of guilt over their prudence. Thirty years later, it is revealing to note what became of the New Dealers. Nearly all of them took jobs where they served the very interests which were the enemies against which the New Deal fought. Many became highly paid corporate lawyers, using their know-how to help their clients avoid attempts at public regulation. Many others served as executives of large corporations. They adopted the life-styles of wealth, power, and success. They became hostile to radicalism. If their adventure with the New Deal had been a combination of idealism, glamour, and ambition, it was ambition which proved to be the lasting element.

But quite apart from personal motives, the consciousness of the liberals had proved inadequate to the task. It was not merely that the New Deal was opposed by Consciousness I; the mind that was actually creating the New Deal fell short. The liberals never imagined how great were the obstacles they faced—the incredibly stubborn opposition of those they were trying to regulate, the lack of true understanding and participation by the workers, the dangers and weaknesses of the reform structure itself. And the liberals were not aware, either, of the degree of America's problems. They knew that much was wrong, but they did not feel it as the youth of today feel it, or see it as fully as it is seen today. They did not adequately sense the plight of the black man, the tragedy of the cities, the irrationality of production of luxuries amid the starvation of public services, the dangers of repression and war. They meant well, but they tried to cure America with half-measures and without personal risk to themselves. After the New Deal ended, the liberals lasted into the 1950's and 1960's, but their day was over.

The final lesson of the New Deal, then, is that social change cannot be accomplished without the support of an appropriate consciousness in the people. Mere political change, mere alterations in the law, in structure, or in government power, cannot accomplish basic reform. The New Deal was accepted as a doctor is accepted, in an hour of fear and need. But America retained its basic, almost childish refusal of serious responsibility, its lack of communal solidarity, and above all its myths. It wanted only to get on with the ball game.

What was the lasting product of these troubled years of disillusionment and reform? The theme that lingered beyond insecurity and beyond idealism was the theme of domination; these years had convinced much of America that its people must be placed under the control of something larger and more rational than individual self-restraint; that individual man must, for the good of all, become part of a system. This theme runs from Bellamy to FDR, from Mabuse to Portnoy, from the muckrakers to the young lawyers of the New Deal brain trust.

The lasting product of the New Deal era was not its humanism or idealism, but a new consciousness that believed primarily in domination and the necessity for living under domination. This consciousness, which grew out of reform, we have called Consciousness II. It is not accurate to call this consciousness "liberalism" or "reformism." Neither liberalism nor reformism were ever given a fair trial in America. Indeed, humanistic liberalism, with a program adequately conceived and followed through, might have given us a viable society for many years after the New Deal. Consciousness II was often associated with "liberalism," but that usage merely altered the meaning of the latter term. For the new consciousness "liberals" cared more about order than they did about liberty.

The New Deal also produced a lasting institutional product to go with Consciousness II—the public state. The hope behind this creation was that now public and private power, like the armies of two great nations, would balance each other, and the result would be containment of both, and safety for the individual. What the theory neglected was the possibility that the two kinds of power might join. And this is what did happen. The final tragedy of the reform movement is that the power it created was amalgamated with the private power already in existence, and with the now overwhelming and terrible power of technology, to form the inhuman structure in which we now live—the American Corporate State.

IV

CONSCIOUSNESS II

We turn to the consciousness that created the Corporate State—Consciousness II. It carried forward the pessimism of the industrial era and the optimism of reform into a new "realism" that described America in very different terms than those accepted by that part of the population who remained unshaken in Consciousness I and its version of the American dream. In contrast, Consciousness II saw an America where organization predominates, and the individual must make his way through a world directed by others.

Consciousness II began where the questioning of Consciousness I began. Thus, there were nineteenth-century reformers who had Consciousness II ideas, and each decade of the twentieth century brought increasing numbers to its ranks. There was much of Consciousness II in the leaders of the New Deal, as well as in the new breed of industrial and labor leaders of the 1930's and 1940's. We have made the arbitrary choice, however, of describing Consciousness II as a phenomenon of the post–World War II years; indeed, as a phenomenon of today, when it has become not merely an abstract set of principles or the values of a small elite group, but a way of life.

Consciousness II came into existence as a consequence of the disastrous failure of Consciousness I. In the twentieth century, Consciousness I had led to monstrous consequences: robber barons, business piracy, ruinous competition, unreliable products and false advertising, grotesque inequality, and the chaos of excessive individualism and lack of coordination and planning, leading to a gangster world.

For many persons, this chaos meant a profound insecurity and sense of powerlessness. In a mass, industrial society ungoverned by any law except self-interest, the individual became the plaything of circumstances and forces beyond his control. A lifetime of hard work could be wiped out by a business failure. The Great Depression brought the whole nation to the brink of disaster. In Germany and Italy, similar insecurity led to fascism. In America, it led to a breach in the existing consciousness, a turn away from individualism. A large number of people continued as Consciousness I, but another group began to develop a new consciousness.

To the newer consciousness, what the realities of the times seemed to demand was the organization and coordination of activity, the arrangement of things in a rational hierarchy of authority and responsibility, the dedication of each individual to training, work, and goals beyond himself. This seemed a matter of the utmost biological necessity; this way of life was what "had to be" if the society was to keep on functioning. Consciousness I sacrificed for individual good; now it seemed necessary to sacrifice for a common good. Discipline and hierarchy were seen as necessary because the society was not yet prepared to offer each person the kind of work he wanted or the chance to perform his work with a measure of independence.

How was the world experienced by the people of these uncertain times? One of our best insights comes from the German filmmakers. Industrialism came very late to Germany, and the transformation was so great that German artists saw what the change implied perhaps more clearly than it was seen in countries that had gradually grown used to industry, technology, and organization. In a series of films made in Germany or inspired by the German films, man was seen in the process of being remade as the slave of machines. His existence was dominated by the city and by vast and terrifying machinery, as Fritz Lang showed in *Metropolis* and *M.* Man died and was reborn as a robot or monster, a theme familiar to us in the Frankenstein and vampire films, beginning with Dreyer's *Vampyr*, and perhaps reaching its ultimate expression when a robot is made over into the form of the heroine of *Metropolis*, in a scene as beautiful and awe-inspiring as anything ever put onto film. In his new form, man was the hypnotized sleepwalker of *The Cabinet of Dr. Caligari*, or the servant of vampires in *Vampyr,* or the mechanical witch of *Metropolis,* controlled by a mastermind such as a sorcerer or the master criminal Dr. Mabuse, the subject of three films by Lang. Man became massman, walking in dreary, mechanical lock step and spending his working hours as a part of the machinery itself—the central vision of *Metropolis.* All the elements of culture that were anti-machine, such as magic, ritual, emotion, and Christianity, were sought and embraced by the German filmmakers, as they were also by the German expressionist painters, but these elements in their work looked to the past, while their vision of the machine-city saw the world that was coming.

American artists were not as aware of the machine, but some of them did sense the bleak world that was being created. Among those who saw it were James M. Cain and Raymond Chandler, who wrote novels of crime and violence set in southern California in the 1930's and 1940's. In *The Postman Always Rings Twice* and *Double Indemnity,* Cain told swift, brutal, sordid stories of crime in Los Angeles, in a setting where lust for money and sex had overtaken all other values. Cain's ideas received more thorough treatment in *Mildred Pierce,* a novel about a woman's search for security and respectability, in which she threads her lonely way through a materialistic wasteland, dominated by the vulgar, tawdry, and ambiguous symbols of the new America.

Raymond Chandler's detective novels, *The Big Sleep, Farewell My Lovely, The Lady in the Lake,* and *The High Window,* were set in an even darker and more grim universe, where no man could trust another, every man (and woman) had his price, his racket, his secret suspicions, and where the only way to exist was by one's own strength and absolutely alone, relying only on a gun, one's wits, expecting nothing from the world but the satisfaction of the game itself, and at the end of the day a gray moment of silent emptiness.

The people and the places in Chandler's universe were grotesque, evil, decaying, ugly. It was a world without beauty, as claustrophobic as the dark world of Dickens' *Bleak House*, without horizon or sky in any direction, without the redeeming warmth of a single brother human being. What could one do but be like Chandler's hero, tough, professional, cynical? The city had become an alien place, not a source of comfort, satisfaction, companionship, and healing. Chandler may not have recognized that this was the city of the machine, but he saw its inhumanity.

The demand that man adapt himself to the imperatives of the new technological state was expressed unforgettably in James Jones' novel *From Here to Eternity*. The hero of the book is Prewitt, a career soldier in the American army. A boy from the harsh mining country of Kentucky, he enlisted when he was seventeen, and the one thing in life he really wanted was to be a bugler. But the army wanted him to box, and wanted him to continue boxing even after he had accidentally blinded a friend; thus Prew found himself in conflict with a great organization. His friends counseled him to "play the game" the army's way, but his stubborn independence led to his being labeled a "bolshevik," and eventually he landed in the stockade, where men were broken and beaten with a brutality like that of the Nazi concentration camps. Out of the stockade, he went to town, killed the stockade sergeant in a knife fight, and stayed AWOL with a girl while his own wounds healed. When Pearl Harbor was bombed, he wanted, more than anything else, to rejoin his company, to resume the profession of soldiering that was, despite everything, his life. But he was shot by military police as he attempted to return. The book ends with army life continuing as before; the army destroys the individual but he cannot live apart from it. The times are past when a man can be independent of the system.

Given these realities, the individual had no choice but to idealize the life of the professional, the life of the man for whom meaning derives from the function he performs for society, whose satisfaction lies in how well he performs his job. It is remarkable how even those cinema sagas celebrating the American past, like *High Noon, Shane, The Gunfighter,* and *El Dorado*, actually express the realities of the professional life. The hero is not a farmer or a rancher, not a man with goals of his own, but a figure who seems weary, tired of life, and merely anxious to be left alone. Like the professional, he comes into being at the call of need; he attains his personal reality by rising to the demands of danger as a professional gun. When the challenge is gone he cannot join the people he has helped; he disappears alone, without having found anything; a man who lived only for the job to be done.

Behind the sacrifice of individuality to organization, there was a deep element of fear. The man who failed to play the game would be destroyed. In Raoul Walsh's film *White Heat* (1949) James Cagney plays a gangster hero whose sole object in life is to satisfy the ambition planted in him by his mother—

to "get to the top." He is hard, tough, and strong, but he is defeated—not by man, but by science, by organizations, by machines. From the beginning to the end of the film, law enforcement organizations use scientific tests, psychology, a hidden radio, a radio-tracking system, and finally a telescopic-sight rifle against Cagney; significantly, the one man he trusts and befriends turns out to be a police informer. Cagney's own triumph comes when, although he dies, he is able to destroy a great industrial complex by fire and explosion.

The modern man's fear of the system in which he lives was seen with extraordinary clarity in Philip Roth's novel *Portnoy's Complaint*, perhaps the finest single portrayal in America of the struggle to adjust to the organization-world. Portnoy's "complaint" is that he finds that his own inner impulses, which he perceives with exceptional honesty, are in irreconcilable conflict with the role that society expects him to play. His mother wants him to survive and excel in society, to "be good," and he does so by pursuing a brilliant career that makes him one of Mayor Lindsay's aides. But the career is propelled by the central fact of his life: that he expects love only for what he accomplishes in society's (his mother's) terms. Good behavior, high grades in school, the editorship of the *Columbia Law Review*, fighting for liberal causes, all bring praise. But even the slightest fall from the designated path threatens exposure and ruin. Even the slightest infraction can destroy him completely. He is constantly living under the fear of some fatal disease brought on by disobeying his mother's warnings; the metaphor of death suggests what will happen to those who do what Prewitt did and fight the system. But Portnoy lacks the courage of Prewitt, or even of Chandler's private eye. Portnoy knows only too well that there is no existence for losers, no reality except the reality of society, that the world is filled with the incredible dangers and perils that his parents warned him about. Life is a desperate competitive footrace; to fall even a step behind is to forego all hope of keeping up. Every decision is a crisis, for any mistake can be fatal. It is necessary to dress properly, to follow all the rules, to placate authority whenever possible. Any slip will be irrevocable. Below the surface of success is an abyss where one can fall, where one becomes a non-person. Courage is out of the question; it is not possible to fight the system because the system is the source of one's existence; the day of individual independence is over, and only one's desires, covered now by guilt and shame, remain. *Portnoy's Complaint* is a Jewish novel only in the sense that the ghetto Jews were long familiar with the terrors of an alien world. It is a psychiatric novel only in the sense that it sees into the internal conflicts that external reality produces.

What the man or woman of the 1930's and thereafter experienced was a world in which there was no life for the individual by himself, no way for him to make an independent search for self, no existence apart from the system. Portnoy's parents had told him the truth about the world.

The categories of people in the general area of Consciousness II are very diverse, including businessmen (new type), liberal intellectuals, the educated professionals and technicians, middle-class suburbanites, labor union leaders, Gene McCarthy supporters, blue-collar workers with newly purchased homes, old-line leftists, and members of the Communist Party, U.S.A. Classic examples of Consciousness II are the Kennedys and the editorial page of *The New York Times.* It is the consciousness of "liberalism," the consciousness largely appealed to by the Democratic Party, the consciousness of "reform." Most political battles in America are still fought between Consciousness I and Consciousness II. Consciousness II believes that the present American crisis can be solved by greater commitment of individuals to the public interest, more social responsibility by private business, and, above all, by more affirmative government action—regulation, planning, more of a welfare state, better and more rational administration and management.

Behind a façade of optimism, Consciousness II has a profoundly pessimistic view of man. It sees man in Hobbesian terms; human beings are by nature aggressive, competitive, power-seeking; uncivilized man is a jungle beast. Freud took a somewhat similar view in *Civilization and Its Discontents.* Hence the vital need for law: without law we would all be at one anothers' throats; "only the law makes us free." Consciousness II is deeply cynical about human motives and good intentions, and it doubts that man can be much improved. It is this philosophy that helps to explain the great emphasis on society and institutions: these are designed to do the best possible job of administering the doubtful and deficient raw material that is "human nature." Believing that the best and most hopeful part of man is his gift of reason, Consciousness II seeks to design a world in which reason will prevail.

At the heart of Consciousness II is the insistence

that what man produces by means of reason—the state, laws, technology, manufactured goods—constitutes the true reality. Just as Consciousness I centers on the fiction of the American Adam, the competitive struggle, and the triumph of the virtuous and strong individual, so Consciousness II rests on the fiction of logic and machinery; what it considers unreal is nature and subjective man. Consciousness II believes more in the automobile than in walking, more in the decision of an institution than in the feelings of an individual, more in a distant but rational goal than in the immediate present.

One of the central aspects of Consciousness II is an acceptance of the priority of institutions, organizations, and society and a belief that the individual must tie his destiny to something of this sort, larger than himself, and subordinate his will to it. "Ask what you can do for your country (and corporation)," says the voice of Consciousness II. He is an "institution man." He sees his own life and career in terms of progress within society and within an institution. An established hierarchy and settled procedures are seen as necessary and valuable. Achievement by character and hard work is translated into achievement in terms of a meritocracy of education, technical knowledge, and position. When he speaks of the vitality and challenges of his life, this is likely to be in terms of "his part" in the challenges of organized society; a young lawyer may actually spend most of his time doing dull legal research in the library, but he feels that his firm represents important clients and issues, and is involved in exciting controversies; it is not his work in a phenomenological sense but the significance of his work that is important to him. He relies on institutions to certify the meaning and value of his life, by rewarding accomplishment and conferring titles, office, respect, and honor. He also looks to institutions to provide personal security in terms of tenure, salary, and retirement benefits. In place of the continuity of life formerly supplied by religion and family, he sees his work living after him in institutional terms; "this organization is his monument."

Belief in the reality of society is carried into political philosophy. Government regulation of private activities, including business, is considered necessary and desirable; likewise government should help individuals and protect them from the risks of an industrial society. Consciousness II insists that "individual interests" are subject to "the public interest." Thus a typical *New York Times* editorial will argue that "private" interests such as the desire of hospital employees for a raise, of oil companies to maintain prices, or protesting students to air their grievances, must be subordinated to "the public interest." A similar philosophy is a strong part of our current constitutional law. In this sense the "liberalism" of Felix Frankfurter, the communism of Lenin, and the patriotism of a policeman's benevolent association are all alike; they insist on the primary reality of the State, not the individual. Consciousness II does not accept any "absolute" liberty for the individual; rather, it regards all individual liberty as subject to overriding state interest.

Consciousness II is deeply committed to reform. We can thank its reformist tendencies for changes in the criminal law, for social security, the movement against racial discrimination, regulation of business, government economic planning, internationalism, an end of corruption in government, public projects like the TVA, collective bargaining, and improvement of work conditions, and so on down a long, honorable, and admirable list. These reforms help to define Consciousness II because they may be seen as part of a battle with the past. Much of the energy of Consciousness II has gone into battling the evils that resulted from Consciousness I—prejudice, discrimination, irrationality, self-seeking, isolationism, localism, outworn traditions, and superstitions; Consciousness II has worn itself out fighting the know-nothingism of an earlier America. Consciousness II believes optimistically in the possibility of social progress (as distinguished from individual progress, which it doubts). Confront men of Consciousness II with any list of evils and the response is cheerfulness: they know what measures can be taken, they see signs of improvement, and they compare the present favorably with the evils of the past which have been overcome. Even today they still believe America's problems can be solved by pushing ahead with material progress, equality, a greater public commitment to social welfare, to rebuilding cities, and to revised domestic priorities.

Consciousness II believes in the central ideology of technology, the domination of man and environment by technique. Accordingly, science, technology, organization, and planning are prime values. Different groups within Consciousness II might disagree —aircraft executives might think the nation should be dominated by machine and computer technology, while professors of English, horrified by this, would think the world should be dominated by rationally critical thought—but the idea of domination is common to both, although neither would necessarily acknowledge that similarity. Throughout all of Consciousness II runs the theme that society will function best if it is planned, organized, rationalized, administered. Thus the Nixon view is that government is a problem in management; a professor of law would see the function of law as "social ordering," and a social scientist would see such problems as traffic jams, air pollution, or inadequate public housing as failures to apply planning and rationality. Consciousness II believes in *control*. Even the broadest civil libertarian outlook is placed in a framework of procedures, supervision, and limits. Consciousness II deeply fears what man would be like, and what masses of people would be like, if not placed under the ascendancy of reason.

There is in all of this a rejection of unfettered diversity and unresolved conflict. Liberalism, of course, supports conflict as a means to the attainment of the greatest possible rationality (the truth of the market place) and it supports pluralism as a means to attain a balance in society. But the emphasis is on the solving of problems, the "cure" of conflict. J. Huizinga, in *The Waning of the Middle Ages,* describes the medieval world as one in which extreme contrasts, inconsistencies, and violent conflict were not "settled," but lived side by side, lending a color to life that order cannot provide. Consciousness II wants conflict-resolution; it is deeply procedural because procedures help get things "settled"; its paradise would be one possessing an appropriate tribunal or authority where problems are "solved." In *Why Are We in Vietnam?* Norman Mailer calls Consciousness II "direct current." Mailer is pleading for "alternating current," for "dialectic," for a world of extremes. Consciousness II, although nominally "liberal," has the potential to become repressive. It welcomes every point of view and tolerates every idea, but it wants everything expressed through proper channels and procedures; it wants no interference with rationalities; it wants no disruption of orderly processes. "Freedom" must not destroy the underlying order that enables all types of freedom to flourish in orderly fashion.

Consciousness II believes in a meritocracy of ability and accomplishment, the object of which is to promote excellence. Rejecting the rigid structures, caste systems, and hereditary aristocracies of the past, it seeks to open society to universal achievement. In this it is much like Consciousness I, but there are differences: II is freer of prejudices and irrationality than I, and II would place the meritocracy within an institutional framework. As Consciousness II might conceive of the meritocracy, the society would be so structured as to produce, encourage, and reward those forms of excellence which are socially valuable: the excellent medical man, the excellent lawyer, the excellent scientist. Consciousness II believes in the uncommon man; the man of special abilities and effort, the man who is intelligent, sophisticated, exciting, and powerful. It believes that this form of "merit" can and should be judged by society, using standards that are external and rational; there is an objective difference between an excellent engineer and an incompetent one. Consciousness II believes that this merit is both an inborn capacity and a moral quality. Since it is a moral quality, or a virtue, it furnishes the appropriate basis for a "democratic aristocracy" in which society's "best" people—judged by rational standards—receive the rewards of money, status, security, and respect. The meritocracy is therefore structured so as to provide an equal opportunity for all at the starting point, but it rejects the idea of equality thereafter, for such equality is at war with excellence. Consciousness II people are tremendously concerned with one another's comparative status, and they often speak of others in terms of their abilities or lack of abilities; he is "able," he is "not very able," he is "first rate," he is a "C student," he is the "executive type," he is "plodding and unimaginative." There is an abstract equality of opportunity, but not an equality of individual human beings.

Consciousness II is thus profoundly antipopulist and, in a large sense, antidemocratic. It is no accident that the most successful Consciousness II individuals surround themselves, not with vulgar material display, but with the signs of elegant style and taste; it is no accident that they show an impatient, intolerant, and disdainful attitude toward individual members of the very groups they are "trying to help"—the less intelligent, the ill-educated, and above all the blue-collar "boob." For "reason" has led Consciousness II to believe in an elitist society—with never a doubt that the standards by which the elite is determined are the correct ones: utility to the technological society. The absolute worth of each individual is, to Consciousness II, a mere religious doctrine, having no application in reality.

One of the central beliefs of Consciousness II concerns work. The belief is that the individual should do his best to fit himself into a function that is needed by society, subordinating himself to the requirements of the occupation or institution that he has chosen. He feels this as a duty, and is willing to make "sacrifices" for it. He may have an almost puritanical willingness to deny his own feelings. Self-sacrifice is regarded as a virtue for two reasons. First, because it serves a higher purpose, that of the state, organization, or profession. Second, because it serves to advance the individual and his family in terms of the rewards that society can offer.

The Consciousness II man thus adopts, as his *personal* values, the structure of standards and rewards set by his occupation or organization. We are not now speaking of the purposes which the organization is designed to achieve, but what the organization defines as standards of individual success. Thus the individual directs his activities toward such goals as a promotion, a raise in salary, a better office, respect and commendation by his colleagues, a title, "recognition" by his profession. Beginning in school, he measures himself and his achievements by the tests, examinations, grades, and other formal hurdles of life. He becomes a projectile, ready to be set in motion by outside energies. His motivations are constantly directed toward the future, because it is not inner satisfaction that moves him, but something extrinsic to himself.

In one sense he is self-sacrificing, but in another sense his life is dedicated to personal success, for having adopted the goals set for him, the Consciousness II individual is fiercely determined to satisfy his ambitions within these terms. Indeed, he often seems to keep pushing beyond rational limits; the exterior goals consume the inner ones, and he has little time left for more intimate personal values. He becomes an oppressive person who does not enjoy himself while at work, who does not seem to have any personal distance from the hurdles that have been set for him. In some cases this even leads the individual to unethical or illegal behavior, which he slips into because it all seems to be part of "playing the game."

With respect to the other values of the organization, its reasons-for-being, Consciousness II may either adopt these without question, or be cynical about them. That is, a lawyer may believe that the companies he represents are doing good in the world, or he may be indifferent to whether they do good or evil, regarding himself as a craftsman or professional, who serves but does not judge. He is a "hired knife-thrower." In either case, he renounces any personal judgment concerning the effect his work has on society, either accepting the claim of the organization or limiting himself to instrumental values such as those of being skillful at his own particular art. His dedication to personal success and to instrumental values may make him extremely zealous in pushing his organization's objectives; he makes, in public at least, a wholly committed salesman of his company's products, enforcer of the law, or advocate of some public policy, and his zeal is not mitigated by the intrusion of any inner values. This is the doctrine of "doing good" by being "tough" and "hardheaded"; it is also the doctrine that "reality" is the future goal that is being pursued and not the things that are at present being done.

A prime characteristic of the Consciousness II person is his disclaimer of personal responsibility for what his organization does or for what his society does. He pictures himself as a person without absolute or transcendental values; he cannot make a personal judgment; he must accept the premises of society. He cites the compartmentalization of his work, his lack of general authority. He says that he must defer to the judgments of experts in other areas where he is not competent; if his company is making a dangerous product, that is a matter within the special competence of Product Design; if his country is making a war, that is the responsibility of political and military experts. It is not for him to "take a stand"; he doesn't know enough; it would be unprofessional. But this is not only a refusal to be responsible, it is a refusal to think independently. For example, lawyers talk about the rationality and equality of the law, but they simply do not get outside the accepted assumptions to think about how the law operates as an instrument of one class in society against another. Accordingly, the public values of Consciousness II can stray far from reality; they simply do not question the assumptions, however unreal, of the system in which they function.

Like Consciousness I, Consciousness II sees life in terms of a fiercely competitive struggle for success. The difference lies in the means of struggle and the terms of success, for with Consciousness II these are defined by organizational or institutional values. This difference lends an air of gentility or public spiritedness to the struggle by Consciousness II. He can claim, and can convince himself, that his struggle is for something other than pure selfishness. His efforts produce good for the corporation or institution, good for the public interest, good for his fellow man, for the more he helps his institution, the more "self-sacrificing" he is, the more he helps himself to get ahead. Of course, this was very much the theory of the Consciousness I struggle too, but in practice the latter was pretty well discredited, while the public-good theory of struggle seems to be affirmed by everything we see around us. And there is a contrast of style as well; Consciousness II does not celebrate his own success with ostentation but with sophistication. Nevertheless, in Consciousness II the struggle does show through from time to time; an excess of zeal, a lack of nicety about means, or a cold and impersonal attitude, combined with driving energy, reveal the true state of things. Below the surface, as with the man of an earlier era, is the jungle, the void, the fear of failure. But the void below the meritocracy is far worse than being "at the bottom of the heap" in earlier days; everything that makes the Consciousness II man feel his own reality is lost. His friends are made through his work; they are unlikely to find anything in common with him after his downfall. In a world where men are recognized only by their credentials, to lose credentials is to cease being a human being. Thus it is that some of the most successful men of our times are also among the most insecure; they have to go on proving themselves as if there were cracks in their stylish floors through which they could still catch glimpses of the abyss.

In sum, the new man's insecurity is greater than that of the old. The new man is tied to uncertain forms and forces over which he feels little control and may at any time be victimized by an impersonal "system"; moreover, when the new man loses, he seems to have less in the way of personal strength —roots, perhaps—to fall back on. He lacks a sense of self that could be sustained despite rejection by the system. And he lacks a community of friends who can be counted on to support him with their affection despite the judgment of society.

Because it classifies and judges individuals according to generalized standards, Consciousness II often fails to see behind the classifications to the unique individual. Upon meeting a person, the first thought is to classify him, the second thought is to judge him, and the third is to find the best way to deal with him. The difference between Consciousness I and II can be felt immediately across a lunch table; I is observant of the particular person who is opposite; II pays almost no attention, and is indifferent to most personal cues and signs of personality. II's conversation, unless he has some particular goal, would be pretty much the same regardless of who was sitting opposite.

Dependence on the meritocracy struggle makes Consciousness II, despite all of his liberal-reformist convictions, deeply cautious and profoundly conservative. He can fight for reform just so long as the fight is in the same direction that organized society is going; beginning in the 1950's he could fight racial discrimination, after 1967 he could oppose the Vietnam War, in 1969 he was for "revised priorities," but he was still following the direction of his organization and of society. And insisting on the use of accepted procedures, he makes sure that nothing he says or does will be perceived by his organization as a threat to its own power. Consciousness II is in favor of many reforms, but he will not jeopardize his own status to fight for them; he will not put his own body on the line.

Between the values of his working life and those of his home life Consciousness II draws a strict line. His home life is characterized by many values which are contrary to those of his job; here he may be gentle, human, playful; here he may deplore what the organized part of society is doing. He is made sick by pollution of water and air, denounces dehumanization in organizations, scorns those who are motivated solely by institutional goals; but these values appear within a closely guarded shelter of privateness. Consciousness II puts all his earnings into an individual burrow for himself and his family; he prefers owning a private home at a ski resort to living at a ski lodge; he wants a private summer house at the beach. This privateness and the "good" values that go with it seem to be related. What Consciousness II does is to "buy out" of the system. Taking no personal responsibility for the evils of society, he shelters himself from them in a private enclave, and from that sanctuary allows his "real" values a carefully limited expression. He does not risk himself or his family by this process. His children get "all the advantages" that he can give them in life's struggle. He does not have to live with his own workvalues.

Thus a crucial aspect of Consciousness II is a profound schizophrenia, a split between his working and his private self. It is this split that sometimes infuriates his children when they become of college age, for they see it as hypocrisy or selling out. But it is schizophrenia, not hypocrisy. The individual has two roles, two lives, two masks, two sets of values. It cannot be said, as is true of the hypocrite, that one self is real and the other false. These two values simply coexist; they are part of the basic definition of "reality"; the "reality" of Consciousness II is that there is a "public" and a "private" man. Neither the man at work nor the man at home is the whole man; it is impossible to know, talk to, or confront the whole man, for that wholeness is precisely what does not exist. The only thing that is real is two separate men.

This strange split, between the man who privately and secretly does good, and the man who publicly follows what organization demands, forms the subject of Kurt Vonnegut's novel *Mother Night*. An American is recruited by U.S. Army Intelligence to pose as a Nazi propaganda broadcaster during the war, publicly broadcasting hate while secretly transmitting signals giving information to the U.S. But after the war the hero finds it is his public self that has become real. The great crime of our times, says Vonnegut, was to do too much good secretly, too much harm openly.

Because of his lack of wholeness, because of his enforced playing of roles and subjection to outside standards, the consciousness of a Consciousness II person becomes vulnerable to outside manipulation. The individual has no inner reality against which to test what the outside world tells him is real. And the Corporate State does not ignore this vulnerability. As we have already shown, the Corporate State needs to administer, to the maximum degree possible, the working and consuming (home) lives of its people. It can do this by rule and organization, but it is far more effective to administer consciousness; no force is needed, no police, and no resistance is encountered. The optimum administrative state is one that administers consciousness, and as Herbert Marcuse shows us in *One-Dimensional Man*, the American Corporate State has gone a long way in this direction.

The apparatus for consciousness creation and manipulation is vast and formidable. We start with the entire advertising industry, which deliberately sets out to influence the values and wants of the people it reaches. The mass media are perhaps an even more important factor; by showing us a way of life, they insist on a particular picture of reality, and by creating that picture of outside events known as "news" they further affect reality. Government makes other direct efforts to influence consciousness, the most important of which is compulsory education. Perhaps the greatest influence of all is the culture and environment that society creates. In the aggregate, the forces working to create consciousness are overwhelming. And it should not be supposed that these forces are undirected. They are directed in at least two ways. First, by what is deliberately excluded. For example, many attitudes, points of view, and pictures of reality cannot get shown on television; this includes not only political ideas, but also the strictly non-political, such as a real view of middle-class life in place of the cheerful comedies one usually sees. Secondly, some views of reality are heavily subsidized while others are not. A much-publicized example of this was the CIA subsidy of certain student organizations: this was explained as aberrational when in fact subsidy of existing consciousness-creating forces is the rule and not the exception. The state does not wish to leave consciousness to chance, and nothing is more subsidized in our society than commercial advertising itself. Given a people who are vulnerable and a machinery with this power, the consequence is that much of Consciousness II is "false consciousness," a consciousness imposed by the state for its own purposes.

False consciousness is most readily described in terms of a lower-middle-class family, one which is just beginning to enjoy the material benefits of society. This is the family whose wants are most vulnerable to manipulation by television: the expensive home appliances, the new car, the boat, the vicarious world of sports. And this is the family where the "falsity" is most apparent; they "see" the countryside in a speeding car, tear up a fragile lake with a power boat, stand in long lines for "pleasures." It is also the family with the most easily manipulated political consciousness. They have been convinced that communism is trying to destroy America, that the Cold War is necessary, that the nation's arms-space-highway priorities are right, that welfare recipients are freeloaders.

Let us imagine a young, attractive couple, both college educated, with a home and several children, he with a profession or executive position in some organization. Their house is furnished in good taste; there are antiques and simple, fine modern things, the art includes some striking original prints and drawings; there are plenty of books. They have small dinner parties with exceptionally good food, wine, and conversation. They love the out-of-doors, ski in the winter, play tennis, and enjoy a small sailboat in the summer (they do all of these things very well), and manage to travel to some off-beat place each year. They read a lot, are interested in politics, are strongly modern in their views, enjoy good movies, music and plays, spend time with their children, have many friends. What is wrong with this picture?

What is "wrong" is clearly not in the interests and activities themselves; any of these things could be part of a true culture or true consciousness. How then have we the right to suggest that with our young couple all of their living is false? Marx and Marcuse distinguish between those needs which are a product of a person's authentic self, and those which are imposed from the outside by society. Why does an individual ski? Is it based on self-knowledge, or on a lack of self-knowledge, on advertising, and other pressures from society? If the latter, then the activity will not really satisfy the self, or enable the self to grow. The activity will have an essential emptiness, even though the person doing it may "think" he enjoys it. We can see many obvious examples of this type of false consciousness in America today, from the unathletic secretary who risks life and limb to ski on an occasional weekend, to the man in the Nehru jacket, turtleneck, or sideburns, to "That Cosmopolitan Girl" whose "favorite magazine" tells her what to cook, wear, and think. Some of what our young couple do may thus be simply a consequence of these imposed standards; they may be just another television couple trying to live the life pictured by the tube. Although much of our culture is indeed that and no more, there is more involved; the falseness of the picture goes deeper.

Our young couple are role-players. They have an image of what is fitting to their roles. And in choosing the activities and interests that make up their life, they are choosing from sources outside themselves;

they are choosing from a preexisting assortment of activities which complement, harmonize with, or add to the role-picture. Their choices need not come out of a popular magazine. They can come out of a sense that a young lawyer has *a*) political interests, *b*) cultural interests, *c*) likes sports, *d*) does things that are offbeat and in good taste. The selection of particular interests and activities does not matter so much. There is a curious interchangeability among them. There is the suspicion that our young couple would like Acapulco just as much as Aspen, camping just as much as sailing, playing the violin just as much as playing the recorder. And each activity also has a similarity of limits—in a sense, they are all blind alleys. Whether it is cooking or tennis or reading, it must be kept within bounds, not permitted to continue expanding until it takes up more than a just proportion. There is a limit to the commitment. Will the young lawyer become a ski bum? Will he sail around the world? That is not part of the picture. And the activities are not integrated into a whole life; like the dichotomy between working life and home life, they have separate existences. All of the young couple's activities have the quality of separateness from self, of fitting some pattern—a pattern already known and only waiting to be fulfilled.

But we are not yet at the heart of the matter. Any experience, no matter why it is entered into, or with what lack of self-knowledge, still has some potential for self-discovery; a person can try Mozart or skiing for all the wrong reasons and yet have something happen to him in consequence. No—there is a deeper falsity in all of the different interests and activities that comprise the life of Consciousness II. It is that not enough happens to our young couple as a result of any experience they have.

If there is one characteristic that is shared by all the different groups we have called Consciousness II —aircraft employees, old leftists, young doctors, Kennedy men, suburban housewives—it is the insistence on being competent and knowledgeable, on having "already been there." The aircraft worker, if he is a weekend camper, knows all about boots, camping equipment, maps, trails, and weather. The young lawyer's sophisticated wife converses about Camus, *The New York Review of Books*, and Mozart at a dinner party, and she speaks with the same knowledge and assurance that the aircraft worker has in his own area of interest. Her husband is an *excellent* tennis player or skier. The professor of law *knows all about* the latest theory of pluralism and the latest development in mergers; he seems to listen at a cocktail party but really does not; there is nothing for him to learn. Mention sex, restaurants, travel, everybody knows all about them. One can't tell them anything; they adamantly resist and belittle any new information or experience.

At social gatherings, the conversation reveals all of this clearly. Sometimes it is a display of what the speaker knows. At other times two people agree on what they know—"we understand" the subtleties of skiing or tennis, they say to each other. There may be an argument about who knows the most. But rarely is there someone who will admit to being overwhelmed by something totally new. Indeed, the key idea is found in the phrase "will admit," as if having one's mind blown were something to be ashamed of instead of something to be happy about. Rarely, then, is there someone who is unprotected and undefended, unprepared for anything that may happen.

Consciousness II has been convinced that man's needs are best met by trying to *dominate* experience rather than being subject to experience. It insists that "real" experience is that which is dominated, not that which comes to the individual who is unguarded and open. It is the ethic of control, of technology, of the rational intellect. But when experience is classified or analyzed, it is also reduced, just as it is reductive to classify a person. When experience is dominated, it has no impact. One learns nothing new, feels nothing new; the sources of life have been dried up; there is a sadness and sterility to Consciousness II. It is like a person whose life is busily scheduled; nothing is permitted to *happen to him;* the whole day proceeds as expected and planned. Consciousness II people are busy people in this sense. The man to whom something can happen must be ready to be diverted from his course and thoughts. A camping trip is full of potential for experience. There may be a sudden storm, the food may have been forgotten, the party may decide to hike all night by flashlight and sleep all day. But nothing can happen on a camping trip with too-competent people. They can take care of any event. Consciousness I also takes pride in competence, ability, and knowledge. But in the American innocent, from Billy Budd to Marshal Dillon, from "just plain folks" to Andrew Carnegie, there always remained a dimension of reverence; many were genuinely religious, for one thing. The camping journals of Consciousness I people sound embarrassingly sentimental and florid, but the quality of wonder is still there.

All that we have said concerning Consciousness II may perhaps best be summarized in terms of its relationship to reality. Consciousness II came into existence as a response to the realities of organization and technology. But it pushed these values too far; it came to believe that the individual has no *existence* apart from his work and his relationship to society. Without his career, without his function, he would be a non-person; hence the terrible fear of failure in the competitive struggle; below the meritocracy is an abyss where people have ceased to exist altogether. Thus there is a loss of a sense of the reality of self, apart from the way in which society judges self. And because of this, a sense of reality about organizations and society is lost as well. No matter what systems, structures, and values they produce, even mass destruction through war, they pass unchallenged as "reality"; the individual has no subjective standard of reality with which to evaluate or oppose the purported reality of efficiency, technological progress, or megadeaths based on some doctrine of political necessity.

Consciousness II is the victim of a cruel deception. It has been persuaded that the richness, the satisfactions, the joy of life are to be found in power, success, status, acceptance, popularity, achievements, rewards, excellence, and the rational, competent mind. It wants nothing to do with dread, awe, wonder, mystery, accidents, failure, helplessness, magic. It has been deprived of the search for self that only these experiences make possible. And it has produced a society that is the image of its own alienation and impoverishment.

V

ANATOMY OF THE CORPORATE STATE

What is the nature of the social order within which we all live? Why are we so powerless? Why does our state seem impervious to democratic or popular control? Why does it seem to be insane, destroying both self and environment for the sake of principles that remain obscure? Our present social order is so contrary to anything we have learned to expect about a government or a society that its structure is almost beyond comprehension. Most of us, including our political leaders and those who write about politics and economics, hold to a picture that is entirely false. Yet children are not entirely deceived, teen-agers understand some aspects of the society very well, and artists, writers and especially moviemakers sometimes come quite close to the truth. The corporate state is an immensely powerful machine, ordered, legalistic, rational, yet utterly out of human control, wholly and perfectly indifferent to any human values.

It is hard to say exactly when our society assumed this shape; it came on slowly, imperceptibly to those living with it day by day. The major symptoms started appearing after the conclusion of World War II, and especially in the 1950's. Those symptoms, such as the Cold War, a trillion dollars spent for defense, destruction of environment, production of unneeded goods, were not merely extensions of the familiar blunders and corruption of America's past. They were of a different order of magnitude, they were surrounded by a growing atmosphere of unreality, and they were all an integral part of a seemingly rational and legal system. The stupidities and thefts of the Grant era were not insane; they were human departures from a reasonably human standard. In the 1950's the norm itself—the system itself—became deranged.

Our present system has gone beyond anything that could properly be called the creation of capitalism or imperialism or a power elite. That, at least, would be a human shape. Of course a power elite does exist and is made rich by the system, but the elite are no longer in control, they are now merely taking advantage of forces that have a life of their own. Nor is our system a purely technological society, although technology has increasingly supplied the basis for our choices and superseded other values. What we have is technology, organization, and administration out of control, running for their own sake, but at the same time subject to manipulation and profiteering by the power interests of our society for their own non-human ends. And we have turned over to this system the control and direction of everything—the natural environment, our minds, our lives. Other societies have had bad systems, but have endured because a part of life went on outside the system. We have turned over everything, rendered ourselves powerless, and thus allowed mindless machinery to become our master.

The American Corporate State today can be thought of as a single vast corporation, with every person as an involuntary member and employee. It consists primarily of large industrial organizations, plus nonprofit institutions such as foundations and the educational system, all related to the whole as divisions to a business corporation. Government is only a part of the state, but government coordinates it and provides a variety of needed services. The Corporate State is a complete reversal of the original American ideal and plan. The State, and not the market or the people or any abstract economic laws, determines what shall be produced, what shall be consumed, and how it shall be allocated. It determines, for example, that railroads shall decay while highways flourish; that coal miners shall be poor and advertising executives rich. Jobs and occupations in the society are rigidly defined and controlled, and arranged in a hierarchy of rewards, status, and authority. An individual can move from one position to another, but he gains little freedom thereby, for in each position he is subject to conditions imposed upon it; individuals have no protected area of liberty, privacy, or individual sovereignty beyond the reach of the State. The State is subject neither to democratic controls, constitutional limits, or legal regulation. Instead, the organizations in the Corporate State are motivated primarily by the demands of technology and of their own internal structure. Technology has imperatives such as these: if computers have been developed, they must be put to use; if faster planes can be produced, they must be put into service; if there is a more efficient way of organizing an office staff, it must be done; if psychological tests provide added information for personnel directors, they must be used on prospective employees. A general in charge of troops at Berkeley described the use of a helicopter to attack students with chemicals as "logical." As for organizations, their imperative is to grow. They need stability, freedom from outside interference, constantly increasing profits. Everyone in the organization wants more and better personnel, more functions, increased status and prestige—in a word, growth. The medium through which these forces operate is law. The legal system is not primarily concerned with justice, equality, or individual rights; it functions as an instrument of State domination, and it acts to prevent the intervention of human values or individual choice. Although the forces driving the State are impersonal rather than evil, they are wholly indifferent to man's needs, and tend to have the same consequences as would a system expressly designed for the purpose of destroying human beings and their society.

The essence of the Corporate State is that it is relentlessly single-minded; it has only one value, the value of technology-organization-efficiency-growth-progress. The State is perfectly rational and logical. It is based upon principle. But life cannot be supported on the basis of any single principle. Yet no other value is allowed to interfere with this one, not amenity, not beauty, not community, not even the supreme value of life itself. Thus the State is essentially mindless; it has only one idea and it rolls along, never stopping to think, consider, balance, or judge. Only such single-valued mindlessness would cut the last redwoods, pollute the most beautiful beaches, invent machines to injure and destroy plant and human life. To have only one value is, in human terms, to be mad. It is to be a machine.

In the remainder of this chapter, we shall attempt to outline the main features of the Corporate State. We shall build our picture out of several elements, but the description is cumulative, for it is the *interrelationship* of the elements that gives the State its extraordinary form. In the case of the Corporate State, the whole is more than the sum of the parts, and the truth is in the whole, not the parts.

1. Amalgamation and Integration. We normally consider the units of the Corporate State, such as the federal government, an automobile company, a private foundation, as if they were separate from each other. This is, however, not the case. In the first place, there is a marked tendency for "separate" units to follow parallel policies, so that an entire industry makes identical decisions as to pricing, kind of product, and method of distribution; the automobile and the air travel industries show this. Second, very different companies are coming under combined management through the device of conglomerates, which place vast and diverse empires under a single unified control. But even more significant is the disappearance of the line between "public" and "private." In the Corporate State, most of the "public" functions of government are actually performed by the "private" sector of the economy. And most "government" functions are services performed for the private sector.

Let us consider first how government operations are "privately" performed. To a substantial degree, this relationship is formalized. The government hires "private" firms to build national defense systems, to supply the space program, to construct the interstate highway system, and sometimes, in the case of the think institutes, to do its "thinking" for it. An enormous portion of the federal budget is spent in simply hiring out government functions. This much is obvious, although many people do not seem to be aware of it. What is less obvious is the "deputizing" system by which a far larger sector of the "private" economy is enlisted in government service.

An illustration will indicate what is meant by "deputizing." A college teacher receives a form from the Civil Service Commission, asking him for certain information with respect to an individual who is applying for a government job. When he fills in the form, the teacher has acted as if he had been "deputized" by the government; i.e., he is performing a service for the government, one for which he might even feel himself entitled to compensation. Now consider a foundation which receives a special tax-exempt status. The foundation is in this favored position because it is engaged in activities which are of "public benefit." That is, it is the judgment of the government that some types of activities are public services although performed under private auspices. The government itself could do what private foundations now do: aid education, sponsor research, and other things which do not command a profit in the commercial sense. It is the government's decision that these same functions are better performed by foundations. It is the same judgment that government makes when it hires Boeing to build bombers, or a private construction firm to build an interstate highway. Public utilities—airlines, railroads, truck carriers, taxicabs, oil pipe lines, the telephone company—all are "deputized" in this fashion. They carry on *public* functions—functions that in other societies might be performed by the government itself.

In the summer of 1970 it was reported that the broadcasting industry was participating in a "crusade" against drug use. At the urging of President Nixon to "get the message across" to young people that drug use is "weakening the character" of the United States, television and radio responded in such diverse ways as adding a drug-addiction problem to the plot line of a daytime serial, delivering editorials against drugs, devoting news programs to the drug "crisis," canceling all programs for an entire day to present twenty-four hours devoted exclusively to the subject of drug abuse, and inserting subtle antidrug messages amid programs of rock music. Since broadcasters get their licenses from the federal government, there may be some question whether this concerted campaign was the purely voluntary action of private businesses. And the fact that the campaign was not limited to announcements but was also incorporated into supposedly neutral entertainment programs shows the extent to which the entire content of broadcasting can become political in nature, and serve to carry out policies of government. Even the most ordinary family or adventure program shows only an approved attitude toward government. If the "Mission Impossible" team undertook an anti-Vietnam war mission, or a comedian made some serious jokes about patriotism, the broadcasters involved would surely feel that they had reason to worry about the loss of their licenses.

Let us now look at the opposite side of the coin: government as the servant of the "private" sector. Once again, sometimes the relationship is formal and obvious. The government spends huge amounts for research and development, and private companies are often able to get the benefits of this. Airports are built at public expense for private airlines to use. Highways are built for private trucking firms to use. The government pays all sorts of subsidies, direct and indirect, to various industries. It supplies credit services and financial aid to homeowners. It grows trees on public forest lands and sells them at cut-rate prices to private lumber companies. It builds roads to aid ski developments.

It is true that government has always existed to serve the society; that police and fire departments help business too; that paving streets helps business, and so do wars that open up new markets—and that is what government is and always has been all about. But today, governmental activity in aid of the private sector is enormously greater, more pervasive, more immediately felt than ever before. The difference between the local public services in 1776 and millions of dollars in subsidies to the shipping industry may be a difference of degree but it is still quite a difference. But the difference is not only one of degree. In the difference between a highly autonomous, localized economy and a highly interdependent one, there is a difference of principle as well as one of degree. Government help today is *essential*, not a luxury. The airlines could not operate without allocation of routes and regulation of landing and take-offs, nor could the television industry. The educational system, elementary school through high school, is essential for the production of people able to work in today's industry. Thus it may be said that everyone who operates "privately" really is aided and subsidized, to one degree or another, by the public; the sturdy, independent rancher rides off into the sunset on land irrigated by government subsidy, past sheep whose grazing is subsidized and crops whose prices are artificially maintained by governmental action; he does not look like a welfare client, but he is on the dole nevertheless.

Regulation itself is a service to industry. The film industry and the professional sports industry have elaborate systems of private regulation, including "commissioners," a system of laws and government, fines and penalties, all designed to place the industry on the best and most united basis to sell its product. Such "regulation" as is performed by such federal agencies as FCC, SEC, FTC, and CAB, is remarkably similar in general effect, but it is a service rendered at taxpayers' expense. Indeed, there is a constant interchange of personnel between the regulatory agencies and industry; government men leave to take high-paying positions with the corporations they formerly regulated; agency officials are frequently appointed from industry ranks.

This public-private and private-public integration,

when added to the inescapable legislative power we have already described, gives us the picture of the State as a single corporation. Once the line between "public" and "private" becomes meaningless and is erased, the various units of the Corporate State no longer appear to be parts of a diverse and pluralistic system in which one kind of power limits another kind of power; the various centers of power do not limit each other, they all weigh in on the same side of the scale, with only the individual on the other side. With public and private merged, we can discern the real monolith of power and realize there is nothing at all within the system to impose checks and balances, to offer competition, to raise even a voice of caution or doubt. We are all involuntary members, and there is no zone of the private to offer a retreat.

One way to appreciate the true nature of the public-private amalgamated State, is to list some examples of power that can be found in the United States:

Power to determine the hour at which employees come to work, the hour at which they have lunch, the hour when they go home;

Power to make *Business Week* available to airline passengers but not *The Nation;*

Power to raise bank interest rates;

Power to wake all patients in a hospital at 6 A.M.;

Power to forbid apartment dwellers to have pets or children;

Power to require peanut butter eaters to choose between homogenized or chunky peanut butter and to prevent them from buying "real" peanut butter;

Power to force all young people who want to go to college to do a certain kind of mechanical problem-solving devised by the College Entrance Examination Board;

Power to require that all public school teachers be fingerprinted;

Power to popularize snowmobiles instead of snowshoes, so that the winter forests screech with mechanical noise;

Power to force all riders in automobiles to sit in seats designed to torture the lower lumbar regions of the human anatomy;

Power to use forest products in constructing homes, making furniture, and publishing newspapers, thereby creating a demand for cutting timber;

Power to dominate public consciousness through the mass media;

Power to induce lung cancer in thousands of persons by promoting the sale of cigarettes;

Power to turn off a man's telephone service;

Power to provide railroad passengers with washrooms that are filthy;

Power to encourage or discourage various forms of scholarship, educational activity, philanthropy, and research;

Power to construct office buildings with windows that will not open, or without any windows at all;

Power to determine what life-styles will not be acceptable for employees;

Power to make relatively large or small investments in the safety of consumer products;

Power to change the culture of a foreign country.

Were we confronted by this list and told that all of this power was held by a single tyrannical ruler, we would find the prospect frightening indeed. We are likely to think, however, that, although the power may exist, it is divided in many ways, held by many different entities, and subject to all sorts of procedures, checks, balances, and controls; mostly it applies only to persons who subject themselves to it voluntarily, as by taking a job with a corporation. But power in the corporate state is not so easily escaped. The refugee from a job with one corporation will find a choice of other corporations—all prepared to subject him to similar control over employees. The television viewer who tires of one network finds the others even more tiresome. Can railroad or automobile passengers do anything about conditions they object to? Do they find alternative means of transportation readily available?

Editorials which denounce students usually say that a student who does not like the way a university is run should leave. But society makes it practically mandatory for a young person to complete his education, and, so far as rules and practices go, most universities are extraordinarily alike. Under these circumstances, it is hardly accurate to say that a student "voluntarily" submitted to university rule. The student's case is the case of the railroad traveler, the peanut butter eater, the man who wants a bank loan, the corporate employee, the apartment house dweller who wants to keep a pet. The integration of the Corporate State makes what was formerly voluntary inescapable. Like the birds in Alfred Hitchcock's apocalyptic film, powers that once were small and gentle become monstrous and terrifying. The better organized, the more tightly administered, the more rational and inclusive the Corporate State becomes, the more every organization turns into a government, and all forms of power take on the aspect of government decrees.

2. *The Principle of Administration and Hierarchy.* The activities, policies, and decisions of a society might theoretically be carried out by a variety of methods —voluntary cooperation by individuals, the physical coercion of a military tyranny, or the psychological conditioning of B. F. Skinner's *Walden Two.* The Corporate State has chosen to rely on the method of administration and hierarchy. So pervasive, indeed, is the principle of administration that in many ways the Corporate State is in its essence an administrative state. The theory of administration is that the best way to conduct any activity is to subject it to rational control. A framework of organization is provided. Lines of authority, responsibility, and supervision are established as clearly as possible; everyone is arranged in a hierarchy. Rules are drawn for every imaginable contingency, so that individual choice is minimized. Arrangements are made to check on what everyone does, to have reports and permanent records. The random, the irrational, and the alternative ways of doing things are banished.

It is worth recalling how this State derived from classic liberalism, and, more proximately, from the New Deal and the welfare state. Liberalism adopted the basic principle that there is no need for management of society itself; the "unseen hand" is all that is needed. The New Deal modified this by requiring activities to be subject to "the public interest." Gradually this came to mean ever-tightening regulation in directions fixed by the demands of a commercial, technological, mass society. Gradually it came to mean the replacement of a "political" state with an "administrative" state. A "political" state, in our present meaning, is one in which differences, conflicts, and cultural diversity are regarded as aspects of pluralism to be represented in the political process and allowed a life of their own within the body politic. Thus political radicals, marijuana users, or culturally distinct groups would all coexist, have political voices, and contribute to the diversity and balance of the nation. This "political" model has also been called the "conflict" model, not because there are actual conflicts, but because conflicting opinions and ways of life are allowed to exist side by side. Administration means a rejection of the idea of conflict as a desirable element in society. Administration wants extremes "adjusted"; it wants differences "settled"; it wants to find out which way is "best" and use it exclusively. That which refuses to be adjusted is considered by administration as "deviance," a departure from the norm needing to be treated and cured. It is a therapeutic model of society, in which variety is compromised and smoothed over in an effort to make everything conform to "the public interest." This society defines that which does not fit "the public interest" as "deviance." Marijuana use is made a crime, and people using it are punished, cured, or "helped." Political radicals are expected to be "responsible"; blacks are expected to be "integrated." The society "knows what is best" for everyone; its massive energies, power, and apparatus are focused on making such that everyone accepts "what is best."

The structure of the administrative state is that of a hierarchy in which every person has a place in a table of organization, a vertical position in which he is subordinate to someone and superior to someone else. This is the structure of any bureaucracy; it represents a "rationalization" of organization ideals.

When an entire society is subjected to this principle, it creates a small ruling elite and a large group of workers who play no significant part in the making of decisions. While they continue to vote in political elections, they are offered little choice among the candidates; all the major decisions about what is produced, what is consumed, how resources are allocated, the conditions of work, and so forth, are made administratively.

Hierarchy takes on particular importance in the organizations where most people work. It declares that, as workers, most men and women must accept the absolute authority and superiority of someone "above" them. The boss is not only empowered to tell a worker how to perform his work, the boss is also treated as a higher form of human being. We have frequently heard criticism of the "childishness" of the average adult American, but hierarchy not only encourages, it demands childishness—the wholesale turning over of responsibility and self-respect to someone in authority. One of the key points in the rebellion of the new generation is rejection of such authority and insistence upon personal responsibility and true personal equality.

Administration seeks to remove decision-making from the area of politics to the area of "science." It does not accept democratic or popular choice; this is rejected in favor of professionals and experts and a rational weighing of all of the factors. Procedures are set up by which decision-making is channeled, and care is taken to define exactly which institution shall make which decisions. For each type of decision, there is someone "best" qualified to decide it; administration avoids participation in decisions by the less qualified. Its greatest outrage is directed toward a refusal to enter into its procedures—this seems almost a denial of the very principle of administration. If followed, these procedures usually produce a decision that is a compromise or balance which rejects any particular choice in its pure, uncompromised form. Choice takes place within narrow limits. A weighing of all the factors produces a decision somewhere in between, rather than one or another "extreme."

Administration has no values of its own, except for the institutional ones just described. It has no ideas; it is just professional management. Theoretically, it could accept any values. In practice, however, it is strongly conservative. Things go most smoothly when the status quo is maintained, when change is slow, cautious, and evolutionary. The more elaborate the machinery of administration, the less ready it is for new, disquieting values. And "rationality" finds some values easier to understand, to justify, to put into verbal terms than other values. It can understand quantity better than quality. Rationality does not like to blow its mind. Administration is neutral in favor of the Establishment.

Public welfare offers an example of the administrative model of society. The object of public welfare, apart from administration, is to protect people against the hazards of forces in an industrial society beyond their control, and the other hazards of life against which neither family nor local community any longer offer help; to provide every person with a minimum standard of security, well-being, and dignity. With the introduction of administration and hierarchy as the means for carrying out public welfare, the emphasis shifts to regulation of exactly who is qualified for welfare, how much is allotted, how it is spent, whether regulations are being followed. A large apparatus is developed for checking up, for keeping records, for making and enforcing rules, for punishing infractions. Some of this may save money, but the money saved is minimized by the costs of administration. Some of this may also serve the purpose of punishing the poor for not working, even though many are unable to work. But the "accomplishments" of administration are almost secondary; after a while what it does ceases to have an outside reference; it acquires an autonomous life of its own.

The tendency of administration, while it may appear to be benign and peaceful, as opposed to the turbulence of conflict, is actually violent. For the very idea of imposed order is violent. It demands compliance; nothing less than compliance will do; and it must obtain compliance, by persuasion or management if possible, by repression if necessary. It is convinced that it has "the best way" and that all others are wrong; it cannot understand those who do not accept the rightness of its view. A growing tension and anger develops against those who would question what is so carefully designed to be "best"—for them as well as for everybody else. Thus it is not uncommon for public school administrators to engage in repression of independent thinking by the students, although the ability to think is presumably an important objective of education. It was reported that at South San Francisco High School an eighteen-year-old honor student, Joe Gettus, would not be allowed to graduate because, while having a smoke in the men's room with his younger brother and a friend, he had burned some cigarette holes in a three-by-five-inch American flag he had bought for a nickel in a school "flea market" sale. Gettus had won two first prizes, one for an essay on the subject of peace and one for painting and mixed media, and received all A's and B's except in physical education, where the teacher flunked him after the incident. (The youth commented about his gym teacher's action, "He thinks he hates me, but he doesn't know, because he really doesn't know me.") Mrs. June Gettus said about her son, "His prime interest in life is getting people to think, and boy, he's getting people in this town to think." Dean of Boys Robert Warfield said that he liked the youth, but that he "lacks discipline" and has "a tendency to over-intellectualize."

At the Del Valle High School in Walnut Creek, California, the students produced a "controversial" yearbook. Among the "objectionable" aspects of the book was a poem by seventeen-year-old Robert Danielson, a star of the school baseball team, commenting on the training of high school athletes. Because of the poem, young Danielson was told by his coach that he would not receive a team letter and was not welcome at the team presentation awards dinner. The coach sought to mitigate this punishment by telling the faculty, "I like the kid . . . I think he's pathetic, but I like him. If I hadn't, he wouldn't have played baseball for me for two years." Meanwhile the principal threatened the faculty advisor to the yearbook, Mrs. Hildagard Buckette, with dismissal. He also announced that in the future the yearbook would be subject to guidelines established by a faculty committee.

In part, the poem read as follows:

I run at the sound of the whistle.
I stop at the sound of the whistle.
I will grovel on the ground at its harsh scream.
The whistle governs my afterlife.
I'm well trained.
The men in the red jackets told me so.
Don't doubt.
Don't hesitate.
Don't reason.
I don't ask questions. . . .

Administration wants the best for everybody, and all that it asks is that individuals conform their lives to the framework established by the State.

3. *The Corporate State Is Autonomous.* What controls the amalgamated power of the Corporate State? We usually make at least three reassuring assumptions. One: power is controlled by the people through the democratic process and pluralism in the case of government, and through the market in the case of the "private" sector. Two: power is controlled by the persons who are placed in a position of authority to exercise it. Three: power is subject to the Constitution and the laws. These assumptions stand as a presumed barrier to the state power we have described. We will deal with the first two in this section, and the third in a later section on law.

As machinery for translating popular will into political effect, the American system functions impossibly badly. We can hardly say that our political process makes it possible for voters to enforce their will on such subjects as pollution, the supersonic plane, mass transportation, the arms race, or the Vietnam War. On the contrary, if there are any popularly held

views, it is impossible for them to be expressed politically; this was demonstrated for all to see in the
1968 presidential campaign, where both candidates
supported the Vietnam War. Even if the political machinery did allow the electorate to express its views,
it is difficult for citizens to get the information necessary to form an opinion.

What we have said with respect to the failure of
the political process is also true with respect to the
"private" economic process which supposedly is governed by a market. There is nothing at all to "stock-
holder democracy" in the control of corporations; it
has long been true that stockholders have no realistic
power in the government of corporate affairs. But
the more important fact is that producers largely
create their own demand for products. This is the
central thesis of Galbraith's *The New Industrial
State*, and it is hard to see how it can be disputed.
Corporations decide what they want to produce,
and they convince people that they want it, thus
fashioning their own market. What we now produce
and consume, the way we use our resources, the
plans we make for future use of resources, are therefore not directed by what the people want. We do not
know if they would prefer to have snowmobiles rather
than new hospital equipment; no one asks them, and
they cannot make their voices heard.

If pure democratic theory fails us in both the public and private spheres, we must nevertheless consider whether a modified version of democracy can
permit large competing interests to achieve a balance which represents a rough approximation of what
people want; this is the theory of pluralism. Here
again, the theory simply does not work out. Robert

Paul Wolff has effectively discussed this type of pluralism in his book *The Poverty of Liberalism* (the same essay also appears in a cooperative volume called *A Critique of Pure Tolerance*). The interests that make up the spectrum of political "pluralism" are highly select; many important interests are entirely omitted. Thus, as Wolff points out, we have recognized the three major religions but no agnostics; we have virtually no representation of the poor, the blacks, or other outsiders; no representation of youth, no radicals. "Pluralism" represents not interests, but *organized* interests. Thus, "labor" means large labor organizations, but these do not necessarily represent the real interests of individual employees. "Labor" may support heavy defense expenditures, repressive police measures, and emphasis on economic growth, but this may not be at all an expression of the true interests of the industrial worker. Likewise the three major religions may fail to represent the more individual spiritual strivings of persons which might take such forms as resistance to the draft. Indeed, at the organizational level there is far more agreement than difference among the "competing interests," so that they come to represent the same type of cooperation as conglomerate mergers produce among interests in the private sphere.

Even if the people had power to give orders, the orders might have little or no effect. Increasingly, the important part of government is found in the executive departments, which are staffed by career men, experts, professionals, and civil servants who have specialized knowledge of technical fields. These persons are not elected, nor are they subject to removal on political grounds. They are thus immunized from

direct democratic control. Congress and the state legislatures, however, have neither the time nor the
specialized knowledge to oversee all of these governmental activities. Instead, the legislatures have increasingly resorted to broad delegations of authority.
Even if a statute tries to set more definite standards,
such as the Federal Power Act, which lists some factors to be considered in building hydroelectric projects, the factors are simply left to be considered and
weighed in the agency's discretion. What really happens is that government becomes institutionalized in
the hands of professionals, experts, and managers,
whose decisions are governed by the laws of bureaucratic behavior and the laws of professional behavior.
These laws mean that decisions will be within narrow compass, tend to the status quo, tend to continue any policy once set, tend to reflect the interests
of the organization. These organizations, then, are
unprepared to respond to any outside direction even
if the people were in a position to give it. The same
is true of the private corporate bureaucracies.

If the people do not control the Corporate State,
is it at least controlled by those who give the orders
—the executives and the power elite behind them?
Such control might not satisfy those who favor democracy or the rule of law, but it would still be control that had to consider the broad trends of public
opinion—still a major difference from no control at
all.

Let us focus on an imaginary organization—government or private (an agency or corporation)—and its
executive head—the personification of the "power
elite." We enter into the paneled executive suite or,
in the case of a more sophisticated organization, a

suite in the most advanced taste, and there we expect to find an individual or "team" who really do exercise power. But the trappings, from the modern sculpture to the console telephone, do not tell the whole story. Any organization is subject to the demands of technology, of its own organization, and to its own middle-management. The corporation *must* respond to advances in technology. It *must* act in such a way as to preserve and foster its own organization. It is subject to the decision-making power of those in middle-management whose interests lie with the advance of organization and technology.

If the organization is a private corporation, the power elite must take much else into consideration; the fact that there are financial interests: bondholders, stockholders, banks and bankers, institutional owners (such as pension funds and mutual funds), potential raiders seeking financial control, possible financial control by a system of conglomerate ownership. This is not to suggest that stockholders or bondholders have any significant part in management, that there is any investor democracy, or that conglomerate structure necessarily means guidance of management. But the very existence of these interests creates certain impersonal demands upon the corporation; for example, the demand for profit, for growth, for stability of income. The manager cannot act without an awareness of the constant demand for profits. Thus a television executive's decision about whether to put on a special news broadcast and "sacrifice" a paying program is made in the oppressive awareness of the demand for profit—a demand which, because it is so institutional and impersonal, literally "cares" about nothing else than profits. The business executive is also required to be aware of many different kinds of state and federal law. The corporation is quite likely to be influenced by another set of relationships to government. It may possess valuable government contracts, subsidies, franchises or licenses, any of which can be modified or revoked. It may be the beneficiary of favored tax treatment that can be changed. It must therefore act in such a manner as to preserve whatever special privileges and advantages it has.

Inside a corporation, there is the important influence of the system of decision-making. Most managements consist of a committee rather than a single head; all students of group behavior know how a committee is limited in ways that a single executive is not. Beyond this, management is limited by the many kinds of specialists and experts whose views must be consulted: the experts in marketing, in business management methods, the technicians, the whole class of people who occupy what Galbraith calls the "technostructure." The structure of any large organization is bureaucratic, and all bureaucracies have certain imperatives and rules of their own. The bureaucracy acts to preserve itself and its system, to avoid any personal responsibility, to maintain any policy once set in motion. Decisions become "institutional decisions" that can be identified with no one person, and have the qualities of the group mind. The bureaucracy is so powerful that no executive, not even the President of the United States, can do much to budge it from its course. Top executives are profoundly limited by lack of knowledge. They know only what they are told. In effect, they are "briefed" by others, and the briefing is both limiting and highly

selective. The executive is far too busy to find anything out for himself; he *must* accept the information he gets, and this sets absolute limits to his horizons. The briefing may be three steps removed from
the facts, and thus be interpretation built upon interpretation—nearer fiction than fact by the time it
reaches the top.

Thus the man in the chic office turns out to be a
broker, a decider between limited alternatives, a mediator and arbitrator, a chairman, but not an origina-
tor. And such a position tends to be utterly inconsistent with thought, reflection, or originality. The
executive cannot come up with reflections on policy,
he cannot be the contemplative generalist, because he
is too pressed and harried by the demands upon
him. Increasingly, it is also inconsistent with the realities of the outside world, as the executive is insulated
from them.

From all of this, there emerges the great revelation about the executive suite—the place from which
power-hungry men seem to rule our society. The
truth is far worse. In the executive suite, there may
be a Léger or Braque on the wall, or a collection of
African masks, there may be a vast glass-and-metal
desk, but there is no one there. No one at all is in
the executive suite. What looks like a man is only a
representation of a man who does what the organization requires. He (or it) does not run the machine;
he *tends* it.

4. *The New Property.* If the Corporate State were
merely autonomous, its effects would be profoundly
harmful to human beings; but the State is *worse* than
autonomous: its machinery is influenced by private

manipulation for power and gain, yet those who use it in this way have no power to influence it in a more positive direction, and ultimately they become captives as well as profiteers. These paradoxical results follow from the development of what we may call the New Property.

With the rise of organization as the governing principle of American life, a change in the nature of private property and wealth necessarily followed. Organizations are not really "owned" by anyone. What formerly constituted ownership was split up into stockholders' rights to share in profits, management's power to set policy, employees' right to status and security, government's right to regulate. Thus older forms of wealth were replaced by new forms. Just as primitive forms of wealth such as beads and blankets gave way to what we familiarly know as property, so "property" gave way to rights growing out of organizations. A job, a stock certificate, a pension right, an automobile dealer's franchise, a doctor's privilege of hospital facilities, a student's status in a university—these are typical of the new forms of wealth. All of these represent *relationships* to organizations, so that today a person is identified by his various statuses: an engineer at Boeing, a Ford dealer, a Ph.D. in political science, a student at Yale.

The growth of status with respect to private organizations has been paralleled by a rise in statuses produced by, and related to, government. The more that government has become "affirmative" in nature, engaging in regulation, allocation of resources, distribution of benefits, and public ownership, the more it has become a status-dispensing organization; indeed, the largest of all such organizations. Characteristic forms of status-wealth dispensed by government are occupational and professional licenses, taxicab and television franchises, airline routes, grazing rights on the public domain, subsidies to businesses and farmers, or welfare payments to indigent families, tax benefits, social security benefits, jobs and offices on the public payroll, and contracts to build highways or defense hardware.

These statuses, public and private, achieve their great importance because they become, for most individuals, the chief goals of life. Instead of seeking happiness in more tangible ways, the Consciousness II person defines happiness in terms of his position in the complex hierarchy of status. A new job, he says, cannot be a mistake as long as it is "a step up," an individual gets satisfaction from "having people under him," a title can compensate for the absence of many other things. The individual feels he must be happy because he has status, as a student or teacher, at a high-class university; if he is "at Yale" he glows with an artificial inward warmth. Statuses involve money, security, convenience, and also power, but these things do not quite express what they mean. They are a substitute self. The organizations of the Corporate State are empowered to confer and take away selfhood, and this fact, perhaps more than any other, explains the State's ability to dominate all of the thinking and activities within it.

In theory, all of these benefits and statuses, whether originating in the government or in "private" organizations, are distributed according to "the public interest" or the interests of the organization concerned, but never simply to advance private interests. An airline route or television channel is given to the applicant who will "best serve the public interest"; the windfall to the successful applicant is supposedly compensated by its services to the public. Likewise a government contract is awarded to the bidder who will best serve the government's interest, or who submits the lowest bid. The theory is extended to taxicab medallions and turnpike concessions; these privileges are valuable because they are partial monopolies, and they are given to the "best" applicants, just as in a private organization the promotions supposedly go to those who most "merit" them and will do the company the most good. On a grander scale, Congress votes subsidies or tax concessions to large groups, such as farmers, or the shipbuilding industry or the oil industry, on the theory that these serve the national interest.

But the whole concept of a society that assumes responsibility for allocating resources, benefits, and privileges is undercut if private interests are able to manipulate the system for their own advantage. If an airline can get a new route, not because of "merit" but because of its political influence in Washington, the allocation system becomes not an instrument of public policy but a vast and corrupt grabbag for the shrewd and the powerful. In turn, this maneuvering alters public policy. The machinery of the State begins to be influenced by these private interests. It is still autonomous, but autonomous in an even more antisocial direction.

This marriage of the machinery of the Corporate State with private profiteering can be illustrated by the television industry. Technology gives us television, and the imperative of technology, unguided by other values, insists that we produce it and use it without attempting to consider what it should and should not be used for, what harm it might do, what controls are essential to its use. When private manipulation is added to the equation, it produces programs expressly designed to win huge audiences so that mass-produced products can be sold, even if this means a degradation of popular taste and consciousness. It is the worst of all possible worlds: uncontrolled technology and uncontrolled profiteering, combined into a force that is both immensely powerful and utterly irresponsible.

This combination of forces bears a large responsibility for much of what is wrong with our society, from universities where the professors care more about advancing their status than teaching, to the oil industry, where the land, sea, and atmosphere are wantonly polluted, to the Vietnam War, which combined the latest in technology with the most venal of private motives in the defense-space industry. But it should not be thought that because private interests can successfully use the Corporate State, they can influence its course in any affirmative manner. On the contrary, individuals or organizations which depend on the New Property lose their own independence of action and thought; some may become rich and powerful, but they are irrevocably tied to the source of their advantages. Those who get few advantages may, however, be equally dependent on the system as it becomes all-pervasive. We can see this most clearly in the case of individuals who are beneficiaries of the New Property.

When status and relationships to organizations replace private property, the result is a change in the degree of independent sovereignty enjoyed by the individual. Private property gave each person a domain in which he could be independent, and it enabled him to tell the rest of the world to go fly a kite. But a person whose "property" consists of a position in an organization is tied to the fate of the organization; if the organization goes down he goes with it. More important, he is subject to the power of the organization, for his "New Property" relationship is invariably conditional. There are conditions to be met for acquiring a status, maintaining it, advancing it, or avoiding its loss, and these conditions significantly affect the individual's independence. These conditions are set by the organization, not the individual, and they may be unilaterally altered by the organization. And except as specifically enacted by law, there are no limits to the conditions that may be placed on status—they may demand anything that serves the needs of the organization. A high school boy must cut his hair or be suspended, a civil servant must refrain from political activity, a college teacher must publish in scholarly journals.

What are the consequences that follow from this conditioning power? It allows the rise of broad new legislative power with respect to individuals. In "The Adventure of the Copper Beeches," Sherlock Holmes was consulted by a young lady who had been offered a position as a governess provided that she would agree to cut her hair short, wear a designated dress at certain times, and sit in a certain chair when requested. These conditions puzzled her enough to seek Holmes' advice, but nobody questioned that the prodigiously stout man with the very smiling face, who offered her the position at his country home, had a perfect right to make these or any other "requests" of a would-be employee. Today, in the public-private state, where organizations are nationwide, and are connected both to other organizations and the government, the smiling request is no longer a private whim but a matter of public concern. If the telephone company, or IBM, beaming with prodigious good nature, asks that employees cut their hair, wear a certain dress, or sit in a certain chair, the fact that such companies have almost monopoly control over various areas of the labor market makes them the possessors of a legislative power never contemplated by the framers of the Constitution, who said that the United States would never be a country where a man could be told whether or not he must wear a hat.

This legislative power may cut deeply into the private life of the individual. Each step forward in job technology and organization means a further refining of job specifications, and today employers justify as fully relevant to the job an official inquiry into a prospective employee's home life, psychological make-up, friends and associates, political and cultural activities, and past history. No part of an employee's life is so private that it could not be deemed, by the accepted process of reasoning, a matter of legitimate concern to his employer. Today's forms issued by organizations such as the Peace Corps and VISTA ask former teachers, employers, and friends to make evaluations of an applicant based on "all they know" of the individual.

Whether in the hands of "private" or "public" organizations, the new legislative power may in many circumstances be exercised without regard to existing constitutional and Bill of Rights protections. A private employer may dismiss a man or a private university may expel a student for an act which, as a citizen, he has a constitutional right to do; the rationale is that these "private" organizations are not limited by the Constitution. The government, which *is* limited by the Constitution, can nevertheless evade those limits when in its capacity as a regulator of statuses. Would-be government employees, candidates for admission to the bar, applicants for radio or television channels, have their opinions, speeches, friends, and associations subjected to scrutiny. Here the theory is that the particular status is "not a right, but a privilege"; if the individual is denied the status, it is claimed, he can continue to exercise his constitutional liberties and therefore the government has not taken away anything protected by the Constitution. By a similar chain of reasoning, a driver's license can be revoked although the driver has not been convicted of any violation, or a franchise can be denied because of arrests, even though they did not lead to convictions.

Power over the New Property leads to all sorts of procedural innovations unknown to the Constitution. Organizations set up investigatory procedures that take no account of the Fourth Amendment's protection against unreasonable searches and seizures, conduct trials where the rules of evidence are unknown, and impose punishments that may violate the principle of double jeopardy—all in the process of determining whether a student has broken university rules, or an employee of the Post Office is a security risk, or a welfare recipient is not qualified to receive one type of payment. It was the entertainment industry that instituted private boycotts and loyalty tests for those suspected of left-wing political views.

All of these invasions of constitutional limitations tend to increase gradually but steadily. Job specifications increase with the technology. Competition for positions increases, and so selectivity increases. More years of training are needed to qualify. And the power of new legislation, over time, becomes encrusted with additions; congressmen tack on a loyalty oath or a no-riot provision onto old-age benefits or student aid; having the power, they do not resist exercising it. Or private employers institute lie detector tests and personality evaluation forms. In this sense the battle over liberty is not waged along a stationary line; the whole battle takes place aboard a moving platform where the passing of time alone brings new erosions of liberty; each time the battle is resumed, it is resumed further down the line. Moreover, a victory may be more illusory than real. Suppose an employee or contractor wins his point. He may nevertheless be denied advancement or denied a new contract when the time comes. The organization may find other conditions which he cannot meet. It is difficult to stop a private employer, or even the United States government, from establishing new conditions and applying them retroactively to past situations.

But will anyone even want to contest the conditioning power of organizations? The Bill of Rights assumes that the individual has an interest that is separate from, and possibly contrary to, that of government. The Bill of Rights is not self-executing. One must *want* to make a speech which displeases the authorities before the right of free speech comes into play; and status works to undermine the separateness of that interest. It makes an individual decide that what is best for the organization is also best for himself; he has the same interest as the conditioning authority. He *wants* to be investigated, he *wants* to have his privacy invaded, he *wants* to fulfill special conditions because the organization's well-being is identical with his own, and he hopes to be the person who uniquely satisfies the conditions for the next rung on the ladder. Under the circumstances, rights are likely to go unused until they cease to be functional.

Now we can see how the squeeze works against individuals in the Corporate State. In the preceding section of this outline we suggested that the organizations in the Corporate State gain external power as choice is reduced; the individual is compelled to deal with them and belong to them. Statuses apply a different but related kind of compulsion; they erode the individual's basis of independence, his ability and desire to "go it alone." They offer him a reward for compliance; they purchase an abandonment of independence. From the welfare recipient to the licensed physician, from the student with a government scholarship to the man with an executive job, individuals have an *interest* in the compliance which the Corporate State demands. Power is the stick and status-benefits are the carrot; when combined they leave few people with the means or the will to resist what is, after all, designed expressly to be in their "best interests."

And the status system strikes even deeper. It destroys the potential for solidarity which would be necessary to reassert control over the Corporate State. One consequence of a status system is a rigid hierarchy. As everyone's property is transformed into relationships, so all relationships are fixed in vertical order. Everyone is above someone and below someone, and this of course gets in the way of community, for people at different levels of the hierarchy cannot join hands. Also, hierarchy results in automatic, clearly defined inequality, so that everyone can feel the differences between himself and those in other statuses. It gets to be in the interest of each status to see that the liberties of those in other statuses are repressed. One man's special status, benefits, and privileges depend upon the proper functioning of the rest of the organization; he wants to see everyone else kept in his proper place. Anyone getting unruly may alter the special laws applicable to someone else. Thus no one has any interest in anyone else's freedom.

A dramatic illustration of how a status system undermines solidarity and the potential for collective action occurred in late 1969 when the drawing occurred for the draft lottery. Students who previously had a strong sense of solidarity found that, helplessly and much against their will, they were divided; a high number and a low number inevitably felt separated from each other. In time many students managed to regain a feeling of closeness to others differently situated, but they all recognized the power of the system to divide them.

The deepest problem concerning statuses has to do with the kind of individual they create. Each person gets increasingly tied to his own status-role. He is forced more and more to *become* that role, as less and less of his private life remains. His thoughts and feelings center on the role. And as a role-person he is incapable of thinking of *general* values, or of assuming responsibility for society. He can do that only in the diminishing area outside his role. Consider an automobile company executive. He can propose public housing as a solution to the urban crisis. But he cannot propose that fewer cars be produced, or that models be kept the same, to save money for public housing. Thus his role prevents him from acting for the community in the one area where he has power to act, and it prevents him from even realizing that his cars are one of the things draining money that should be used for cities. As long as he is in his role, he cannot act or think responsibly within the community. Outside his role, if there is any outside, he is virtually powerless, for his power lies in the role. Thus a nation of people grows up who cannot fight back against the power that presses against them, for each, in his separate status cubicle, is utterly apart from his fellow men.

What we have said concerning individuals who are dependent upon the New Property carries over to organizations. The large corporations which enjoy privileges as television licensees or holders of airline routes may get rich off the government, but they cannot and do not contest the government in any area; they are afraid of the government or even of an individual congressman or commissioner at the same time that they are using the government for their own purposes. They have no interest or will to express independent values. Their exclusive interest is simply in government favors. In this way they contribute to the autonomy and ungovernability of the Corporate State.

5. *Law: The Inhuman Medium.* Law is supposed to be a codification of those lasting human values which a people agree upon. "Thou shalt not kill" is

such a law. The Corporate State is a distinctively legalistic society. It utilizes law for every facet of its activity—there has probably never been a society with so much law, where law is so important. Thus it might be expected that law would represent a significant control over the power of the Corporate State, and a source of guidelines for it. But law in the Corporate State is something very different from a codification of values. The State has transformed it.

During the New Deal period the law was gradually changed from a medium which carried traditional values of its own to a value-free medium that could be adapted to serve "public policy," which became the "public interest" of the Corporate State. This produced law that fell into line with the requirements of organization and technology, and that supported the demands of administration rather than protecting the individual. Once law had assumed this role, there began a vast proliferation of laws, statutes, regulations, and decisions. For the law began to be employed to aid all of the work of the Corporate State by compelling obedience to the State's constantly increasing demands.

One area in which this can be demonstrated is the field of constitutional rights. The first point that must be made is that despite the vast growth of corporate power the courts, except in the area of racial discrimination, have failed to hold that corporations are subject to the Bill of Rights. A mere statement of this fact may not seem very significant; corporations, after all, are not supposed to exercise the governmental powers with which the Bill of Rights was concerned. But this has been radically changed by the emergence of the public-private state. Today private institutions do exercise government power; more, indeed, than "government" itself. They decide what will be produced and what will not be produced; they do our primary economic planning; they are the chief determinants of how resources are allocated. With respect to their own employees, members, or students, they act in an unmistakably governmental fashion; they punish conduct, deprive people of their positions within the organization, or decide on advancement. In a sweeping way they influence the opinions, expression, associations, and behavior of all of us. Hence the fact that the Bill of Rights is inapplicable is of paramount importance; it means that these constitutional safeguards actually apply only to one part (and not the most significant part) of the power of the Corporate State. We have two governments in America, then—one under the Constitution and a much greater one not under the Constitution. Consider a right such as freedom of speech. "Government" is forbidden to interfere with free speech, but corporations can fire employees for free speech; private organizations can discriminate against those who exercise free speech; newspapers, television, and magazines can refuse to carry "radical" opinion. In short, the *inapplicability* of our Bill of Rights is one of the crucial facts of American life today.

But does the Bill of Rights afford protection even where it directly applies? The Supreme Court decisions of the last few decades are not reassuring. In its adjudications the Court gives heavy weight to the "interest of society." It defers to what the legislature-executive-administrators have decided. The commands of the state are to be overturned only if there is no "rational" basis for them or if they contravene an express provision of the Constitution, and that provision is not outweighed by "the interest of society." The result over the years has been that virtually any policy in the field of economics, production, planning, or allocation has been declared constitutional; that all sorts of decisions classifying people in different and unequal statuses for tax or benefit purposes have gone unquestioned; that peacetime selective service has been upheld; that free speech has been severely limited.

A second area where law has been made to serve the state is that of federal regulation of economic activity. Here, if anywhere in the law, one might expect control to be exercised over corporate power. But the story is the same as the story of constitutional law. In the first place, most regulation is either very superficial or does what the regulated industry really wants to be done anyway. Regulation polices the outlaws, prevents unruly competition, limits entry into a field, and in effect rationalizes and stabilizes industry. Gabriel Kolko, in *The Triumph of Conservatism*, suggests that regulation began performing this function as long ago as the so-called Progressive Era; and surely regulation performed largely this function under the New Deal. Food in interstate commerce must be properly labeled, inspected, and not adulterated. Stocks must not be sold in a misleading way. These are regulations with which any industry can feel comfortable. Moreover, regulation has to a large extent been taken over by personnel representing the thinking and interests of those supposed to be regulated.

The inadequacy of regulation shows most clearly

in the decisions made concerning allocation of valuable resources. Consider the television channels, owned by the public and licensed free of charge to various applicants (who can make a fortune out of them, and then sell them for millions of dollars). The FCC could have distributed these channels to a wide spectrum of applicants; there could be stations controlled by blacks, by the poor, by students, by universities, by radicals, by groups with various cultural interests. The opportunity was there. What did the FCC actually do? A large number of stations, the most desirable of all, were given to the three giant networks, which proved a crucial aid to the networks in establishing domination over the entire industry. Most of the remaining stations were given either to already established powers in the mass communications field, such as newspapers (with the result that in a given town the principal station would be given to the principal newspaper, so that the sources of information in the town tightened rather than loosened), or they were given to giant corporations. Moreover, the FCC failed to make any adequate provision for truth, objectivity, or balance in the programs of those to whom it turned over the airwaves. Has anyone ever been able to see a program prepared by the Black Panthers, or migratory workers, or student draft resisters, or New Left economic critics, or women's liberation groups presented on a major network? Yet, at the same time, the law actually forbids any of these unrepresented groups to attempt to broadcast their views without a license. Regulation, proceeding strictly according to law, thus had the effect of giving a television monopoly to the power groups in the Corporate State, and excluding all others *by law*.

The role of the law with respect to the Corporate State, and particularly with reference to technology, can be further illustrated by the circumstances surrounding the introduction of chemical Mace as a police weapon. Developed by a private company whose motivation was presumably to make a profit and expand its market and organization, it was purchased by many police departments and presently sprayed in people's faces, causing temporary and/or possibly lasting injuries, plus that more profound injury to the nation as a whole that comes from the use of technology in a way that dehumanizes both policeman and victim. The law authorized the company to market this product, and the police to adopt it and start using it on human beings, without: any tests or studies by a scientific or government agency; the kind of review by the Food and Drug Administration required for other drugs used on people; approval by any legislative body; any vote by the public; any disclosure of information concerning the properties of Mace; any information on long-term effects of Mace, or its effects on people with special infirmities or allergies; setting any general standards as to what weapons are appropriate for what circumstances; requiring any special training for the use of Mace. At the same time, the law gave Mace its full protection and sanction. The law bars any redress to victims, any lawsuit for injuries, any criminal proceedings against the police—unless the most unusual circumstances are present. Thus the use of Mace has the full power of the law behind it, and those who oppose its use have never been given a chance.

While furthering the power of the Corporate State, the law has also served the function of advancing private interests. As the nation has become a legalistic society, law has increasingly become the medium in which private maneuver for power, status, and financial gain could take place. It has become a huge game board, like Monopoly, on which expert players make intricate moves to positions of advantage. The game of law is played with all of the legal powers of government to provide benefits, subsidies, allocate resources and franchises, and grant special exceptions and favors. It is played with the whole property-status system in which a move from one status to another provides different and increased benefits. It is played with all the duties imposed by law on citizens, including the tax laws and the draft. Lawyers are the professional strategists for this game and vast amounts of energy and activity are poured into playing it.

The legal game board builds up into structures that embody, *in the law itself*, almost every inequity, injustice, and irrationality that has become accepted in our society. Among the greatest examples are the federal tax laws and the draft. The tax laws are surely one of the most intricate and remarkable structures of inequity that the human mind has ever devised. There are hundreds of pages of inequities; special privileges of every imaginable sort. It seems accurate to say that the one overriding principle of the tax laws is that inequality and special favors are the rule that governs all. If possible, the draft law is even worse. For it sends some young men off to risk their lives and lose long years which might be spent in ways of their own choosing, while others are privileged to escape any military service. We need not linger here on facts that are so well known; the point is that the tax structure and the draft are not unusual examples of how the law works; they are entirely characteristic examples of what is true of the law as a whole.

Viewed in a broader perspective, it can be seen that for each status, class, and position in society, there is a different set of laws. There is one set of laws for the welfare recipient, one for the businessman. There is one set of laws for the government employee, another for the congressman. There is one set of laws for the farmer, another for the writer. These differences are not limited to any particular area or subject matter; for example, the constitutional right of privacy is treated differently for a businessman or farmer than for a welfare recipient. A person receiving Medicare is required to take a loyalty oath; others are not. If "law" means a general rule to govern a community of people, then in the most literal and precise sense we have *no* law; we are a lawless society.

As administered, the law becomes lawless in an even deeper sense. A motorist is stopped by a policeman who is on the lookout for a stolen car of that description. The motorist soon proves he is driving his own car, but in the course of events the officer calls the motorist by his first name (obtained from the automobile registration) in a way which the motorist deems insulting. "Please call me Mr. ————," the motorist says. The officer says, "You want to be arrested?" "For what," says the motorist. The policeman says, "I can arrest you for having a dirty license plate, or for a faulty windshield wiper, or for failing to signal when you pulled over, or disrespect to an officer, or jaywalking." The driver realizes that at best he will lose several hours, perhaps be subject to a fine, a record, even a jail term if the magistrate is in a vindictive mood. He apologizes profusely to the officer.

When the heavyweight champion Muhammad Ali refused to submit to induction into the army, the New York State Boxing Commission, a public body operating by authority of law, revoked his title. The Commission held no hearing at which Ali presented his case. It did not wait to see whether the courts would convict Ali of a crime or hold that, by reason of his religious views, he had a right to refuse induction, or that his draft board was illegally constituted. In Seattle the legal authorities started proceedings to revoke the license of a G.I. coffee house because it supposedly encouraged anti-war thinking among young G.I.'s; the license official said that he did not want such activities around the Seattle area. Through the law, his arbitrary personal view became a governmental act.

Behind this lawless use of law lies the fact that the greater the quantity of legal rules, the greater the amount of discretionary power is generated. If a licensed pharmacist is subject to fifty separate regulations, he can be harassed by one after another, as soon as he proves himself to have complied with the first. One school of legal philosophers has long advocated a society in which precisely drawn laws would give everyone the freedom of knowing his exact rights. But in practice, experience has shown that the greater the number of laws, the greater the resulting discretion, and the more lawless the official part of the state becomes. Laws that are widely violated, that represent cultural differences, such as the marijuana laws, especially lend themselves to selective and arbitrary enforcement.

For blacks, for anyone with long hair or nonconforming dress, and even for youth in general, the law and the police have become something to be automatically feared. The long-haired youth who drives a car is likely to be stopped, searched, and harassed by police over and over again because of his appearance alone. Blacks have experienced a similar arbitrary discrimination for years. Youth in general find curfews and other laws specially designed to "keep them in their place." All of these groups feel the law to be their enemy in two ways. First, because of the way it is enforced against them. Second, because in a larger sense it is constructed against them; tax favors, subsidies, and privileges are denied them and given others; special penalties are reserved for them alone.

What we fail to realize is that there is a basic pattern to this kind of lawless law. When police lawlessness is revealed, such as the "police riot" in Chicago or unnecessary brutality at a university, everyone is shocked as if this were an *aberration* in our society. But the police have always been brutal and lawless to the powerless; we know this from how blacks were and are treated by the police in the South, and from the way young people, the poor, blacks, and outcasts are treated in the North. The cry of police lawlessness misses the point. In any large city the bureaucracies are also lawless; the building inspectors make threats and collect bribes, the liquor licensing authority is both arbitrary and corrupt, the zoning system is tyrannical but subject to influence. An individual in a small town criticizes the mayor and the zoning board rezones his house, the assessor raises his taxes, the police arrest him for minor violations, and the sanitation department declares his sewage system unsafe. Impossible? No, it has all happened to unpopular and powerless people. An aberration? Not at all. It is not the misuse of power that is the evil; the very *existence* of power is an evil. Totalitarianism is simply enough power, of whatever sort, to exercise full control over those within the system.

The point is this: there can be no rule of law in an administrative state. The ideal of the rule of law can be realized only in a political-conflict state which places limits upon official power and permits diversity to exist. Once everything is subject to regulation, the rule of law is inevitably lost, for the rule of law cannot stand as an independent principle of society; it is always tied to the question of power. The real issue in any society is the degree of power. Is that power divided or massed? Is it controlled? In a managerial society, where the individual is subject to the vast regulatory power of the state, the rule of law becomes an empty, hollow concept.

With the advent of deep cultural conflict in the United States, the law has lost any pretense of neutrality and become a major element used by one side in the struggle. The way law is employed in the ghetto, in cases involving war protesters, and in drug-possession cases among the young has made almost the whole new culture "illegal." During the summer of 1970, nearly every attempt to hold an outdoor rock festival anywhere in the United States was subject to repression by legal means. An instructive example was the Powder Ridge Festival, supposed to be held at a ski resort in Connecticut on the weekend of August 1. A judge declared the whole festival to be a "nuisance" because of the traffic congestion it might create, and issued an "unappealable" injunction against it. Of course, the rock fans responded by coming anyway, perhaps in part to show their contempt for this species of law. Equally instructive was a recent action by the Board of Regents of the University of California. Ignoring the recommendations of faculties and administrators, the regents delayed promotions for two professors deemed to be left wing and at the same time gave extraordinary and unrequested salary raises to two professors who had been vocal in a way that appealed to right-wing sensibilities. Both actions carried with them, of course, the full sanction of the regents' legal authority.

One further thing needs to be said concerning the function of law in the Corporate State. In any society, there is some medium that intervenes between the individual values, choices, and needs of people and the social structure that results. In a primitive society, this mediator is the cultural-social tradition; it provides a society that is encrusted with many uses of the past, but in a long-range sense reflects the beliefs and values of the people in it. Beginning with the market system and the industrial revolution, a new mediator appeared: money. As Marx said, money became the pimp between man and his values. Money did not, of course, provide as accurate a reflection of socially felt needs as the old culture did; you only got what you paid for, and so there commenced the terrible erosion of values that we discussed in Chapter II. But money was not totally unresponsive to values either; perhaps it reflected 50 percent of them; it enhanced some while neglecting others, but it remained true that what an individual or society wanted, it could (if it could pay for it) succeed in getting.

As we have described the American Corporate State, it is a society very different from both a primitive culture and from the early market system. It is a society which is entirely indifferent to human needs and values, which can be wholly irrational, which can indeed make destructive war on its own people. What medium could possibly furnish a way for human needs to emerge so utterly distorted and ignored, and yet keep the people believing that it was "their" society?

Law is such a medium. Far more than money, law is capable of intervening between man and his humanity. Why? Because law is a medium that is capable of being wholly external to the self. Primitive culture is a reflection of self, modified by time and tradition. Money is a medium which is compelled to reflect the self if the individual happens to have enough of it. But law can be given any form at all; it is capable of being made the servant of interests wholly indifferent to man. Thus it is perfectly suited to the Corporate State. And law has a second great advantage: it is the very means by which standards are carried forward by any human community. When law is employed to serve the Corporate State, the people do not know what has been done to them, for law gets into the individual's mind and substitutes its external standards, whatever they may be, for the individual's own standards. We are taught that it is our moral and civic duty to substitute the law's standards for our own. It is a virtue to obey the law, a sin to ignore it in favor of one's own personal desires. That doctrine serves a community well as long as law is formed in a human image. But what if the law becomes the betrayer of the people? Its use then is diabolical. The people's best instincts are then used to disable them from fighting an enemy; they are told it is morally right to surrender. Thus the people are led to deny their own inner values in favor of law which has become, unknown to them, corrupt, unjust, and antihuman, the servant of an enemy of man—the Corporate State.

Diabolically, law can teach that what is wrong is right, that what is false is true. It does this by supplying the sole normative standard in a society become so complex, so confused, so divided, where people know so little about each other, that they can have no other standard. And so we have today the fact of law that says to a young American, "Thou shalt kill," and a people who believe that it is their moral duty to obey such a law. When a "not" was accidentally left out of one of the Commandments in an early Bible, it was called the Wicked Bible; today it is our law which has become wicked, and which has robbed us of the ability to know what is just and what is human.

Behind the law stands that even more basic element of the Corporate State, "reason." It is a state built upon "reason." But just as what is denominated as "law" has been distorted to fit the ends of the state, so reason itself has been distorted to become merely an expression of the state's values. The "reason" of the Corporate State leaves out so many values, ignores so many human needs, and pushes its own interests so singlemindedly that it amounts to this: the state has called its own insanity by the name of reason.

Ultimately, what the Corporate State does is to separate man from his sources of meaning and truth. To humans, the cosmos cannot be a source of truth. Nor can an entity such as the state. For human beings, the only truth must be found in their own humanity, in each other, in their relation to the living world. When the Corporate State forces its "public interest" truth as a substitute for man's internal truth —for the truth man creates—it cuts him off from the only reality he can live by. We say a man is mad when he believes he is Napoleon, or kills someone because an outside voice told him to do so. A society is mad when its actions are no longer guided by what will make men healthier and happier, when its power is no longer in the service of life. It is this fact that stands back of the fury and rebellion of youth. That anger is based on much else besides. But perhaps its deepest basis is the sense that the State has cut man off from his sources, cut him off from his values and from knowledge. The State is the enemy not merely because of oppression, injustice, and war, but because it has become the enemy of life itself.

VI

THE LOST SELF

What kind of life does man live under the domination of the Corporate State? It is the life that was foreseen in *The Cabinet of Dr. Caligari, Metropolis,* and *M,* a robot life, in which man is deprived of his own being, and he becomes instead a mere role, occupation, or function. The self within him is killed, and he walks through the remainder of his days mindless and lifeless, the inmate and instrument of a machine world.

The process by which man is deprived of his self begins with his institutionalized training in public school for a place in the machinery of the State. The object of the training is not merely to teach him how to perform some specific function, it is to make him become that function; to see and judge himself and others in terms of functions, and to abandon any aspect of self, thinking, questioning, feeling, loving, that has no utility for either production or consumption in the Corporate State. The training for the role of consumer is just as important as the training for a job, and at least equally significant for loss of self.

Job training in school consists of learning goal-behavior and an accompanying discipline and repression of unrelated instincts and interests. Goal-behavior is simply the substitution of outside ends for inner objectives. In the classroom, the goals set for the child include memorizing and being able to repeat certain information and opinions, completing papers and tests according to prescribed standards, and conforming to certain rules of deportment. The more senseless the goals the better, for that child is best prepared who will pursue any goal that is set with equal effort.

Consumer training in school consists of preventing the formation of individual consciousness, taste, aesthetic standards, self-knowledge, and the ability to create one's own satisfactions. Solitude, separateness, undirected time, and silence, which are necessary for consciousness, are not permitted. Groups are encouraged to set values, inhibiting the growth of self-knowledge. Since activity and initiative are the key to finding one's own standards and satisfactions, the child is taught passivity, so that it must depend for satisfactions on what is provided by the society. Thus the child is taught to depend on the fun of cheering for the basketball team, rather than spending the same two hours searching for some individual interest.

While learning to be a producer and a consumer, the child is also trained in how to go about making a substitute-self, one that will get the maximum approval and rewards from the State, a self that will get along better than the real self, the self that might-have-been. The child learns to play a role, to dress, talk, behave, and enjoy things in a certain way, and at the same time to judge others by their success in playing roles. The child also learns to base relationships with others on criteria fixed by the State; other boys and girls can be rated on a fixed objective scale. Further, the child learns that life as defined by the State is not an experience-in-common but an individual position on a scale of relative positions, so that individuals must compete for places in life; "life" consists of a position-achieved, and not in living-as-process. Accordingly, the student is trained to submerge his personality in a series of organizations, teams, groups, and classroom situations; he is compelled to accept the judgment of his peers on many issues, and to believe that "social acceptability" should be a major personal goal.

School is intensely concerned with training students to stop thinking and start obeying. Any course that starts with a textbook and a teacher and ends with an examination runs this danger unless great pains are taken to show students that they are supposed to think for themselves; in most school and college classes, on the other hand, thinking for oneself is actually penalized, and the student learns the value of repeating what he is told. Public school is "obedience school"; the student is taught to accept authority without question, to respect authority simply because of its position, to obey not merely in the area of school regulations but in the area of facts and ideas as well. He is told to accept hierarchical authority—that principals, deans, "adults" have the right to make decisions concerning him without consulting him or being responsible to him in any way. Everything that happens is decided by someone other than the student—the curriculum (some of which may even be dictated by state law), and all other school activities; what apparent freedom the students have, such as publishing their own newspaper, is like the "freedom" of a prison newspaper; it can be suspended at any time. Democracy, while praised in theory, is rejected in practice by the school. The student is trained away from democracy; instead, he is most elaborately trained in joining a hierarchy. Every organization he belongs to has a hierarchy similar to that which he will encounter in the outside world. From the school paper to the camera club there is a president, secretary-treasurer, and underlings. In a structure such as the school newspaper, almost all of the subtleties of the corporate executive suite are reproduced and practiced. In short, democracy and independence are among the greatest sins in public school.

From the outside, reading textbooks, writing papers and essays, doing homework, engaging in classroom recitations and discussions, may have all the appearance of work that is good for the mind. But a closer look (and this is true of college as well as high school) shows how little thinking is really going on. This is child labor, an ordeal that both keeps the child off the streets and trains him in the carrying out of prescribed tasks. A history examination reveals it all: it asks for names, dates, and conclusions found in the textbook or outside reading. The real questions on the test are: "Did you do the job that you were told to do?" "Do you remember what you were told?" "Have you learned to carry out a job carefully and accurately?"

"Did you have the self-discipline to do this job despite all the temptations and other activities that offered themselves?" "Can you sit longer and concentrate harder than the others in the class?" The youngster who gets A's is well on his way to being suitable material for the Corporate State.

One of the great purposes of the school is to indoctrinate the inmates. Vast powers are set to work on remolding their thinking. Indoctrination is not the same as teaching. The purpose of teaching is to help the student to think for himself. The purpose of indoctrination is to compel him to accept someone else's ideas, someone else's version of the facts. It is indoctrination whenever the student can get a bad mark for disagreeing. Indoctrination may take many forms. There may be a blatant course entitled "Democracy versus Communism." Even if there is not, the usual courses in American studies, history, and civics will present a strongly biased point of view. As we have just begun to learn, the bias may not only be political, it often is racial as well. The school tries to force-feed a whole set of values and attitudes: about advertising, business, competition, success, and the American way of life. And this is carried on amid a pervasive atmosphere of dishonesty and hypocrisy. No one will admit that America might be a bad country, that the textbooks might be boring and stupid, that much of what the school does may not be in the best interests of students, that there could be other ways of doing what routine requires.

The productive side of the American State is organized as a meritocracy, a hierarchy of jobs or roles for which the individual is trained and fitted. His training, abilities, character, opinions, and loyalties, that is, the whole of his public, exterior self, must be shaped to this end. Most people who describe the American scene would prefer to emphasize the "voluntary" nature of the process; the individual *chooses* to seek and qualify for a position. But from the point of view of the process as a whole the "choice" to join organized society in some capacity does not really exist, and all of the arrangements we will describe, educational, legal, and otherwise, are designed to make it imperative for an individual to fit himself into the hierarchy. No measures, including use of the penal laws, are neglected in prodding lagging "volunteers." The meritocracy process produces two major consequences. First, it creates a working force for the machinery of the State. Second, for all but those at the top, it creates a condition of "inferiority" in which the individual is looked down upon by society and looks down upon himself because he is "not as good" as someone more successful. It is the meritocracy that makes the worker, white or black, into a "nigger" who despises himself.

A key to insight is to understand what is meant by "merit." The standards of "merit" are set by each organization or profession and its needs. The man best qualified flies the airplane, or serves as a doctor or automobile repairman. We would not want to fly in a jet piloted by the least qualified man. But we must recognize some further aspects of this. The word "merit" is used in a purely functional sense. It means only functional usefulness, it implies no ethical or humanistic judgment whatever, and to a considerable extent its standards are an "accident" of technology. At one stage of technology a big man may be valued, at another stage, a small man or a man with a rapid heartbeat, etc. These matters to a large degree lie outside the control of the individual, who is fortunate or unfortunate as the circumstances dictate.

In school, the meritocracy shapes the whole structure of education. The object is not simply to train each child for a function in the State, but to begin the process of arranging everyone in a hierarchy of statuses, a process which will be completed many years later. Accordingly, school is full of devices for measuring and comparing children. Tests—academic, psychological, physical, and social—dominate the curriculum. The tracking system, in many public high schools, separates students into "ability groups" for their training. The end of the high school training process comes with the State's decision: who goes to a good college, who goes to a bad college, who goes to the white-collar occupations, who is destined for the factory or the filling station. Except for those born to wealth or hopeless poverty, this classification is the most important thing that happens to a person in our society; it determines almost everything else about the kind of life he will have. It determines a man's entire standing in the community; the amount of honor, gain, and respect he receives; indeed, his entire value as a human being. It also determines his relationships to others, friendships, how he lives, his interests except for an ever-narrowing private area which in many cases vanishes into nothingness by middle age. "Merit" also constitutes the way in which a man forms a knowledge of himself; it becomes the key to his identity, self-respect, and self-knowledge. He learns to say "I *am* . . . a lawyer / auto worker," etc.

The opposite side of "merit" is doing one of society's undesirable jobs—that of a blue- or white-collar worker. For these jobs, the most important requirement is not any affirmative form of training, although that is of course necessary, but a negative form of training—training in giving up those sides of human nature that are incompatible with the job. No person with a strongly developed aesthetic sense, a love of nature, a passion for music, a desire for reflection, or a strongly marked independence could possibly be happy or contented in a factory or white-collar job. Hence these characteristics must be snuffed out in school. Taste must be lowered and vulgarized, internal reflection must be minimized, feeling for beauty cut off. All of these processes are begun in school, and then carried into later life in the case of those who are destined for the lower half of the nation's productive force.

What the school determines to accomplish it does so in a constant and total atmosphere of violence. We do not mean physical violence; we mean violence in the sense of any assault upon, or violation of, the personality. An examination or test is a form of violence. Compulsory gym, to one embarrassed or afraid, is a form of violence. The requirement that a student must get a pass to walk in the hallways is violence. Compelled attendance in the classroom, compulsory studying in study hall, is violence. We do not suggest that all violence is an evil, or that all of it could be avoided, but the amount of violence in a high school is staggering. There are more subtle kinds; humiliation, insults, embarrassments, and above all, judgments. A judgment, unasked for, is an act of violence; if one met a man at a party, and the man said, "I'd pronounce you approximately a B-minus individual," one would recognize how violent the act of grading or judging really is. It ceases to be violence only when it is made affirmative by affection and concern, emotions that rarely exist in a high school system.

The authority exercised by the school is in the purest sense lawless, in that the school authorities have virtually unlimited discretion. They make and change the rules, they provide whatever procedure there is for deciding if the rules have been violated, they determine punishments (backed, if necessary, by the law). There is no rule of law by which the student can assert any rights whatever. As in any total institution, all of the many different powers of the school can be brought to bear on an individual, so that he can be flunked and also removed from an athletic team if both are needed to ensure compliance. And the school's power extends out into the indefinite future. For the school can make possible, or thwart, the prospects of a job or a college education. Given black marks in high school, a student may find himself crippled for life, unable to get into a good college, unable to pursue a desired career in consequence. It is as if a prison had the authority to permanently maim or cripple prisoners for disobeying the rules; the school's jurisdiction lasts only three or four years, but its sentences can last a lifetime.

While the school's authority is lawless, school is nevertheless an experience made compulsory by the full power of the law, including criminal penalties. (The option to go to private school does exist for families that can afford it, but this is not the students' own option, and it is obviously available only to a few.) School has no prison bars, or locked doors like an insane asylum, but the student is no more free to leave it than a prisoner is free to leave the penitentiary.

Thus at the core of the high school experience is

something more terrible than authority, indoctrination, or violence—it is an all-out assault upon the newly emerging adolescent self. The self needs, above all, privacy, liberty, and a degree of sovereignty to develop. It needs to try things, to search, to explore, to test, to err. It needs solitude—solitude to bring sense to its experiences and thereby to create a future. It needs, not enforced relationships with others, rigidly categorized into groups, teams, and organizations, but an opportunity to try different forms of relationships— to try them, to withdraw, to re-create. The school is a brutal machine for destruction of the self, controlling it, heckling it, hassling it into a thousand busy tasks, a thousand noisy groups, never giving it a moment to establish a knowledge within.

After a person has been classified by the meritocracy he is fitted into the personal prison that each individual carries with him in the form of a role. Roles are nothing new to the world—peasant, knight, and bishop had roles in the Middle Ages; medicine men and warriors have roles in a primitive tribe. But roles have changed somewhat; they are ever more highly specialized, and they grow constantly more pervasive, cutting deeper into every side of an individual. The basic process which is going on during all the years of schooling is learning to become the kind of person society wants, instead of the kind of person one is, or would like to be. At an elementary level, this is seen in the student's attempting to become "academic" when his real interests are mechanical, sensual, or just plain undeveloped. At a higher and more tragic level, one can observe the violent alienation of law students from their prior selves. Finding themselves in law school for many possible reasons, they discover that they are expected to become "argumentative" personalities who listen to what someone else is saying only for the purpose of disagreeing, "analytic" rather than receptive people, who dominate information rather than respond to it; and intensely competitive and self-assertive as well. Since many of them are not this sort of personality before they start law school, they react initially with anger and despair, and later with resignation as their self-alienation becomes complete. In a very real sense, they "become stupider" during law school, as the range of their imagination is limited, their ability to respond with sensitivity and to receive impressions is reduced, and the scope of their reading and thinking is progressively narrowed.

Training toward alienation, from elementary school onward, reaches its climax when the student is forced to make his choice, first of a college major, then of a career. Surrounding these moments is a gradually built-up picture of man as a creature who has one single "right" vocation in life, the vocation for which he is "best fitted," and for which he can be aptitude tested and trained. The choice is surrounded by great anxiety and doubt, particularly because the student may find that his own nature fails to conform to the expected norm. He may find that he is seriously interested in music, surfing, and astronomy, that no career can encompass these interests, and that consequently he is faced with having to give up a part of himself. Often he has an "identity crisis" at this point, and it would only seem fair to say that the crisis is really not of his making at all, but one forced upon him by society's demand that he give up a portion of the identity which he has already formed. This sort of "choice" can only be a sad and desperate moment. For a young person is not only asked to give up a large portion of the "identity" he already has in favor of something unknown and perhaps far less satisfying; he must also give up all the as yet undiscovered possibilities within him, and thus commit a part of himself to death before it can be born and tried out. When a college student decides on medicine, he puts out of his mind the chance that he might learn about literature and discover a special affinity there; he will never give that potential in him a chance, but for a long time he will wonder about it.

In discussing Consciousness II, we dealt with role-playing in the context of false consciousness—the modern young couple whose activities and tastes are formed outside themselves, so that they ski or collect antiques because of values they accept from their roles. But role-playing can also be viewed as a set of limitations on each individual—our concern here. The role-prison drastically restricts such fundamental aspects of personality as relationships with others, personal expression, modes of thought, and goals and aspirations. Indeed, it does so with such total effectiveness that we are usually not at all aware of the prison we are in.

The deepest form of role-constraint is the fact that the individual's own "true" self, if still alive, must watch helplessly while the role-self lives, enjoys, and relates to others. A young lawyer, out on a date, gets praised for his sophistication, competence, the important cases he is working on, the important people he knows, his quick and analytical professional mind. His role-self accepts the praise, but his true self withers from lack of recognition, from lack of notice, from lack of appreciation and companionship, and as the young lawyer accepts the praise he feels hollow and lonely.

If the professional is imprisoned by his role, the policeman, nurse, salesman, secretary, and factory worker are even more enclosed by the relationships, thoughts, and goals prescribed by their occupations. On the job, most of what happens is sterile, impersonal, empty of experience. An airline ticket salesman, a stewardess, a pilot, a baggage handler, a telephone reservations girl, a plane mechanic, an air controller, are all expected to be mechanical people, thinking their own thoughts and expressing their own feelings as little as possible, putting in an entire working day that is dictated by the functional requirements of their jobs.

For both the professional and the nonprofessional, regulation does not stop with the job itself. Job requirements merge into requirements of the society as a whole. These broader and vaguer restraints are difficult to perceive, we are so accustomed to them. We are often aware of some of the particulars of this direct supervision, such as laws against the use of drugs, but as in most matters where the Corporate State is concerned we do not see the whole design. We think that the state has intervened to prevent certain excesses: murder, theft, drug addiction. But the pattern is not a series of negatives or prohibitions imposed on otherwise unregulated private lives for the good of the community. Instead, the state has undertaken to define, within rather strict limits, the life-style of its citizens with respect to sex life, culture and consciousness, and political thought and activity.

The prescribed way of life can be summarized quite easily. Sex life shall consist of a monogamous marriage; extramarital sex, premarital sex, sex exchanged between two couples, communal sex, homosexuality, and polymorphous sexual expression are all rejected. Cultural life shall include anything produced and prescribed by the machine, but it may not include even minor deviations such as long hair, marijuana, nude swimming, vagrancy. Political life shall be limited to loyalty to the Corporate State, enforced by loyalty oaths, internal security laws, and restrictions on speech and expression; for example, life is made distinctly unpleasant for the man who wishes to contend publicly that "our form of government" is wrong. All of this repression is upheld under the legal doctrine, mentioned earlier, that "the national interest" prevails over any "individual interest." And it is all enforced by an elaborate system of official surveillance, including wiretapping, eavesdropping, invasions of privacy by police searches, police photography of demonstrators, congressional investigations, and all of the other methods with which we have become familiar.

The full force of these restrictions can only be appreciated when they are seen not merely as a pattern, but as a seamless web in which each restraint augments all of the others. The individual feels pressure from the meritocracy, from the rules concerning him, from the organization he works for, from the draft and public welfare, from regulatory laws. Anything he does is likely to be the subject of notice by some official agency. Significantly, the law makes little distinction between the criminal and non-criminal areas; a "narcotics addict," for example, might be subject to "involuntary civil commitment" rather than "criminal punishment." In other words, the law is not particularly concerned with distinguishing between whether an individual has breached some rule or whether he is in need of affirmative correction; criminal and civil laws are simply different means to produce the desired result. And there is cooperation among the different agencies of pressure; thus, from time to time one notes in the newspaper that some political dissenter, not easily reached by any specific law, has been attacked by permitting some portion of the character information on file concerning him to be "leaked" to his enemies; for example, New Orleans District Attorney Garrison, who persisted in questioning the official version of President Kennedy's assassination, was suddenly made the subject of newspaper stories based on a highly "confidential" army psychiatrist's file concerning him. Or a college professor in upstate New York fighting the marijuana laws is faced with loss of his house due to cancellation of his fire insurance by "private" insurance companies. Or a hippie group living in a small town is driven out by zealous enforcement of zoning laws. This pervasive official power over individuals gives that special gray, oppressive feeling of totalitarian countries that appears in Kafka's *The Trial;* one may have obeyed all known laws, but still the authorities are watching.

One of the ways we can perceive this surveillance most clearly is in the use of the criterion of "character" when individuals are selected for college, graduate school, employment, and promotion. "Character" means the individual's personality, habits, friends, activities, politics, opinions, associations, and disciplinary and police record. All of these are thought by an increasing number of organizations to be an appropriate subject for investigation in order to reach a decision on an individual's "merit." In many cases these matters are thought to have an importance equal to the individual's "ability" and "achievement." Surveillance of character has become pervasive in our society. Most colleges and graduate schools and large private employers investigate applicants' character, and the federal government has elaborate procedures and many thousands of people occupied full time with character investigations. Where the government is concerned, the chief emphasis is upon making sure of political loyalty. Most agencies that determine qualifications for the various professions and occupations, such as the committees governing admission to the bar, licensing authorities for physicians, taxi drivers, boxers, television station owners, real estate brokers, liquor dealers, and wilderness guides consider character an important element in determining their actions.

What does "good" character mean to all of these official investigators? First, that the individual has never violated, or been accused of violating, any laws, regulations, or rules of any private organization. Second, that the individual is not rebellious against the Corporate State, or against the specific objectives of organizations or against duly constituted authority, public or private, or against the conventions of life. Third, that he is a "team" man who goes along with the group, does not think or act with undue independence, and acts in ways that are approved by others. Fourth, that he is not emotionally unreliable or undesirable. Fifth, that he has commended himself to his superiors at various stages of his life and in the various institutions through which he has passed.

To ascertain "character," organizations make use of police and other official records, questioning of the applicant himself, and statements by school authorities, former employers, friends, and enemies. These sources of information are carefully and permanently kept secret from the applicant, who has no opportunity to refute anything reported concerning him. No adequate effort is made to ascertain the truth or reliability of statements made about an individual. A college teacher, for example, may fill out dozens of forms each year without having anyone check the basis for his opinions. Persons asked to supply information are not limited to reasonably objective facts, but invited to answer such questions as "cooperation with others," "ethical standards," "appropriateness of dress," "language and conduct," "ability to react constructively to criticisms, suggestions, advice," "emotional stability." Although few teachers, school authorities, or former employers know individuals in their school or organization very well, they are told to answer the questions on the basis of whatever opinions or information they have.

The information and opinions concerning an individual's character are filed away and continue to be available down through the years. Nothing in the file is ever changed or disclosed to the individual, so that his character-on-file takes on an independent existence that may have an ever more remote relationship to the real individual, assuming that it ever did resemble him. The rule of most organizations is, when in doubt, don't take a chance. Thus, a file that suggests an individual may be a "risk" constitutes a permanent disability to him. The consequences to the individual of this stress upon character are profound. Beginning with childhood, he learns that he must trim his sails, be prudent, please those in authority, avoid experimentation and trouble, and try to force his individuality into the rigid mold of "good character" prescribed by the State. The State, not content with dictating his working life, has thus intruded deeply into his private life and private personality.

The personality that emerges from all of this processing is, in the language of the new generation, "uptight." Uptight means rigid, tense, afraid, narrowly limited. But the concept of uptightness, as developed by the new generation, carries a far deeper critique of the American personality. In part, uptightness might be defined as how much of society a person carries around within himself. The uptight person is concerned with goals, with competence, with coping, with managing the past and the future. He is a person with a coating or crust over him, so that he can tolerate impersonal relations, inauthenticity, loneliness, hassling, bad vibrations. He is preoccupied with the nonsensual aspects of existence, so that he has little capacity to receive or give out sensual vibrations. He is a person who can successfully handle the frustrations, difficulties, traumas, and demands of the Corporate State, and by that very fact is diminished in his humanity, tense, angry, and tight as he confronts the world. Anyone who can function efficiently in an airport or large hotel is uptight, because he has to be.

One place this tension can be felt with the greatest immediacy is in a "nice" "clean" suburb, preferably upper middle class, such as can be found outside any city in America. Here the casual walker *feels* the managerial world. He is watched with suspicion, whether on Main Street or on a residential street. Police cars cruise by slowly, inspecting him carefully; five minutes later the police are back, passing the stroller with an even slower, more deliberate scrutiny.

Housewives look out from their windows, as if spying an unexpected patch of dirt in an otherwise spick-and-span house. Storekeepers and other "solid citizens" follow him with their eyes down the center of town. Is this small-town America, with its typically suspicious provincialism? No, this is Darien, Bethesda, or Paoli, and its residents are sophisticated people, men who work in the big city, women who went to college. Is the walker just a bit paranoid? He would answer that he feels no such paranoia in a city, or in the real country, or in a lower-class suburb, or in a high-class suburb that is also a college town. It is the business-managerial suburb that can tolerate nothing strange, different, unknown; it is here one feels the intensity of the demand that every individual be regulated and controlled in "the national interest."

To the description we have given so far, we must add the impoverishment of the individual in his relationship to the public community. In the first place, the individual finds himself with no meaningful work to do—his job is increasingly frustrating, artificial, and purposeless. In the second place, he finds himself powerless to take action that would have any meaningful impact on society, and on the social evils which are increasingly apparent. Thus, he is not only deprived of "private" experience, he is deprived of a man's role in society. Appearances cannot remove the fact of his impotency, or give him a sense of manhood in the public realm.

In the years following World War II the evils afflicting America were visible to all, and reflected in much of the art of the time. American painting showed the desolation of urban life, and the movies were even more vivid in their depiction of alienation, violence, and claustrophobia. Such films as *A Place in the Sun* or Sam Fuller's *Pickup on South Street* showed that the dehumanization of life and environment was seen and felt by many people. This being the case, it was demeaning that no one was able to act. At the very end of *Casablanca*, a film made when America had just entered World War II, Humphrey Bogart is a man who can still change fate by taking action. Perhaps *Casablanca* was the last moment when most Americans believed that.

The individual was placed in the position of seeing much that was wrong in his society but remaining personally aloof. He could not be passionate; he could not be moral. He might have private feelings but publicly, and especially in his work, he went along with the system. Writing in 1967, Arthur Miller called the present age the Age of Abdication (*The New York Times*, December 23, 1967); it is equally an age without a public life. Sadly, many of those who took no public stand undoubtedly felt deeply concerned, but there was no communication between like-minded people, no solidarity which would have made effective action possible. To take a public stand meant being picked off, one by one, without even the satisfaction of having done any good. To perceive evil was to feel utterly alone.

For the individual of the Fifties and Sixties, deprived of his political and public manhood, denied work of which he could be proud, the Corporate State provided substitute images of the heroic life: the cowboy, the gangster, the detective, the virile romantic hero. Rare indeed was the popular entertainment which attempted to show that an individual could be proud of his job or, except in war, proud of his contribution to society. He must watch the deterioration of his community as a spectator in the bleachers, a non-participant in the great events of his times.

The product of the system we have described is the "new man" of the technological age, a man suitable for operating machines and working within organizations. He is a man who permits himself to be dominated by technique, by propaganda, by training, by advertising, by the state, all to the end that he shall be as perfectly suited as possible for playing his part. He is an artificially streamlined man, from whom irrationality, unpredictability, and complexity have been removed as far as possible. He is oversimplified in the service of reason; he tries to control himself by reason, and the result is not man but a smoothed-down man.

In John Barth's novel *End of the Road* we meet a young couple who attempt to "understand" each other perfectly, in verbal terms, disallowing all mysteries and contradictions. They want to be able to see right through each other, without any obstacles such as arbitrary or irrational fictions. What they achieve is a reductive and shallow view of each other. They banish uniqueness, expose everything that is hidden, assault every last corner of privacy, and end up as people without depth. Like overly functional architecture, they deny man's artistic need to elaborate his surroundings by carving them with designs that suggest the unknowable. Striving to know the past and the future perfectly, they have all but eliminated the richness of present experience. Adaptation to the machine not only precludes complexity, it prohibits personal growth. The individual can, of course, grow in the direction of increasing his specialty. But any other growth has a definite disutility. A person who continued to grow after he had chosen his occupation might want to change jobs or occupations in middle life; he might want to change wives; he might demand that other people relate to him in new ways; he might question his place in the hierarchy, and question his dedication to his present goals. Even if he is in one of the learned professions, he cannot grow, he becomes ever narrower. His human self is covered over by his alienated existence.

Consider a social event among professional people—a dinner, cocktail party, garden party, or just a lunch among friends. Everything that takes place occurs within incredibly narrow limits. The events are almost completely structured around conversation. No one pays any sensual attention to the food, the mind-altering experience of the drink, or to the weather, or to the nonverbal side of personality; the people do not listen to music together, or lie on the grass and look at the sky together, or share food, or sit silently and exchange vibrations. They do not talk about philosophy or subjective experience. They do not strive for genuine relationships, but keep their conversation at the level of sociability, one-upmanship, and banter, all of which leave the individual himself uncommitted, and not vulnerable. Above all, there is no exchange of brotherhood and love. Why not? There is no law against any of these possibilities, no employer forbids them, no file threatens to expose them. Professional people are so deeply in their roles that they simply cannot imagine any of these other possibilities; they may look sophisticated and free, but they are painfully stereotyped and constricted; to get them to stretch out on the floor and listen to music is to ask the impossible; for even if they wanted to, they could not bring themselves to do it freely.

Nor is this constraint limited to personal relationships and expression; if one overheard the conversation it would be clear that the modes of thought and purposes of a professional group are as limited as if thought-control had been imposed. They are dedicated to a certain pattern of "rational" thought, they limit their view of the world to their own specialty, and in fact they appear impervious to new ideas altogether, merely continuing to think in established channels for the rest of their lives, never allowing their minds to be startled into new realms after reaching maturity. If told there was a new philosophy or religion coming into prominence, few would be willing even to hear what it was about. Similarly, they allow their goals to continue to be guided by the tests, rewards, statuses, and honors which their world provides, never questioning these as valid goals. In short, what seems to be the freest class in American society turns out to be locked into a cage from which even the desire for real freedom seems to have fled; the party is a dull affair.

The end result of this personal and public impoverishment is a hollow man. Look again at our middle-class, professional people's party. Their goals—status, promotion, institutional approval, and a correct image for the outside world—are hollow in terms of personal satisfaction and meaning. They work under terrible stress, which prevents them from finding more genuine meaning and is likely to drive them to ulcers, heart attacks, or the psychiatrist's couch. In Marx's sense, they are alienated from their determinate selves, alienated from their work, and alienated from their needs.

A few of them even go to plastic surgeons to change their faces, but many have done something plastic to their inner selves. Many have several different and separate selves, different roles which are not integrated and prevent anyone from confronting the individual as a whole. They have surrounded themselves by things, and rendered themselves passive in the process; it is as if they have given up the power to change and grow and create, and things have acquired this power instead; things change and dance, and the individual sits motionless, besotted, and empty. For he who can neither act to fulfill his own genuine needs, nor act to help his society in its dire need, has no genuine existence. The existentialists believe that man exists when he acts; Orestes, in Sartre's play *The Flies*, does not exist until he assumes responsibility for his country and himself. And so the party we have been watching is a party to which no real selves are invited to come, a social event for alienated selves. "I'd like you to meet Dr. Smith's alienated self," the host politely says to the alienated self of another of his guests. Nobody minds, so long as no real selves have been invited.

But the real tragedy of the lost self in America is not that of the professional middle class, who have had all the advantages, but the tragedy of the white-collar and blue-collar worker, who never had any chance. The meritocracy has placed them low on its scale, convincing them that they have little value as people. The productive state has demanded output from them all their lives, draining them of life, creativity, vitality, and never giving them a chance to be renewed. Competition has made them fearful and suspicious of their fellow men, believing that every other man is not a brother but a threatening rival with a knife at the throat of his adversaries. Imprisoned in masks, they endure an unutterable loneliness. Their lives are stories of disappointed hopes, hopes disintegrating into the bitterness and envy that is ever present in even the most casual conversation of the worker. If they had an individual excellence or greatness, in some area, it has been passed over by society; they are Joan Baez or Bob Dylan, working in a bank or a filling station until their minds and bodies have forgotten the poetry that once was in them. They are driven by outside authority, not merely that of the state and their employer, but by the nameless authority that says "it must be done this way," the authority of what Heidegger called "the they." Caring nothing about their work, nothing about what happens to them, they face a prospect stretching all the way to retirement, another form of death. But death is with them already, in their sullen boredom, their unchanging routines, their minds closed to new ideas and new feelings, their bodies slumped in front of television to watch the ball game on Sunday.

If anyone doubts these words, let him look at the faces of America. Stand at a commuter train station and see the blank, hollow, bitter faces. Sit in a government cafeteria and see the faces set in rigidity, in unawareness, in timid compliance, or bureaucratic obstinacy; the career women with all their beauty fled, the men with all their manhood drained. We do not look at faces very often in America, even less than we look at ruined rivers and devastated hills.

What have we all lost? What aspects of the human experience are either missing altogether from our lives or present only in feeble imitation of their real quality?

Let us take our list off the yellow pad where it was jotted down one fine morning in early summer.

Adventure, Travel The Yukon, the Hebrides, a blizzard, fog on the Grand Banks, the lost cities of Crete, climbing a mountain on rock and ice in elemental cold and wind.

Sex Experiences with many different people, in different times, circumstances, and localities, in moments of happiness, sorrow, need, and comfortable familiarity, in youth and in age.

Nature The experience of living in harmony with nature, on a farm, or by the sea, or near a lake or meadow, knowing, using, and returning the elements; Thoreau at Walden.

Physical Activity Chopping wood, carrying a boat, running, walking, climbing, experiencing heat and cold, swimming, building a house, paddling a canoe.

Clothes Clothes to express various moods, and to express the body, its strength, its shape, its sensuality, its harmony with the rest of nature. Clothes for fun, for work, for dignity.

Morality Having a moral stand with respect to something happening to oneself, to others, or to society; maintaining that stand, and giving it expression.

Bravery
Worship
Magic and Mystery
Awe, Wonder, Reverence
Fear, Dread, Awareness of Death
Spontaneity
Romance
Dance

Play

Ceremony and Ritual

Performing for Others

Creativity   In more primitive cultures, creativity and art are part of everyday life, and each person has an opportunity to exercise his creative side.

Imagination

Mind-expanding Drugs

Music as a Part of Daily Life

Multimedia Experiences   Music, light, smell, dance, all together.

Alterations of Time   Staying up all night, getting up before dawn, sleeping all day, working three days straight, or being wholly oblivious to measured time.

Seasons   Observing the four changes of season by stopping other activities for a while and going to some place where the change is fully visible.

Growth, Learning, Change   Constantly learning new things, experiencing changes of feelings and personality, continually growing in experience and consciousness.

Harmony   Enough time and reflection to assemble various experiences and changes into a harmony within the individual, relating them to each other and to earlier experiences.

Inner Life   Introspection, reflection.

Responding to Own Needs   Staying in bed when the need is felt, drinking a milk shake on a hot afternoon, or stopping everything to watch a rainstorm.

Own Special Excellence   Having enough independence to disregard other people's standards of excellence, discover one's own special excellence, and then pursue it.

Wholeness   Being completely present with another

person, or completely given to some experience, rather than being partially withheld as most roles demand.

Sensuality   Being sensually aware of all the stimuli at a given moment; smell, temperature, breeze, noises, the tempo of one's own body.

New Feelings   Experiencing feelings or emotions qualitatively different from those previously known.

Expanded Consciousness   Experiencing previously unknown kinds of awareness, new values, new understanding.

New Environments   Experiencing a new total environment long enough to make adjustments to it and understand its terms (such as six months in the tropics).

Creating an Environment   Taking whatever elements are given, natural, human, and social, and making a unique pattern out of them as one's own creation.

Conflict, Disorder

Suffering, Pain

Challenge

Transcendence

Myth Making and Telling

Literature, Art, Theatre, Films

Bare Feet

Aesthetic Enjoyment of Food

New Ways of Thinking

Nonrational Thoughts

New Ideas

Ability to Listen to Others

People: Perceiving Them Non-verbally

People: Seeing the Uniqueness of Each One

People: Creativity in Relationships

People: Exchanging Experiences

People: Exchanging Feelings
People: Being Vulnerable with Them
People: Friendship
Affection
Community
Solidarity
Brotherhood
Freedom.

In Ken Kesey's remarkable book *One Flew Over the Cuckoo's Nest*, the rowdy, full-blooded hero finds himself, although perfectly sane, confined to a mental hospital ward under the jurisdiction of "The Big Nurse." The Nurse is determined to "cure" McMurphy, the hero, of his refusal to accept the system of the hospital, and his efforts to get other patients to reassert their independence and sense of life. Slowly, the claustrophobic, suffocating net is drawn closer around McMurphy, his struggles are taken as evidence that he is insane, and "for his own good" he is subjected to mind-damaging shock treatments. When he still resists conforming to the total supervision and madness of the hospital, the Big Nurse has him lobotomized, leaving him a blank and helpless vegetable. Kesey's book is about the American working man, deprived of his virility, his manhood, and his intellect by the system we have described. It is no wonder that the book has created an extraordinary impression upon today's young people. High school, the office, and the factory prepare a bleak fate for our youth. Indeed, the saddest thing of all in America is probably the fate of most of its teen-agers. For at sixteen or seventeen, no matter how oppressive the Corporate State, there is still a moment when life is within their grasp. There are a few years when they pulse to music, know beaches and the sea, value what is raunchy, wear clothes that express their bodies, flare against authority, seek new experience, know how to play, laugh, and feel, and cherish one another. But it is a short, short road from Teensville to Squarestown; soon their senses have been dulled, their strength put under restraint, their minds lobotomized; bodies still young, cut off from selves, walk the windowless, endless corridors of the Corporate State.

VII

"IT'S JUST LIKE LIVING"

When man allows machines and the machine-state to master his consciousness, he imperils not only his inner being but also the world he inhabits and upon which he depends. He permits himself to be forced to exist in a universe that is, in the most profound sense, at war with human life.

We are slowly becoming aware of what is happening to our environment. More and more individuals and groups speak out against the destruction of the natural world. But as yet we do not see that this destruction has an imperative logic behind it. The Corporate State draws its vitality by a procedure that impoverishes the natural world. It grows by a process that we shall call "impoverishment by substitution." It is not a question of mistaken priorities or lack of awareness or even of greed. The "progress" of the State is rooted in destruction of existing values.

Most discussion concerning our environmental crisis assumes that it is just a case of neglect or of excess. Perhaps the most frequent view is that we have lagged —that a combination of the Vietnam War and inertia have permitted problems to grow out of hand. A second view is that we are guilty of a moral failure, that in our rush to acquire and grow, we have not paused to tend to deeper qualitative values; we have simply not assumed moral responsibility for how things are used—the ends to which new technology and systems are put. Under a third and related view, our problem is the doctrine of *laissez innover*, permitting the introduction of any and all technology without controls, priorities, or values. A fourth view emphasizes a more general failure to plan—a failure to agree in advance on goals and then to provide for them. A fifth view, perhaps the most pessimistic, suggests that our success itself leads to loss of meaning, that affluence and progress bring ennui and surfeit, that the trouble with our children is that they have too much.

All of these views "blame" man but they do not take account of the uncontrolled forces that dominate the Corporate State. What is the logic of these forces? What do they, if left to themselves, tend to do with man's natural world? Up to now we have stressed their indifference to man's values. But this indifference does not mean that the forces lack a pattern of their own. They want to exploit, for their own purposes, the natural and human resources that are available. They want to substitute for whatever exists something of their own manufacture. And they want to prevent man from becoming aware of what is happening to him.

The logic of exploitation was first described by Marx in the context of early capitalism. He saw it as the means by which a surplus was built up for the ruling classes. In the Corporate State the concept is both broader and more impersonal. It is a failure to pay the "hidden" or social costs of economic progress and production. By emphasizing costs instead of the "value" of labor or resources, the concept is freed from the narrower idea of market value. The broader concept is described by E. J. Mishan in *The Costs of Economic Growth*. It applies both to human labor and to the physical and social environment. By placing the two side by side, we can see exploitation in its larger dimensions.

Suppose a man is employed to work in a coal mine, and after twenty years he develops an occupational illness of the lungs. The costs of his illness, to himself and his family, in terms of direct expenses, losses of opportunity for his children, and more general deprivation and suffering, are part of the "hidden" costs of mining coal. If they are not included in the man's salary, or otherwise paid for by the producer, they fall upon the individuals concerned and upon society, and the social gain represented by production of coal is actually offset by the uncompensated loss of health, education, happiness, and psychological stability. For example, we may have more coal but also more juvenile delinquency if the miner's children are uncared for at home; the real costs of coal include crime, more policemen, courts, community insecurity. Perhaps, by some measurement, the production of coal still represents a net gain, but it will be far less of a gain than is usually assumed, and may actually, by other standards, be a net loss.

Just as the mining of coal has its unexamined human costs, so it has "hidden" environmental costs. To call them "hidden" is simply to show how our awareness has been dulled, for they assault one's senses and one's feelings. And to call them "environmental" is also an inadequate description, for environmental costs are really indirect human costs. What we are referring to is the destruction of landscape by mining, the denudation of hills and valleys, the pollution of streams and of air, the degradation of cultural life by long hours, physical exhaustion, lack of education, and the destruction of community. The cost of coal includes making the world a more depressing place to live in, and this should be measured against the energy coal gives off.

Many of the "hidden" costs of production are directly related to that "paradox," the continuation, and even growth, of poverty and inequality in the world's most affluent nation. Consider simply the factor of education. Technological progress means that more and more education is required for productive work; education becomes more and more expensive. The need for a more expensive education is therefore a cost of technological advance. If it is not paid for out of profits of technology, the burden is placed directly on the inadequate resources of individuals and communities, and technology is thus subsidized by a segment of the population which, unable to obtain a suitable education, falls into or remains in poverty. In this sense, Marx continues to be right; these people, by their poverty and deprivation, are helping to pay the costs of the latest advances.

Today a man gets poorer simply by standing still. There is a general rise in prices, a gradual inflation each year. One of the important costs of a rapidly growing and changing economy is the risk that each individual bears—that he and his training or job will become obsolete. Such an economy has many victims, but it does not pretend to pay more than a tiny fraction of the costs, although they are just as much costs of production as the physical industrial accidents which once were treated the same way. An example of another type of cost for the individual is the growth of large cities. Living in an urban environment is far more expensive than in a small town. And at the same time so many country pleasures are lost that the urban worker needs expensive substitutes—television, for example, instead of a Sunday afternoon ball game with local friends. Since one of the consequences of "growth" is to make the simple product complicated, individuals are constantly having to pay more for a "better" product—color instead of black-and-white TV, homogenized instead of regular peanut butter. There is no logical place to end this catalogue, but there is a moral place—with the human costs of the draft and war. A man drafted into the army loses some of his most productive years. Some of his best opportunities for education are passed by, his family loses his support, and if he is injured or killed, the loss is incalculable and irreparable. Yet individuals—poor ones especially—are required to pay these costs of the defense and war policies that are one consequence of uncontrolled power. In short, we can say that the same power that turns out America's affluence also creates our social problems of poverty and wealth. Poverty and inequality are part of the cost of the well-being we enjoy. They are not an accidental consequence or some unfinished business, but a built-in part of the structure itself.

What we have said so far is more of a description than an explanation. Why does our society consistently fail to pay the costs of its own growth? For Marx, the explanation lies in the accumulation of surplus capital. For Mishan, it is a question of inadequate economic theory; a failure to recognize the true costs of production. But there is a more general logic to the process we have described. As Galbraith points out in *The New Industrial State,* our economy is long past satisfying the most pressing needs of the society. Today, continued growth depends upon creating new wants, developing new goods and services. In large measure, this is done by a process of *substitution.* One cannot sell anything to a satisfied man. Ergo, make him want something new, or take away something that he has and then sell him something to take its place. Take away man's appreciation of natural body odors and then sell him deodorants and perfumes. Remove adventure from daily life and substitute manufactured adventure on television. Make it hard for an adult man to enjoy physical sport and give him a seat in a stadium to watch professionals play. Give him less time to cook and sell him instant dinners. It has always been contended that the logic of commerce is improvement: make a *better* mousetrap and everyone will profit. But that is only what some optimists hope will be the *result* of commerce. The *logic* of commerce is simply to sell, whether the product is better or worse. Pollution of a beach is of course an accident; only a paranoid would see it as a plot to sell swimming pools. But failure to safeguard footpaths does sell cars.

Technology has its own reasons for removing things from the culture (these have been described by Herbert Marcuse in *Eros and Civilization*). Unregulated sex, play, music, and dance do not go well with the model worker-consumer who must single-mindedly work when he is supposed to work, and consume mass-produced products when he is expected to consume. Carefully designed substitutes for the natural pleasures are less troublesome and more profitable.

The substitution phenomenon can be seen at work in the case of our neglected public services. We have "no money" for urban public schools, although they have obsolete plant and equipment, lack adequate teaching staffs, and suffer from broken windows, unheated rooms, hopelessness, and despair. We have "no money" for improving the urban environment, "no money" for public libraries and museums, "no money" for the Job Corps or other youth programs. We have "no money" for all of the tasks which we know are necessary if the society is to be kept from tearing itself apart. Where is the money, then?

Plainly, the money is not in the municipal or state treasuries. Is it in the suburbs? Suburban areas do have better schools and services, and yet most of the money in the suburbs comes from the cities. It is clear that the arbitrary boundaries of municipalities leave the suburbs free to avoid the city's social problems and provide for themselves with all the insularity of the Long Island Sound town that thinks it has the "right" to limit beach privileges to residents because they live there, as if the suburb could exist for one minute without the city to support it. But suburban public services, while pleasant by city standards, are hardly excessive; they are merely adequate. They could not be stretched to cover, on the same level of quality, the millions of city residents as well.

It is widely thought that money for the poor and the cities is actually to be found in the federal government's vast expenditures for war and weapons, plus its lesser but nevertheless huge subsidy programs to industry. But even if our military-industrial spending, industrial subsidies, and other unnecessary public expenditures came to one hundred billion dollars a year, it would not be enough. Consider simply the matter of public education. Suppose we estimate that there are 35,000,000 children from deprived backgrounds who now get a substandard education, and who would require a relatively high quality of education if they are to enjoy anything approaching equality of opportunity in later life. Estimating the cost of such an improvement in their present education by private school standards (far less than college costs), we could suggest $3,000 per year per child, or $105,000,000,000 annually. In short, the entire one hundred billion dollars obtained by the most optimistic estimate of what could be gotten from the federal budget would be used up in providing for the educational needs of these children. Not a cent would be left for other types of education, including colleges, adult education, the education of less deprived children. And yet other billions, hundreds of billions, would still be needed for capital expenditures for dilapidated schools, for urban housing, transportation, medicine, for the adult poor, for the aged, and so forth down the list. We repeat, the entire federal budget would not be enough.

By now it should be perfectly clear where the money is: it is not in the "public sector" at all but in the "private sector"—the consumer economy where most of our resources are now expended. "The money" is now being spent for consumer goods. It is being spent on all of the things, large and small, that make up the affluent American way of life—automobiles, appliances, vacations, highways, food, and clothing. All of these things have reached beyond any standard of necessity to higher and higher standards of luxury. It is here that we must, if we wish, tighten our belts. So long as vast social deprivation exists, we do not "need" cars that become obsolete, vacation trips to Europe, electric dishwashers, supersonic planes, or even television entertainment. We not only do not "need" them, we cannot afford them.

It is possible to make the above statement and to mean by it no more than a moral point—that we should all think of our poor brothers, etc. But if we treat the question of priorities as a moral issue we misunderstand the way in which priorities are established in our society. They are very definitely not established by individual moral decisions. They are decided by the exercise of power, power controlled by the most massive forces in our society. There is no individual choice involved. But where are those forces? Where is the power that says that we must spend our money, not on our social needs, but on luxury and waste? This power must be highly visible, for it is one of the most important influences in our society. As we look around, we do not immediately discern it. Where is the command that says "ignore the needs of society"? Look again—it is there.

The most powerful, the loudest, and the most persistent command in our society is the command to buy, to consume, to make material progress, to "grow." The voice of advertising urges us to buy, buy, buy—and it never lets up. And the voice of advertising is only the most obvious of the forces that include the mass media's portrayal of a "way of life" in their programs and stories, the rhetoric of businessmen and politicians praising economic "progress" and "growth," and the overwhelming influence of American high schools and colleges in portraying a materialistic way of life as a desirable form of existence, individually and nationally. What are these voices saying? As we seem to hear them, they say "buy," "consume," "enjoy," "grow," "advance." But this is only half their message. The other half—just as real as if it were spread in full-page newspaper ads, or spoken imperatively by firm, confident television announcers—is this: "Don't spend money on city schools, on hospitals, on the poor." "Ignore the pressing needs of society." "Don't think about what's inadequate or impoverished in our communal life." "Forget the blacks, forget the poor, forget the most elementary demands of decency and justice." If we actually heard and saw such ads, we would be incredibly outraged; yet we *do* hear them and see them, and we heed them.

If it is true that the logic of our economy is what might be called "impoverishment by substitution," this explains what is happening to our world, but it does not explain why we are all so blind both to the process and to the consequences. Not only do we fail to see rather obvious relationships, such as that between the availability of electric toothbrushes and the shortage of good schools, but we fail to see the impoverishment of our lives by the "progress" of our economy. There is a pattern to this blindness too, and it is related to the logic we have already described.

In the first place, the substitution phenomenon

tends to dull our awareness, even though the substitute may fail to perform the vital functions of the original. Football on Sunday TV is not the same as physical play, but it serves as a placebo to lessen our awareness of loss.

It is not substitution alone, but the management of consciousness that necessarily accompanies substitution, that offers an explanation for our unawareness. To demonstrate this, let us borrow some thinking from Marshall McLuhan. A young boy asks his father, "What do you do, Daddy?" Here is how the father *might* answer: "I struggle with crowds, traffic jams, and parking problems for about an hour. I talk a great deal on the telephone to people I hardly know. I dictate to a secretary and then proofread what she types. I have all sorts of meetings with people I don't know very well or like very much. I eat lunch in a big hurry and can't taste or remember what I've eaten. I hurry, hurry, hurry. I spend my time in very functional offices with very functional furniture, and I never look at the weather or sky or people passing by. I talk but I don't sing or dance or touch people. I spend the last hour, all alone, struggling with crowds, traffic, and parking." Now this same father might also answer: "I am a lawyer. I help people and businesses to solve their problems. I help everybody to know the rules that we all have to live by, and to get along according to these rules." Both answers are "true." Why is the first truth less recognized than the second?

McLuhan's answer is that a medium itself tends to be overlooked because it has no *content*. A light bulb, he says, has no content. The *content* of the father's day is being a lawyer, the purpose of his activity. The medium, however, is the father's actual activities dur-

ing the day. And, as McLuhan says, the medium is the
message, although we don't know it. Translated into
more general or cultural terms, it might be said that
we are trained to be aware of the goal of our activities,
but not to be aware of what is actually happening.
What are we doing? Going from New York to San
Francisco. Ask again. Sitting five abreast, bored and
anxious, re-reading the airlines brochure, cramped, isolated, seeing and thinking nothing. What are we
doing? Preserving freedom in Southeast Asia. Ask
again . . .

It is apparent that we are far less aware of some
sides of our culture than of other sides. It is this differ-
ential awareness that is revealed when we all know
that a jet travels from New York to San Francisco, but
we are "surprised" to learn that a jet makes a great deal
of noise. At the most simple level of explanation we
could say that we are taught to be an instrumental
people; we think of the purposes or goals of some
activity rather than of the activity itself; where a plane
is going, what a lawyer is trying to accomplish, what
the future results of a telephone conversation will be.
A businessman, to use a familiar illustration, is persuaded to think of profits, not of what it takes to make
them, or what the effect of making them is. We are
numb to some things, other things are repressed, and
our consciousnesses are so managed that certain things
are simply omitted from the culture. The ordinary
man's suit eliminates his body from the culture during
the working day; during a conference one conferee has
no awareness of another's body. On the other hand, if
businessmen dressed in the Renaissance clothes that
we see on the Shakespearean stage, the body would
again come back into their culture. In somewhat the

same way, our awareness of the hours spent on the plane is "taken out of the culture."

When it comes to the question of what we have lost, consciousness again fails us, for the forces that manage consciousness insist that more of our needs are satisfied than ever before. Hence, today man is only dimly aware of his biological needs. Food is a need we recognize, but is contact with the open spaces of nature also a basic need? We might not be able to recognize the symptoms of its loss, even though the symptoms may themselves be highly visible. Scurvy was an illness that troubled seamen on long voyages. Everyone knew that food was a biological need but no one knew that orange juice (or Vitamin C) was a biological need, and so there was no association between scurvy and diet. Today we have plenty of symptoms without causes: mental illness, psychopathic personalities, crime, and anti-social behavior. Are these the scurvy of today, caused by a lack of contact with the land or sky, or by lack of work for the hands, or physical exercise, or something else that our civilization has eliminated as nonessential? We may well be unaware of our losses, even the most critical of them. Certainly there is much evidence that when a primitive culture is destroyed or transformed, as by civilizing the Polynesians or Eskimos, all sorts of unforeseen things happen; it is not only the visible culture that is lost. Similar cataclysmic changes would be even harder to detect in our own lives. And it should be added that if human needs are often invisible, human possibilities, never having seen the light of day, may die without anyone's noticing. Our culture might smother human possibilities without anyone's ever hearing a cry.

The whole logic we have been describing—exploitation, substitution, numbing of awareness—may be seen at once in the phenomenon of Disneyland. Economic progress destroys nature, adventure, traditions, and the local community. A plastic substitute is constructed and admission is charged. Advertising and promotion then work to convince the people that they are really experiencing Main Street, The Wild West, the history and adventure of America. As the families flock to the clean, sunny, happy enclosure, how many of them realize that something precious has been taken from them, that they are being charged for a substitute that offers only sterile pretense in place of real experience? How many find the chief experience at Disneyland to be a sense of *loss* of all that they are "seeing"?

If substitution is the pattern by which the Corporate State has created a world, perhaps we can now look and see what that world has cost us. Perhaps we can throw off the numbness enough to take a more accurate measure of our losses. We can start with poverty and the allocation of resources, and continue through environment, work, culture, and community.

When we turn to the subject of poverty and allocation of resources, it is best to talk in concrete terms, for the subject is too frequently buried in statistics. In New York City, on Sixty-seventh Street, east of Second Avenue, there is a public library that serves the neighborhood. It is small, seedy, inadequate; the books are greasy, the chairs, lighting, and tables are poor, the whole building has an air of shabby neglect. When seen recently, it was obvious that nothing had been done to it in the twenty-five years since it was seen previously, and probably for much longer. Yet in these same twenty-five years, towering apartment houses have been built in the neighborhood, involving expenditures of many millions of dollars, and chic shops, restaurants, and theatres have appeared. Twenty-five years have brought an explosion in publishing, in knowledge, in education, in the need for adult education. They have brought new culture and arts. And so, the wretched library which has stayed the same for twenty-five years (except for the inevitable deterioration of age) has actually fallen far behind. It is much less valuable to the neighborhood now than it was then, and even then it was pitifully inadequate.

The library on Sixty-seventh Street symbolizes one of the costs we have paid for the nearby new apartment houses, with all of their gadgets, appliances, and luxuries devoted exclusively to private good. This particular cost is in enlightenment: fewer people know the poets, fewer people understand national affairs, fewer people can make responsible decisions concerning their city, fewer people can get a better job, fewer people know about nature, art, science, or astronomy, fewer people lead a rich and satisfying life. How absurd, how outrageous, that we cannot improve this library by the price of a Cadillac, or a power boat, or a hotel lobby! Yet this kind of impoverishment is visible everywhere. Across the street from the Sixty-seventh Street Library is a high school, overcrowded and ugly, that has not received any visible attention in twenty-five years. Two blocks west is a unit of the City University, which recently suffered a *cutback* in funds, despite the growing demand on facilities of higher education. Also two blocks west is a police station so old it seems to date from the Tweed era; it breathes a stench of neglect and corruption in the administration of justice which anyone who has to go to court soon finds out for himself. Two blocks from the library is one of the aspects of city life we are most conditioned to—the subway. There again, if we had fresh eyes, we could see the incredible shabbiness, heat, crowding, and debased atmosphere. If we traveled further, we would encounter hospitals, museums, welfare centers —all starving for money that has been spent instead on the surrounding luxury.

All of this decay and neglect of the public facilities which could make possible a degree of equality of opportunity and amenity for the poor is simply the obverse face of the ever-increasing expenditures for private purposes that are seen in every middle-class home. And the trend is clear. Each year still more is spent for private use by the fortunate portion of the country; the gross national product rises steadily; and each year there are yet more drastic cutbacks in expenditures for the community purposes we have described. The decay is spreading; more and more institutions feel the strain; even symphony orchestras are trapped in the spiral of rising expenditures for new kitchen utensils and garden implements. But the sufferers are not institutions but people; the people who are already at the bottom of the ladder, and, above all, the young people whose hopes die in an overcrowded, dingy, and stultifying school.

If we leave the subject of allocation of resources and public services, and proceed to the physical environment in which we live, the problem is again one of *seeing*. Some aspects of the environment created by the Corporate State are not at all difficult to notice; they make a violent assault upon the senses. Noise, whether of jets, supersonic planes, or tote gotes on a forest trail, attack us all. Air pollution causes people to cough and cry, and airport or automobile congestion causes acute misery and anxiety. In the same way, we are aware of the increase of crowding, of long lines, of enforced orderliness, of the disappearance of space between people. We have a large capacity to get used to such discomforts, but the technology seems to force us faster than we can adapt. Thus those who have barely adapted to the interior of a hundred-passenger jet must face the prospect of a five-hundred-passenger jet, with people sitting ten abreast. We are also aware of violent alterations in the environment which change our accustomed way of life. Freeways cut up our cities and our countryside, developments encroach upon the seashore and level the hills, ugliness is strewn everywhere, neon glares obscure the night, huge buildings block the sun. We walk a favorite woods path only to encounter the desolation of bulldozers, blasted tree stumps, and destroyed vegetation. In these instances of assault, where there is little offsetting satisfaction, it can readily be understood why people are starting to realize that they are being pushed, shoved, and hassled.

But there are other kinds of environmental change that are not so obvious. A good example is a modern, high-rise apartment house. Life inside is enclosed by small, identical rectangles that provide not a wasted cubic foot of space for the occupant, nor an irregular angle or cranny where his thoughts can find refuge. Fresh air is not welcomed; it is filtered through an air-conditioning system. The sounds of weather are muffled, but the grating sounds of other occupants penetrate through the thin, uninsulated walls, ceiling, and floors. Long hallways remind the occupant that he or she is only a number on an identical metal door. Some apartments are located near elevators, incinerator shafts, or other maintenance facilities, and so are subject to disturbance from these sources. Everyone is dependent on elevators; these prevent one from going for a casual look outside. A pretentious lobby and guard make sure that no occupant can expect the knock of an unexpected friend. Safe in his apartment, the occupant has no contact with the life of the street, with wind or weather, with the seasons, or with the land.

Of all the changes that have happened to man, perhaps the deepest and least understood is his loss of the land, of weather, of growing things, and of the knowledge of his body that these things give. We do not know much about man's ecological needs, but we readily assume that he has none that need to be taken seriously. We construct office buildings with windows permanently sealed to shut off the weather, and school buildings without windows at all; from time to time models of underground houses are shown, some with painted landscapes displayed behind mock windows. We deprive man of exercise or use for most of his muscles. We feed him with substances that have no comprehensible relationship to any living or growing things, or to any work or effort on his part. We insist upon so much waste that man never establishes any knowledge of the properties of particular objects, whether clothes or food; everything is thrown away before it acquires any meaning. And man is wholly, utterly, irretrievably deprived of any sense of place. Most people are forced to move several times during their lives, and even if they stay in the same place, the environment is constantly being altered, so that it can no longer be recognized.

We do not know what all of this means to man. In the spring, on the first soft, breezy, gently stirring day after a long winter, man feels a pang, an ineffable longing. Could it be that he is not wholly without the need for land, place, and folk memories? Man used to spend a thousand years in the same place, his roots went down deep; he built his life around the rhythms of the earth and his mental stability upon the constancies of nature. Can a hundred years change his physiology enough so that the need for these rhythms and certainties no longer exists? We know almost nothing of the origins of mental illness and character disorders; we know still less about the sources of happiness, satisfaction, and stability.

One thing that is certainly lost is the ability to adapt to physical circumstances. A storm can now disable a city; this is said to be because our technology is so interdependent and therefore so vulnerable. But it must also be true that human beings have ever less ability to cope with any new circumstances, they are ever more passive, they cannot make do, or do without a meal, they cannot walk, and many streets and bridges are now built without sidewalks. In a deeper sense, the ability to cope is related to some kind of environmental stability. One learns to cope with the idiosyncrasies of an old car or an old fireplace, but one cannot learn anything useful about constantly new appliances. In its turn, this inability to cope produces anxiety.

In the very end of Kubrick's great film *2001: A Space Odyssey* there is an image of what man has lost by way of nature and place. The space traveler is in what appears to be a hotel or motel room, expensive and plastic, with a gleaming bathroom and elegant meals served to him. But there is nothing in the room that he can do anything with, no work, nothing that asks a reaction. There is no time, place, or change.

From the production of an environment intended to be good for people, such as the apartment house, it is only a short step to the production of an environment intended to harm people. Once the State begins to control environment, it is as natural to act against people as for them, where policy so requires. Thus the same power that produces air-conditioning produces poison gas, defoliating agents, chemical Mace, or does research on germ warfare. For we have shown that in the Corporate State, power is not controlled by any human values and is indifferent to such values. So it is that we produce weapons of destruction with the same efficiency that we produce jets and apartment buildings; so it is that in the Vietnam War we systematically assault the environment of a whole nation—the growing things, the wildlife, the communities—as policy requires. The bombed ruin of Vietnam, the planned sterility of an apartment house, the "accidental" destructiveness of jet noise over a residential community, are all forms of the substitution phenomenon we spoke of earlier—the substitution of the artificial for the natural environment, whatever the consequences for man.

A third aspect of the world of the Corporate State concerns work. There is no need for us to go back over the broad problems of work in an industrial society, dealt with so fully by Marx and by so many social scientists since his day. Certainly the Corporate State has made great progress in lightening the burdens of work, eliminating child labor, and providing machines for some of the more mechanical tasks. The special problem of the Corporate State concerns the artificiality of much work that is now done—another aspect of the substitution phenomenon.

High school or college teaching illustrates what is happening. The basic task of a teacher is to teach students, and a related task is to pursue his own scholarly interests and keep his own mind alive. But the Corporate State has forced many teachers to spend much of their time and energy on artificial administrative activities, and activities created for them to serve administrative purposes. College teachers have endless committee and faculty meetings devoted to such problems as new appointments, promotions, curriculum, and admissions. They attend panel discussions, symposia, give speeches, and participate in professional conventions in many parts of the country and even in foreign countries. Their advice or assistance is sought by outside organizations ranging from presidential commissions to local community groups. And above all, they are continuously engaged in "research and publication," activities that require half or a third of any college teacher's time. And this is not the self-renewal and search for enlightenment that a teacher needs, it is a high pressure, forced type of "production" (as it is accurately called), designed to satisfy criteria for promotion and tenure. Teaching continues, of course, but the average professor does not have the time for the sort of personal concern for students that would constitute teaching in a more old-fashioned sense of the word.

It is clear that there has been a substitution of one kind of work for another. Has there been a loss in the process? We first ask the question from the teacher's point of view. We put to one side the professional prestige he gets, the salary he receives, the status he

achieves in the society. In accordance with the Mc-
Luhan principle, we are interested in the work itself.
Committees represent little gain. They supply neither
the satisfaction of creative work nor appealing personal relationships. Panel discussions, travel, and professional gatherings offer new places and new people.
But the trips are hasty and tiring, the contact, both
with places and with people, tends to be superficial
and non-repeating, and it is hard to see how such ex-
cursions, however diverting, could be central to anyone's working life. As for "research and publication,"
writing is a deeply satisfying activity for the person
who wants to do it for its own sake, but the "research
and publication" that most college teachers now do is
simply a different thing altogether. More like a Ph.D.
dissertation than anything else, it is artificial writing,
often published before the teacher has anything he
wants to say. Usually it disappears into the graveyard
of a dull and dusty scholarly publication; the author
will be lucky if he gets one or two letters from people
who have read it; it can hardly be said he is communicating with any audience, professional or otherwise.
The article becomes an item in various indexes and
bibliographies. In short, except for the teacher who
has a truly creative moment, the stuff of his working
life will be impersonal, frustrating, and unsatisfying,
and only the goals of prestige and status will keep him
going. The loss, on the other hand, is of the teaching
relationship itself. Teaching, whether of kindergarten
children or graduate students, can be one of the most
rewarding kinds of work, for a genuine working community can be formed in which all gain. What has
happened is that organizational demands have substituted something artificial for something real. Of

course, students and society itself are also the losers.

The pattern by which real work (work that is satisfying and personal) is transformed into something artificial and empty is visible all through those jobs which are under the influence of technology and organization. In the medical profession, there is an acute shortage of doctors to care for people; so acute that many hospitals use foreign-trained doctors for their staffs, and many localities are wholly without medical care. It is a commonplace observation that personal care by doctors has drastically declined. What has happened? One thing is that the available doctors have been lured into the organizational vortex—research, technology, administration, professional activities—and hence have no time to practice. This aspect of the problem is much the same as the problem of teachers. A second problem is the increasingly costly, time-consuming, specialized, and demanding education, with its diminishing satisfactions. If one is going to lead an organizational-technological life, there are better places to lead it than medicine. The great lure of medicine, its personal side, participation in the crises of life, helping people in a vital way, is lost in the process.

From work we move to culture. There is much that we could say about the shabbiness and tawdriness of American mass culture, about neon signs and hotdog stands, but it has been well said elsewhere, and is of no special concern here. Our concern is with culture and consciousness. Culture in America provides one more manifestation of the concept of impoverishment by substitution. Because of the substitution phenomenon, one of the prime characteristics of American culture is that the genuine is replaced by the simulated.

When the radio gives us five minutes of news, there is staccato noise or music in the background, sounds of explosions, fighting, or catastrophes to simulate excitement; we are not allowed to find excitement in the news itself. It is possible to buy premixed peanut butter and jelly, and frozen "Japanese-style" vegetables. Restaurants in shopping centers offer "Chinese" or "French" food that is an ersatz version of the real thing. Deodorants obliterate the smells of the human body, and then perfumes and sprays coat the body with a manufactured smell. The problem with this ersatz culture is that all that is meaningful in the experience is lost in the substitution. Homemade ice cream is an experience that makes an impact on consciousness. When something is put in its place, the ability to experience the genuine is reduced. In this sense, fake Chinese food is worse than none, for it deadens our curiosity and makes our ignorance more stubborn.

A second aspect of the culture of the Corporate State is that it is imposed from outside, not developed from the people themselves. It is like those suburban real estate developments with a "theme" such as adjacent golf or an artificial lake; the "theme" is a promotion technique which simply makes it harder for the inhabitants to know their own minds.

Another characteristic of the culture is that it is designed so that it can only be experienced passively, and this passivity is profoundly impoverishing to the individual. A room in an expensive motel is a good example of impoverishment: a huge glass window with imposing draperies, wall-to-wall carpeting, air-conditioning, television, but nothing whatever to do—no books to read, no fire to be built in a fireplace, no place to cook, no records to be played. One can only sleep or let oneself be served, emerging with a flabby and diminished sense of self.

One of the natural urges of man is to *perform* for his friends by playing a musical instrument, singing, dancing, acting, or cooking. It is a mode of communicating and relating that is very different from conversation, and, to judge by primitive societies, at least as important as conversation. Passive culture almost completely denies performance. A young couple, out on a date, feel this; there are many passive amusements available, but nothing, aside from sex, for them to *do*; the date does not help them to find out about each other, or to express themselves.

The function of the arts and of culture in general should be to raise consciousness, but the culture created by the Corporate State has just the opposite effect; it numbs the individual's ability to be conscious. Piped-in music is a perfect example, for one learns to "not hear it" and indeed must develop this shield, for the music is inescapably present in all sorts of places. But the ability not to hear is a form of deafness that cannot readily be cured, and the deaf individual finds he cannot hear music when he wants to listen. Equally numbing, as Henry James pointed out, is the effect of constant rapid cultural change, and the frantic pace at which all culture is experienced. A hasty French meal, a new building going up to replace one just twenty years old, coast-to-coast travel in a few hours, new models of cars and appliances before the character of the old is known—all of these diminish meaning, sensitivity, and awareness. It is only a matter of degree from the numbness of piped-in music to an army exhibit at the Chicago Museum of Science and Industry where (according to *The New York Times*, March 19,

1968) children were invited to enter a helicopter for "simulated firing of a machine gun at targets in a diorama of the Vietnam Central Highlands." The targets included a Vietnamese hut, and the exhibit provided a light that flashed when a "hit" was "scored." (The exhibit was closed after a protest sit-in.) Robert Jay Lifton, in his book on Hiroshima, *Death in Life,* has described numbing as a consequence of the atom bomb; numbing is also a consequence of our domestic culture. But it is numbing not only to existing experience; the denial of *possible* experience measures the full impoverishment caused by the Corporate State culture. Adventure, challenge, danger, imagination, awe, and the spiritual are banished by this culture, which tries to make everything safe, bland, and equally delightful.

Perhaps the greatest and least visible form of impoverishment caused by the Corporate State is the destruction of community. Man's greatest need, after food and water, is for a circle of affection; man is a communal animal and he craves his kind. But even though we are starved for community in our world, we may not realize it. We can see a physical effect when a bulldozer rips up a hillside, but today our experience of genuine human community is so limited that we are hardly aware of our loss, and the substitutes provided keep us so busy that emptiness is drowned in busyness. Actually, the erosion of community is one of the major effects of the industrial revolution, and such consequences as the destruction of villages and the effects of harsh competition have already been discussed. Our concern is with the continuation of that process by the world of the Corporate State, and with the operation of the substitution phenomenon: the substitution of false communities for real ones. For example, the Corporate State continues the destruction of neighborhoods, replacing them with offices or apartments, and the neighborhood people are compelled to look to new forms for a sense of belonging. These are provided by institutional and occupational groupings: a job with a corporation and membership in an occupational group. However, neither an institution nor an occupational group affords people an opportunity for communal experience; they are, in Kurt Vonnegut's word, granfaloons, false associations, because the relationships are shaped to serve ends outside the individual. A retail jewelers' association or a swim coaches' association may have meetings, publish a magazine, and give its members an identity, but the relationships exist on a false basis. This is not perceived because the organization keeps everyone so busy.

It is ironic that the form of community most praised and cherished by American society, the family, has probably suffered the greatest destruction at the hands of the Corporate State. Technology has deprived the family of almost all of its functions. The family has no work to do together, no mutual education. The State wants the family to be a unit for consumption, to exist for the purpose of watching television, using leisure products and services, and living the life of false culture. The State wants its consuming units as small as possible; were it not for certain biological necessities for which substitutes have not yet come into use, the solitary individual would be the best possible unit for the State's purposes. As it is, the State's domination is shown by the fact that old people are separated from the rest of the family, condemned to uselessness and isolation, perhaps to a "leisure community," aunts and

197

cousins have suffered the same fate, and the "family" has been reduced to the "nuclear" grouping of parents and young children. Technology has created a youth culture, consisting of education for positions in the system, plus a special consumer status, and the result is that children cease to be part of the family by the time they reach high school. This leaves the parents themselves—although they are also separated to a significant extent by the husband's job and the wife's increasingly specialized functions. A nuclear family is, quite evidently, not a large enough unit to supply the warmth, security, and familiarity of a communal circle of affection. Two is better than one, but it is not enough. But when the couple searches for something more, they cannot find it. Friday and Saturday dinner parties, with their hours of sterile conversation, provide no warmth for any of the participants; if warmth, fondness, affection, and companionship were food, a person could go to dinner and cocktail parties nightly and soon starve.

What has the State provided to take the place of the circle of affection? First and foremost, "love," "sex," and "romance" to be pursued in frenzied fashion beginning with puberty, and with the aid of countless commodities, but strangely depersonalized and unsatisfying. Next, a host of "activities," from skiing to collecting antiques, that can be carried on by the smaller units. Next, groups and organizations, which take much time and bring people into proximity, if nothing else. Finally, a theory that the process of living consists of using things, instead of being with people. Thus we have the consumer theory of the family, summed up by an ad for *TV Guide* (*The New York Times*, September 10, 1968), which asserts that "Nothing makes

markets like a marriage. There's new business in raising a family. All together, it's big business: appliances
and house furnishings to stepped-up insurance and
bigger cars . . ." Perhaps our society is also developing
a theory wherein children are treated as things too—
adult toys—for the vacancy in their parents' lives. The
substitutes, and there are many more, have succeeded
in making us unaware of what we have lost. We do
not see the loss of community as well as we see a
beach ruined by black crude oil. The substitutes are
lively, expensive, and attractive. Sometimes the chill of
loneliness is felt, but its cause remains unknown.

In any large city, the geography of the middle class
divides itself roughly into a country of the marrieds
and a country of the singles. Both are, spiritually, anti-
communities which keep people separate and alone.
The country of the marrieds is mostly suburban, plus
individually owned houses and some apartments in the
city. It can be experienced best at a shopping center.
The essence of the shopping center is that there is no
place for people to do things together, except the
stores and places of commercial entertainment—restaurants and movies. The shopping center is not a center, but a hollow, an emptiness, for none of the things
that make people more human have a place there—
such as opportunities to play, to perform, to create.
These anti-communities have parking lots for centers,
temporary space for separately encapsulated people.

But it is the country of the singles that most clearly
expresses the isolation that the modern State imposes.
If this country has a physical location, it is in large
apartment houses, often modern and gigantic in scale,
cut up into units of one and two identical rooms, units
of precise isolation. Except for the lobby, the elevator,

and perhaps a laundry room in the basement, there are no places where people might get together even if they wanted to. Each individual's moments of despair, of boredom, and of happiness occur in antiseptic separation; each meal is cooked separately by each individual, each book is read, or record is listened to, separately. Even if the building has a hotel-like atmosphere, and provides "club" facilities for tenants, such as a swimming pool or rooftop cabana, it makes no difference, for the anti-community is spiritual even more than it is physical. For the singles in their twenties and early thirties, the spiritual anti-community is expressed through dating and the search for a spouse or for affection from the opposite sex. This adult dating is distinguished from the younger kind by the brutally quick appraisals that the partners make—of each other's status, prospects, personality, intentions. It is like computer dating without the intervention of the computer, for all the same questions are asked. As the date proceeds on its inevitable way, from restaurant to entertainment to late evening drink, the parties are carefully totalling the advantages and disadvantages—someone to have dinner with occasionally versus the chance of meeting someone better, someone interested in marriage versus a lack of any real spark of excitement, someone presentable to be seen with versus the absence of rapport or even companionship beneath appearances.

On a Sunday the sense of anti-community in a city is perhaps strongest, for this is the day when work does not furnish a focus for life, when there is nothing to prevent one from "doing what he wants," when a day badly spent is one's own fault, not someone else's. Pleasures, more than anything else, require company.

So Sunday is the cruelest day; people on benches, or on walks looking at stores that are closed, or traveling to a park or the zoo, or just sitting at home; on Sunday each person or family must separately make what it can of the world.

In later years, for people who are still single, particularly women, the pretense of dating is dropped, and there are occasional dinners at a restaurant with "the girls," a slow accumulation of unfashionable clutter in the apartment, a gradual increase of aches and pains that make the doctor's office, the pharmacy, and the medicine cabinet new centers of living. Now the anti-community consists of this: that the cares of life must be borne singly, by each person, that the joys are not acknowledged because they cannot be shared, and that the institutions that must finally receive each individual—nursing homes, hospitals, "convalescent" centers—become more noticeable, take a step closer, and shadow the days as they wait their turn.

Looking back over the discussion in this chapter, it is possible to see that man has created his present society by exploitation not merely of the natural resources of his world—the land, the forest, and the air—but by exploitation of the riches of his entire culture. Whether it is affection, music, dance, work, or religion, they have been ravished by an expanding technology. Marx saw exploitation in terms of the rewards of human labor, but we can see it in terms of *all* of the values of our society. Technology and the commodity system have done more than erode our visible environment and assault our senses; they have deprived us of many of the most basic, sustaining elements of life, the things which nurture us and the things which offer the greatest openings for human possibility.

We have described the system of impoverishment by substitution in enough detail to suggest how it is that most of us, although intellectually aware of our losses, have been convinced that these are not inevitable consequences of the Corporate State, but malfunctions which can be fixed by making the State run better; and how we have had our consciousness dulled to the point where we are only aware of the losses intellectually, if at all, not intensely, angrily, and desperately. What needs to be added is simply that here, as elsewhere with the Corporate State, the process is cumulative. Again, the whole is more than the sum of the parts. We live in a world where the genuine has been systematically replaced by the artificial. Youth is prolonged by studying, so that young, energetic, and restless bodies are confined to chairs in lecture halls and libraries, memorizing facts, writing papers and cramming for exams far past any point of value. Women drive station wagons, attend organizations, and engage in a rush of activities all day long. Over the years we have gradually got used to an ever-more frantic pace of living, a constant acceleration of experience, where men eat, talk, and think faster and faster, until a memorandum read on a plane while eating a precooked lunch becomes the normal way of life. One of the great new activities is security. A profession of security men has grown up, numbering hundreds of thousands of persons, who protect us from ourselves. But the greatest new activity is, of course, technological war and preparation for war. The manufacture of arms is one of the largest businesses, the study of strategy one of the prime mental efforts. The energies, resources, and minds of Americans are lavished upon this as upon nothing else. A world that is artificial is also one that is life-less, and a society that sets out to manufacture an artificial world ends as a manufacturer of death.

It is all epitomized by Astro Turf, the new artificial football field developed by Monsanto, with nylon tufts that are "better than grass," a shock-absorbing pad beneath that "can't turn to mud even if it rains buckets," no dirt so that "uniforms stay clean and bright the whole game long," a grass-green color that the coming of winter cannot fade, and better footing than earth can provide. This is how we are using our resources while the poor get poorer; this is how we are losing our knowledge of land and living things.

The forces of technology and commodity, allowed to have their own way without guidance or control or intervening values, have created a culture which is profoundly hostile to life. It is claustrophobic, confin-ing, stifling, anxiety-creating, because the horizons of life—for community, work, creativity, consciousness, adventure—are all walled in. In this artificial world, on a beautiful spring Sunday, there may be nowhere to go—no woods or fields or shore undefiled by noise, high-tension wires, developments, construction, de-struction. In this world, to one beginning a life, there are no open roads for the body, the mind, or the spirit, only long, hard, paved freeways to nowhere. For amid all the promises of science and knowledge, of discov-ery, wealth, and freedom, life, instead of being ex-panded, has been narrowed and become miserly; and humans, knowing the possibilities of a rich and varied banquet, are forced to live in deprivation, hollowness, and despair. To a young person, the Corporate State beckons with a skeleton grin: "Step right in, you'll love it—it's just like living."

VIII

THE MACHINE BEGINS
TO SELF-DESTRUCT

With its massive and concentrated power, the Corporate State seems invulnerable to reform or revolution.
Nevertheless, in the last few years the State has been
beset by deep troubles from within, from many different groups of angry and dissatisfied people. How is
this possible, when the State's position is so unchal-
lengeable, and its critics are so weak, divided, and
lacking in a plan or theory of how to proceed? It is our
theory that the State itself is now bringing about its
own destruction. The machine itself has begun to do
the work of revolution. The State is now generating
forces that will accomplish what no revolutionaries

could accomplish by themselves. And there is nothing the State can do, by repression or power, to prevent these forces from bringing it down.

It has been the prevailing belief among most political theorists that the State could satisfy its own people. The more thoughtful of these theorists would acknowledge that the State has profound flaws, that it causes enough destruction to furnish motivation for a dozen revolutions. But these flaws are not enough to bring the machine to a halt so long as people accept them, so long as people are convinced that despite our troubles we are better off than we have ever been. Establishment thinkers believe that the State can make reforms at a rate sufficient to satisfy most demands. Some thinkers on the Left agree. Herbert Marcuse wrote in *One-Dimensional Man* that the State would be able to administer happiness and provide enough gratification to keep people pacified, happily unaware of and unconcerned about their loss of freedom in the industrial machine. Gadgets, entertainment, sex, leisure, and even some harmless dissent and "radical culture" are all means the State can employ to keep a real rebellion from ever getting started. Marcuse is no longer so pessimistic, but many other New Left thinkers believe that nothing short of revolution can dismantle the State.

In 1965 this seemed plausible indeed, and supported by almost all available facts. But today, with five years' additional perspective, it is clear that the Corporate State cannot possibly do what the theory expects of it. Keeping people happy and pacified, under either the Establishment or the Marcuse thesis, requires a government that is intelligent, flexible, sophisticated, able to understand what needs to be done, and then put its understanding into effect. Such a government would have to be one that its leaders could control and direct. It is the very essence of the Corporate State that no one can control it, either for the beneficent purpose of preserving human values, or for the Machiavellian purpose of pacifying the people within it.

We have spelled out many of the reasons why sophisticated and flexible social control is, as a realistic matter, impossible. The political system is too rigid, vested interests have too powerful an ability to prevent change, and the whole theory of government-as-management prevents new initiatives or ideas. The present federal government, as well as most large corporations, seems wholly to lack even a single person in a responsible job who has the insight to know what needs to be done. If Marcuse's theory of pacification were actually working, the Corporate State would legalize marijuana to keep young people happy. The fact that the State is plainly incapable of taking this step so far, no matter how much it would help preserve its power, shows how little chance there is of administered pacification.

But it is not only the State's inability to manage that is causing its self-destruction. There are forces at work directly undermining the State, contradictions in its structure that are tearing apart the social fabric. The chief of these, which we will soon discuss, are eroding the motivation of the worker, the satisfaction of the consumer, and the willingness of all citizens to put "the public interest" ahead of their own immediate desires.

The heart of the State's power lies in its ability to maintain its people in a condition of false consciousness. It could indulge in any irrationality, so long as that false consciousness was preserved. What has now happened is that the State has finally begun to act in the one way that must be fatal to it—it has begun to do things which pierce the illusions and myths of Consciousness I and II. While these illusions were intact, there was no limit to the State's power. But like some almost-human machine in a science-fiction drama, its madness has turned back on it, and it has begun to self-destruct. With every possible means available to keep people from seeing the truth, it has started to force the truth on them. For the most part, the State's piercing of Consciousness I and II have so far produced only bitterness, cynicism, despair, and fury at some unseen foe. But where the arrows of truth reached those who were most strongly endowed with hope and vitality, they led not to mere disaffection, but to something even more dangerous to the State—a new consciousness.

We first turn to the creation of dissatisfaction in the worker-consumer. The Corporate State depends upon two human elements: a willing worker and a willing consumer. These are its two vulnerable spots. Consciousness II supplies the motive power: the individual works for the public interest and for status and advantage within the system; he consumes according to the dictates of false consciousness, and then must work even harder, and so the wheel turns. This makes the system heavily dependent upon the continuance of a consciousness ready to work and consume. We have shown, in the two preceding chapters, that in reality work and consumption in our society are artificial, oppressive, and unsatisfying; Consciousness II keeps people unaware of this impoverishment. But this unawareness will not necessarily last forever; the Corporate State is actually on perilously thin ice.

The State works hard to keep the worker-consumer contented. But this is the contradiction under which it works: the overly persuaded consumer may no longer be a willing worker. To have consumers for its constantly increasing flow of products, the Corporate State must have individuals who live for hedonistic pleasures, constant change, and expanding freedom. To have workers for its system of production, the State must have individuals who are ever more self-denying, self-disciplined, and narrowly confined. In theory, they are supposed to accept the discipline of their work in order to enjoy the pleasures of consumption. But the theory is all wrong. For some people it is wrong in fact, because hard work does not leave time or energy for outside enjoyment. For some people, it is wrong in principle, because if they are persuaded to believe in the principle of hedonism, they find it hard to hold on to the principle of service. And for a very large group of people, it is simply impossible on a personal level; they are psychologically unable to go back and forth between self-denial and pleasure.

Once a man has been sold on skiing, boating, foreign travel, gourmet cooking, and the pleasures of status, he can no longer believe in his work. The factory worker looks up from his conveyor belt, the lawyer looks up from his books, and both see crisp sparkling snow and secluded beaches; they are likely to lose, not gain, enthusiasm for their work. Thus there is a great subversive, revolutionary force loose in America, manufactured with all the famous efficiency of the Corporate State.

When the consumer-worker contradiction touches

blacks, it produces the angry militancy of those who believe they have been left out of something. When it touches blue-collar workers, it makes them angry too, but since they believe in the Corporate State, they find someone else, like the communists, to blame for their dissatisfaction. And when it hits middle-class youth, it helps to produce a rejection of the whole ethic of the middle class.

The great selling point of America is "freedom." America is a "free" country; it is part of the "free world," in contrast to the communist world. But what is really meant by this freedom? Imperceptibly, it has come to mean consumer freedom. Consumer freedom is freedom to travel, ski, buy a house, eat frozen Chinese food, live like a member of the "now generation"; freedom to buy anything and go anywhere. For work, on the other hand, there is no longer any concept of freedom at all. Most of the repression of self we discussed earlier—the meritocracy, loyalty, character files, employment regulations—occurs in connection with work; the worker does not live in a "free country." But can consumer freedom be turned off at the office door?

The consumer is stirred to other desires besides freedom. Let us focus for a moment on advertising. It is only the visible portion of a much deeper consumer ethic, but its visibility allows us to study it. Most advertising attempts to sell a particular commodity by playing upon a supposed underlying need, such as sex, status, or excitement. Buy our automobile and you'll get all three, the ads say. But in trying to sell more and more commodities by the use of these needs, advertising cannot help but raise the intensity of the needs themselves. A man not only wants a car—quite independently, he also wants more sex, status, and excitement. Advertising is designed to create, and does create, dissatisfaction. But dissatisfaction is no mere toy; it is the stuff of revolutions.

Generally, it is assumed that the American economy is capable not only of creating wants, but also of coming reasonably close to satisfying them. But if one creates a desire for sex, status, and excitement, and then sells a man an automobile, the desires are likely to remain unsatisfied. The wants created are real enough, but the satisfactions are unreal. A newspaper ad shows a drawing of a group of young people at a beautiful beach; they are beautiful also, and happy, healthy, and carefree besides. It stirs desires in the desk-bound reader. He hardly notices that the ad is for beachwear.

In *The New York Times* of March 4, 1969, there appeared a two-page spread, showing a magnificent, dreamy, misty island scene, fog hovering over exotic mountains, a shallow area of water in the foreground, with a couple meditatively contemplating the scene; the caption says, "The time is now. The girl is your wife." What was for sale? An airplane ride by Pan Am. What was stirred up? The longing for relaxation, absence of work, for new experiences, for closeness to nature, companionship, sensuality, romance, love, mystery, awe, far horizons, freedom from work and from routine. The ad creates a desire to be a beachcomber on some deserted island, a desire for escape, romance, idleness. In short, the very ideal of the hippies, bare feet and all.

Behind the worker-consumer contradiction lies a related problem for the State. American society no longer has any viable concept of work. A Father's Day ad for corduroy slacks says: "For a man's happiest hours"—meaning, for the hours when he is not at work. We are no longer expected to find work happy or satisfying. There is, for example, no advertising designed to create pride in craftsmanship or in a worker's self-discipline. Nor is anyone convinced that he should work for the good of the community. Instead, the belief is created that one works only for money and status. This puts a heavy burden on money and status, a burden they are no longer able to carry.

Money and status offer satisfactions that are primarily relative; one must be relatively well off compared to others. But American society is increasingly organized in terms of hierarchy. This means, to the average worker, an end to the American dream of equality and democracy. On the job, there is a rigid caste system, and for the older man, the chances of rising seem dim. Yet a position in the hierarchy becomes more and more not merely a measure of one kind of ability but a measure of the whole man. America still has a pitiless view of the loser. When a whole society is hierarchical and the shape of the hierarchy is a pyramid, only a few can enjoy the satisfaction of being in superior positions. If everyone is to find satisfaction in his actual position, he must have a good deal of faith in the fairness and justness of his lot. Of course, one's position in the social order never was the result of justice, but the more rigid the hierarchy, the more visible the injustice. Our hierarchy is now almost as formal as that of the Middle Ages, but now we do not have God to justify it, and we have the subversive voice of television constantly telling everyone to "move up a notch." A hierarchy in a land that bills itself as a land of equality and opportunity is an inherently unstable structure. Add that many of the decisions determining status are seemingly unfair and unrelated to merit, that the criteria for appointment and promotion tend to be artificial or absurd, that those who judge merit are themselves open to increasing question, and that there is a manifestly unequal starting point for most people in society. The consequence is that one's status, far from being something to keep one at work, becomes a source of intense dissatisfaction with one's work.

Increasingly, this shows in the kind of strikes that occur and the kind of demands that are made. Today many workers are demanding something, not fully articulated, that goes far beyond a mere economic demand and encompasses the wish for greater status. Newspaper interviews with dissatisfied policemen and municipal workers have shown this clearly; New York City's troubles with its municipal employees quite clearly stemmed in part from a dissatisfaction with status. Nothing could be clearer than that the strength of George Wallace's appeal in 1968 was due to his support of the industrial worker's yearning for higher status. In an article in *The New York Times* (October 24, 1968), Sylvan Fox wrote that New York City policemen had rejected an excellent wage settlement because they wanted something more: recognition from the community. One police official was quoted: "They are turning their backs on material things and going after other things—ego things."

Critics of Marx, and of New Left theorists who follow Marx, insist that Marx was wrong because in America people are contented with their work. In Marx's theory, the exploited industrial worker derived no satisfaction from his labor, but was spurred on solely by hunger and other wants. Today there may be fewer "exploited workers" in a purely economic sense; the bulk of workers have white-collar jobs or unionized jobs where they receive a fairer economic return. But, increasingly, all work is done for external reward alone; it has no inherent satisfactions. Jobs themselves are increasingly absurd in that they are unrelated to any discernible social need; if the backbreaking quality of early industrial labor has lessened, the evident meaninglessness of pushing papers has increased. Today people are dissatisfied with their working lives exactly as Marx predicted; they have been kept from rebellion by material and psychic rewards and by a false consciousness. Should these illusions fade, the true alienation of the working force would be apparent.

Is there not one kind of worker rebellion that is already visible? We refer to the indifference with which so many people do their jobs. The young lawyer refuses to work the traditional late hours, or to check his work with the traditional care. An automobile has to be brought to the shop three times before repairmen can be persuaded to fix what ails it. Craftsmanship of all kinds is declining. Some policemen are reported to make a regular practice of sleeping on the job. In many offices a general malaise prevails; as much time as possible is wasted on coffee breaks and lunch time, and there is little in the way of dedication, standards, or even competence. The same thing can be seen in schools and colleges, where work encounters a broad passive resistance, and in factories, where there is a sullen discontent. Somehow, the inner machinery that drives the working force has begun to fail. This is a great and spontaneous rebellion, once we begin to see it as such.

The most revealing indication of how completely

America lacks a meaningful concept of work is the movies. Some merely portray men in their moment of romance or leisure, others treat the worker-husband as a figure of inept comedy. Almost every portrayal of a man at work shows him doing something that is clearly outside of modern industrial society. He may be a cowboy, a pioneer settler, a private detective, a gangster, an adventure figure like James Bond, or a star reporter. But no films attempt to confer satisfaction and significance upon the ordinary man's labor. By contrast, the novels of George Eliot, Hardy, Dickens, Howells, Garland, and Melville deal with ordinary working lives, given larger meaning through art. Our artists, our advertisers, and our leaders have not taught us how to work in our world.

When advertising paints a picture of consumer hedonism and freedom, and work is considered only a means to that end, the machinery of the Corporate State begins to work toward its own destruction. Consider the hereditary poor. Advertising intended for an audience that can afford what it offers also works (with perhaps even greater effectiveness) on those who cannot afford it; it inflames the desires of the poor without offering them any satisfaction at all. Perhaps the poor are "better off than they ever were before," but they can hardly be expected to be satisfied after watching television. A continuous display of better living is paraded before them. Rich people know that not every day is filled with sports and glamour; they even know that the person who has everything might not even want all these things. The poor have no way of knowing this; television advertising is far more effective with the unsophisticated. Is there any wonder that we have riots? Television might justly be called a riot box; it raises a fury of dissatisfaction and mocks those who watch it. But even the well-paid, highly motivated executive, after a demanding day, may feel troubled emotions if he views a TV scene of surfers. The screen tells him to work harder so he can vacation in California. But perhaps he senses, in some almost unconscious way, that the harder he works, the less likely it is that he ever will surf; in fact, real surfers don't work at all.

If television is a riot box for the poor, who can say what it is to the ordinary middle-class worker, who has many of the advertised products but lacks the sensuality and freedom they are supposed to bring? The one thing that we can be sure of is that the aim of advertising is to create dissatisfaction, and if the American middle-class is still somewhat satisfied, television will keep on trying to subvert it.

The consumer ethic has a special message, and a special meaning, to youth. Since we will be devoting a separate chapter to the new generation, a few words must suffice here. The American economy has done these things: it has greatly prolonged the period of youth, partly because of the need for more technical training, partly because of the paucity of jobs; it has made a separate consumer market out of youth in order to sell more products; it has made youth widely aware of one another in order to stimulate sales by example; it has subjected youth to the stimuli of constant changes, possibilities, and opportunities. Here advertising is dealing with an unformed group in the society, and they are likely to be far more sensitive to the invitation to live *now* than their more settled elders. Thus, advertising is capable of creating a maximum of dissatisfaction, and a minimum willingness to accept the drudgery of life, in the volatile "youth market." They listen with a different ear, and it has made them promises that the rest of us have not heard.

Thus it is that the Corporate State itself is generating rebellion. The FBI may look high and low for a conspiracy, but it will never think of looking to television, the advertising industry, and other creators of the consumer ethic. It is a rebellion that will keep on coming whether or not the rebels or the Left do anything; if they feel lazy, they can sit by and watch it happen. And no matter how many warnings it gets, there is nothing the State can do to stop its suicidal course. The State *must* keep on creating dissatisfaction; it has no choice. Every adult knows that encouraging youth to drive their cars fast is an invitation to tragedy, but the *Wall Street Journal* (October 31, 1968) reported that for 1969 auto manufacturers were making a direct appeal to youth to buy cars with "a mean streak," that "belt out enough torque to leave two black lines right out to the horizon"; that is, "No more Mr. Nice Guy" but "the class bully." And a film, *Wild in the Streets*, invited teen-agers to put LSD in the water supply, take over the country, and cart all people over thirty away to thought-remolding camps. That advertisement and that film are truly subversive, but the world's largest and most scientific security force will not be able to catch the perpetrators, or slow the revolutionary effects of their incitements.

If the willing worker is one-half of the motive force of the Corporate State, the other half is the willing consumer. Consumer dissatisfaction is, of course, far behind work dissatisfaction. The whole economy is designed to satisfy consumers, while it neglects the working side of life. The very idea of consumer rebellion in the world's greatest consumer society seems as unthinkable as malnutrition in a supermarket. Neverthe-less, the first signs of consumer revolt are beginning to appear. They will increase; but let us take note of some of them as of this writing. They are small signs, but they are portents.

On the New York commuter railroads, which con-stantly break down, people have been known to refuse to pay their fares. When the telephone company changed to digit dialing, there were minor rebellions. There have been local revolts against prices in super-markets, and mutterings against the airlines. One day in New York a subway train broke down, and the passengers were asked to get off and board another train. But the people, silently and quite spontaneously, simply sat there and refused to leave. Small signs, but ominous.

Two forms of consumer revolt are already very common: against inadequate public services and against assaults upon the environment. A much-publi-cized example of the former was the Ocean Hill–Brownsville school revolt in New York, where parents objected to the quality of education their children were getting. Rebellions of various kinds by welfare recipients have become common. Much more frequent are campaigns against intrusions into the environment by freeways, airports, offshore oil wells, pesticides, and bulldozers. In a direct sense, these may not seem to be consumer revolts, for objection is made not to a service or product itself, but to its side effects. But freeways, airports, and pesticides are intended to serve the gen-eral public, and when their side effects arouse deter-mined public opposition, it must be concluded that, for many people, the service is no longer acceptable on the terms offered.

The really significant consumer revolt is, as we have

said, yet to come. The potential is vast. Our society produces products that are unreliable or unsafe, that break down and cannot be readily serviced, or are unusable without another product that is unavailable (an automobile without parking space). Some products are showing a noticeable deterioration in quality, others can be frighteningly dangerous in the wrong hands (an oven cleaner that can damage the eyes). Technology of all sorts has proved surprisingly vulnerable to breakdown. At the same time, inflation has made it more and more difficult to purchase anything, and families feel they are literally growing poorer year by year.

We showed earlier how many of our consumer goods are produced by draining resources away from vitally needed social services. This is beginning to undermine the value of the consumer satisfactions themselves. What good is a $250,000 cooperative apartment if, due to the decay in schooling and job training, a robber waits in the hallway or elevator? A luxurious suburban home, if one is a prisoner in it, surrounded by locked gates, private watchmen, and beware-of-the-dog signs to ward off the discontented populace? Shopping in the city if one is likely to get caught in a breakdown of the subway, commuter rail services, or in a giant traffic jam?

Most of the matters we have mentioned would be comparatively trivial if consumers were hardy and self-reliant, and able to keep their needs under some sort of control. But just as we are producing workers who are increasingly unwilling to work, so we are producing consumers who are increasingly dissatisfied, no matter what they get. The manufacturing part of the economy wants a consumer who is passive, has little ability to endure discomfort, and has constantly rising needs. Such a consumer has little ability to substitute one satisfaction for another if the necessity arises; the same mental quality that makes him desire a specific brand makes him unable to find another way to spend a holiday if the planes don't fly. Like a spoiled child, he is ever more difficult to please, ever more filled with complaints. If his gourmet meal aboard an airplane is delayed, he has no capacity to enjoy some diversion until things are put to rights. He is a potential rebel because advertising has taught him to be one.

The rebellion becomes more likely because the "satisfactions" which the consumer learns to enjoy are actually less and less satisfying. An airline that holds itself out as transportation can provide genuine satisfactions; one that focuses the consumer on the food, drink, and service aboard is offering satisfactions so artificial that they can hardly be expected to hold the consumer for long. In the same way, a power boat on a lake is less satisfying than a canoe; the pleasure is "used up" faster. In a story called "The Midas Plague," Frederik Pohl, a science-fiction writer, has imagined a time when consuming even the most excellent products will be so burdensome that the "poorer" one is, the more he will be forced to consume by the State, with a quota of required consumption allotted to each unfortunate individual. The hippies, at least, have anticipated Pohl's fears by rebelling against all consumer goods. Their rebellion seems quixotic until the other portents we have mentioned are recalled.

The end product of the over-pampered consumer society may well be a person who reacts against pampering, a rootless and truly liberated individual, one who ultimately threatens the Corporate State. Suppose a boy or girl is brought up in a plastic home, with rugs and furniture that have no more individuality or character than the furnishings of an expensive motel. Such a child will have very little attachment to his surroundings. The child of a home with genuine character develops loyalties, but the child of a plastic home is equally "at home" anywhere; he might as well be "on the road"; he feels no special connection to anything or any place. From a slavish and passive dependence on consumer goods, which his parents may never throw off, the child of the plastic home may suddenly find he can ignore all consumer goods, and in that moment, he is liberated.

The doubts of the worker and the consumer, basic as they are, are only specific examples of a breach of credulity and consciousness that is even deeper and more general. Perhaps this general doubt can be illustrated by the effect of television on the younger generation in terms of myth and reality. The youngster of earlier generations discovered reality by exploring outside his own front door. He encountered the world of the farm or of city streets, tested it, and found out about horses, cows, and pumpkins, other youngsters, stores, and traffic; the knowledge he gained did not play him false. Perhaps in old age, retelling his experiences, he turned them into myths, but they were myths that were fashioned out of his own reality.

With the child of television, the process is reversed. Our society insists that children first be taught the prescribed mythology, in school, in films, and earliest and most universally, on television. The television-world is what our society claims itself to be, what it demands that we believe. But when the television child finally encounters the real world, he does not find families like Ozzie, Harriet, David, and Ricky, "Father Knows Best," or "My Three Sons." He does not find the clean suburbs of television but the sordid slums of reality. He does not find the high-minded statesmen of the screen, but politicians who are mediocre, small-minded, and corrupt. He does not find perpetual smiles or the effervescent high spirits of a Coke ad, but anxieties and monotony. And when he stops believing in this mythic world, the breach in his credulity is irreparable. Society and television ask total belief; when their picture of the world is unmasked, the result is total unbelief. The child of an earlier generation could get some unsettling shocks without coming to disbelieve everything, but the faith that is now taught is so complete it cannot survive a shock. The child becomes a skeptic of everything. He sees right through every form of posture and pretense; he believes nothing he is told; he experiences that crucial feeling of the new generation, betrayal. In the words of Joni Mitchell's famous song, he has found that all things, clouds, love, and life, must be seen "from both sides now." "Ice cream castles in the air, and feather canyons ev'rywhere" have become clouds that "rain and snow on ev'ryone. So many things I would have done, but clouds got in my way. . . . It's life's illusions I recall. I really don't know life at all." The words and the melody are light and sentimental, the theme of youthful disillusionment is timeless, but it is a great mistake not to recognize that this is one of the songs of revolution.

Every society has troubles, failures, contradictions, and rebellions, but these do not necessarily lead to upheaval. A vital question is how the society responds to its problems. Although we have pointed to problems that are profound, including impoverishment of environment and self, and the contradictions just discussed, there is a great deal that the Corporate State could do to avoid, moderate, or at least defer the consequences. We are all aware of measures that could be taken with respect to environment, poverty, and the cities, and there are also steps that could be taken to make schools and jobs less oppressive. Nevertheless, the fact is that our society seems incapable of doing the simplest and most obvious things to save itself; instead, it has fallen into a pattern whereby it aggravates the very problems that threaten it. The pattern that our society has fallen into is one of rigidity and repression. The State fails to take even the most obvious action to avert trouble, and then takes violently repressive action against the symptoms; the repression is, of course, self-defeating. We can best show how this works by some examples, but it may be helpful to suggest first how this pattern develops.

The basic causes of rigidity have already been discussed. The structure of the State provides no way to control it; all forms of control have been systematically eliminated. The larger and more cumbersome bureaucracy becomes, the less capable it is of flexibility. The more policy is written into law, the more difficult that policy is to change. As the State increasingly demands "loyalty" from its employees, all of the opponents of a given policy are fired or frightened into silence, and no one is left in a position to reverse that policy.

Whether by accident or design, the present Republican administration illustrates to an extreme degree the elimination of differing points of view from the councils of policy. The President and the members of his Cabinet are representatives of the executive class of the business community. There is not a man among them who has the remotest chance of understanding the radical needs of the country, and therefore no one to press for the kinds of action that must be taken. Men who have spent their whole lives in the business-political world, whose friends are all drawn from that world, who have little time to discover radical books or spend long hours with people profoundly unlike themselves, can hardly be expected to comprehend the black ghetto or the drug movement. Without anyone in government who does understand these things, there is no one within the system who can help the State to deal affirmatively with its problems. There is no one who can be a statesman, no one to act with initiative, no one who can be a force for renewal.

Perhaps the most immediate cause of the rigidity-repression pattern is the fact that repression seems to be so much easier than any other solution and so much less expensive; it takes so little thinking, appears to raise so few questions, and apparently does not disturb any American myths. It is the old American idea of getting rid of evil by forbidding it. Thus in 1965, Senator McClellan introduced a bill "To outlaw the Mafia and other organized crime syndicates."

Solving problems by repression instead of coping with them produces a tense and claustrophobic society. A typical clean, medium-sized American city becomes an uptight place; everyone is afraid of criminals or communists or naked people. The police are watching; everyone gets a sense of surveillance. As the laws get tighter and more pervasive, all sorts of people get caught in the net. Even highly placed and influential public figures are not immune; a deal that looks bad, or an unfortunate personal escapade, can bring a kind of random disaster simply because the society is so tense that all violations, no matter what the circumstances, are threatening.

The problem of strikes by municipal employees offers an example of the rigidity-repression syndrome and its self-destructive effects on the State. In New York state, for example, strikes by public employees are forbidden by law. However, the continuing failure of the federal and state government, and ultimately, the people, to provide adequate sources of municipal revenue means that New York City cannot pay its employees enough to keep up with inflation and comparable pay for private employees. The dilemma is a real one; strikes by municipal employees can be a disaster for the public. But passing a law against strikes, without taking measures to solve the underlying problem, infuriates the workers and lowers respect for legal authority without effectively preventing disruptions. When newspaper editorials pompously tell the workers that a law is a law and must be obeyed, the only effect is to radicalize the workers by convincing them that law is merely the tool of their enemies. The State is then one step closer to its own downfall.

Consider the urban ghetto riots and their aftermath. We know from the studies that have been made of these riots that they were virtually unconscious in nature; happening spontaneously, they expressed accumulated rage and frustration, but with no particular focus or design. Despite overwhelming evidence that what was needed was less police harassment and improvement of basic living conditions, the government not only failed to act affirmatively, it increased existing repression and at the same time made it more difficult for sympathetic persons to hold positions where they could influence government to a wiser course. Failure to act affirmatively is illustrated by the action of the New York state legislature in actually cutting welfare. Additional repression is illustrated by police training in anti-riot tactics. Removal of opposing voices is illustrated by legal action against such leaders as LeRoi Jones and Eldridge Cleaver, and the introduction of special "loyalty" requirements for workers in the government's antipoverty programs. The net effect was, of course, to increase, focus, and activate black consciousness in people who had for so many decades endured the injustices of the State, demonstrating to them that the American myth was not for them.

Surely the case of marijuana offers the most clearcut example of the rigidity-repression syndrome at its most self-defeating. Accept any prevailing theory of government and marijuana ought to be legalized: the conservative doctrine that the individual should be free of government regulation; the liberal-reformist doctrine that controls are to be used only when science justifies them; the theory suggested by Marcuse that contemporary government can buy off dissatisfaction by allowing pleasures that pacify. Take an approach that is simply practical and realistic: the laws against marijuana are ineffectual, unjust in their erratic enforcement, tend to break down respect for law, and at the same time radicalize those people, particularly young people, who are threatened with criminal penalties for what they regard as a perfectly acceptable private practice. Nothing so directly threatens the stability of the State, then, as the present marijuana laws, yet the State persists in the suicidal course of trying to enforce them. Such a process may produce a good many arrests in the short run, but in the long run it promises only self-destruction for the State itself.

What comes of all of this, the contradictions and the efforts at repression, is, in time, a destruction of the social fabric itself. We can see this beginning to happen all around us. Curiously enough, it is not the dissenters from society who take the lead in breaking the social fabric, but elements in the Establishment itself. We can see many signs of this in the series of strikes, confrontations, non-negotiable demands, and other power tactics which to many groups now seem to be the only available means of getting anything done. Thus, municipal unions believe that they must ignore both the law and the "public interest" to get what they want by striking and causing the disruption of some vital service. Blacks and other minorities are increasingly certain that only militant power will accomplish anything for them. The New York state parkway police on Long Island, in an effort to win a pay raise, began issuing a sharply increased number of traffic tickets to motorists (*The New York Times*, November 19, 1968). More and more, people seem to feel that only coercion or raw force can accomplish anything. And of course, as belief in the system erodes, it is only pure force that does make anything work.

The most serious injury to the social fabric occurs when the law itself turns lawless. This, too, is happening, not only in the subtle way we discussed previously, but in a way that is recognized by everyone. Police begin to punish demonstrators, not arrest them for legal trial. General Hershey sought to do the same thing, by using his power to draft people and send them to Vietnam. The federal government, ignoring its own laws and directives, eavesdrops and wiretaps whenever it pleases. High school teachers and students are bullied for unpopular views. Antiwar coffee houses for G.I.'s are subjected to deliberate harassment by law enforcement officers. Informers are used more and more frequently, creating suspicion and mistrust. One hears continually of incidents where police bully someone: a police officer, stopping a young motorist, asks for his license and then tears it up in the boy's face; police are suspected of planting narcotics in people's homes when a raid fails to discover any; in New Jersey, state police, unable to find any evidence against a reputed mobster, turned to harassment, such as shining headlights into his bedroom nightly, in an effort to drive the man out of the state (*The New York Times,* January 25, 1969).

But obviously every time a policeman tears up a boy's license another radical is made. At the State University at Stony Brook, Long Island (hardly a radical institution), repeated police harassment over drugs, including use of informers, caused students to go on a rampage in which they pelted police cars with rocks, upset other police cars, set fire to a security guard shack, broke two hundred windows, and, when the fire department arrived, stoned the fire trucks too (*The New York Times,* May 14, 1969). Thus the State, caught in the fatal syndrome of rigidity and repression, finds itself piercing the old consciousness at an ever increasing rate by its harassment of people, while its failure to cope with underlying problems gives a steady supply of fuel to new discontent.

Official lawlessness, government corruption, public hypocrisy, and the other tendencies we have discussed do not produce an effect on the social fabric that is measurable. Their impact is not really visible at all.

The impact really begins to be felt when the people of a society simply begin to disbelieve. When they speak of a courthouse as the "Hall of Injustice," when they think that justice and equality have been subordinated to mere power, when their credulity about "the public interest" is breached, the whole basis on which the authority of the State rests is eroded. Authority is then reduced to force, and no society can long continue on that basis.

One possible sign of the decline of belief is the increasing tendency of young school children to steal whenever they can get away with it. They regard anything that seems to be a part of "the system"—a supermarket, the phone company, a gas station—as legitimate game, but in personal relationships they remain perfectly honorable. Somehow, they need to "kick the system." Most adults refrain from such random acts, not merely because they fear getting caught, but also because they do not see how any system or society could run if everyone simply attacked it whenever they could. But to these youngsters, there is no society to believe in, only a system that must be fought, if only to give oneself a sense of reality.

If the pathology of rigidity and repression had been limited to domestic concerns, it is possible that the Corporate State might still be generally unchallenged, despite all that we have said, for it takes a great deal to make people question their own society. But the pathology extended outward, to create the Cold War, with its progeny, the defense establishment and Vietnam. Nothing else has done so much to destroy Consciousness I and II. It is a story worth retelling from our special point of view.

Every country has foreign enemies, imaginary or

real, a defense-military establishment, and an occasional war, necessary or unnecessary. The two world wars illustrate these statements as they apply to America before it became the American Corporate State. These statements are not meant to be cynical, they are simply historical. They are made to establish a standard of normalcy against which to measure the Cold War and Vietnam. For this latest war is an utterly different phenomenon; a monster incarnated out of the madness of the State.

The war represents that form of madness in which logic is carried to fantastic extremes. Suppose a motorist is about to park in a convenient spot on the street when another car pulls into the place ahead of him. The first man might feel justified in yelling indignantly at the second man. But suppose the first man pushes the logic of justification to extremes. He plants a bomb in the second man's car so that the victim will blow himself up when he steps on the ignition. The first man then goes to the second man's house and, using chemicals, burns down the house, burning to death the second man's wife and children. The first man then poisons the family dog, which escaped the holocaust. Thereafter he acquires a huge supply of weapons for further attack or defense.

When we encounter this kind of logic in real life, we quickly recognize it for one of the forms of insanity. There is a hilariously funny Laurel and Hardy sequence in *Big Business*, in which, beginning with a trivial incident, they systematically wreck a man's house while he wrecks their car; it is funny, but the laughter is uneasy. Poe built his famous story "The Cask of Amontillado" on just this kind of madness—insults leading to a hideous revenge. There are many examples in literature and in recent history, but none so extreme, not even the examples we just gave, as the Vietnam War.

Starting with an initial political-ideological dispute, in a country on the other side of the globe, we have butchered, burned, and mutilated men, women, and children, laid waste a country, and meanwhile created a science-fiction fantasy of weapons capable of destroying the entire world, building more, more, and more weapons until the nation has wasted its own cities, schools, and needs in the effort, impoverishing its people and communal life for this single purpose.

This mad logic is accompanied by a curious detached quality: the war is merely one more artificial, manufactured product of the Corporate State. It is unattended by genuine emotions, genuine needs, genuine dangers, or even genuine fears. It is a game—an extension of war games played by the military, strategy games played by intellectuals in the White House basement, sales promotion games played within a business organization. It has the artificial quality of a business, too: profits and huge organizations needing the war to expand. The war has the special quality of manufactured, artificial, Disneyland "reality."

The "need" for the Cold War and the Vietnam War has been created like the "need" for that other characteristic product of the Corporate State, a new, high-powered car. At the bottom of each creation is a fragment of truth: maybe we do need a defense force of perhaps 100,000 or 200,000 men; and we do need transportation. But the modern car, its high power, its relationship to status, to sex, to aggression, its tremendous size, its extravagant consumption of fuel, its instant obsolescence, its fabulous expense, its indispensability to even the poorest family—all of that is the imaginary made real, just as the threat from a primitive people ten thousand miles away is imaginary. If the war were really necessary to serve the needs of imperialism, it would be less horrible than it actually is—an intellectual creation, a "new product."

And the war carries with it all the habitual falseness of television advertising. It is for "freedom" even though it is attempting to perpetuate a dictatorship. "Elections" are held that are obvious fakes. "Agrarian reform" is promised but never takes place. It is a "moral" war fought by a country which supports blatantly immoral regimes all over the world, a "defensive" war by a country whose offensive military bases ring the world.

All of this insanity, artificiality, and untruth are the commonplace stuff of the Corporate State. We see them on all sides: the supersonic plane, the fifty-story building, the teaching machine for the schoolroom, premixed peanut butter and jelly. None of them bring on rebellion. It is the misfortune of the Corporate State that, unlike its other products, its venture into foreign policy has produced real blood, killed real babies, burned real homes. It is the State's misfortune that the war has produced atomic weapons which really could destroy all life. And it is doubly the State's misfortune that in order to market this product it requires the unwilling bodies of our own youth. The Vietnam War is the Corporate State's one unsalable product.

The Corporate State is trapped by its own product. Years of subversive hunts, of loyalty oaths, and congressional investigations have eliminated from positions of power in the State virtually every person who might know how to get us out of the war. And the failure of newspaper and television to carry facts that would help us extricate ourselves, the insistence on teacher and student patriotism in the schools, CIA subsidies of public opinion—all have prevented public discussion from offering the State any help to escape. The State has, as we have said, no brakes.

And so the great significance and irony of the Vietnam War is this: the Corporate State could engage in almost any activities, no matter how impoverishing to life, so long as it did not pierce the consciousness that accepted the whole scheme of things. The war seemed another such activity and, indeed, it did not pierce the consciousness of many of the middle class, who continue to accept it as "necessary," just as they accept pollution, automobile deaths, or chopping down the redwoods. But the war should not have been offered to our young people. They were the wrong market. And when they began to be killed, their parents were the wrong market too. The war did what almost nothing else could have: it forced a major breach in consciousness. The breaches in consciousness caused by the consumer-worker contradiction or the rigidity-repression syndrome were significant, but they were slow acting and might have taken indefinite time. It might have been years before marijuana and riots catalyzed disillusionment. The war did that with extraordinary rapidity. It rent the fabric of consciousness so drastically as to make repair almost impossible. And it made a gap in belief so large that through it people could begin to question the other myths of the Corporate State. The whole edifice of the Corporate State is built on tranquilizers and sleeping pills; it should not have done the one thing that might shake the sleeper awake.

IX

CONSCIOUSNESS III:
THE NEW GENERATION

Beginning with a few individuals in the mid-nineteen-sixties, and gathering numbers ever more rapidly thereafter, Consciousness III has sprouted up, astonishingly and miraculously, out of the stony soil of the American Corporate State. So spontaneous was its appearance that no one, not the most astute or the most radical, foresaw what was coming or recognized it when it began. It is not surprising that many people think it a conspiracy, for it was spread, here and abroad, by means invisible. Hardly anybody of the older generation, even the FBI or the sociologists, knows much about it, for its language and thought are so different from Consciousness II as to make it virtually an undecipherable secret code. Consciousness III is, as of this writing, the greatest secret in America, although its members have shouted as loudly as they could to be heard.

We must pause over the origins of Consciousness III, lest it seem too improbable and too transitory to be deemed as fundamental as Consciousness I and Consciousness II. One element in its origin has already been described: the impoverishment of life, the irrationality, violence, and claustrophobia of the American Corporate State. But how did this corporate machine, seemingly designed to keep its inhabitants perpetually on a treadmill, suddenly begin producing something altogether new and unintended? The new consciousness is the product of two interacting forces: the promise of life that is made to young Americans by all of our affluence, technology, liberation, and ideals, and the threat to that promise posed by everything from neon ugliness and boring jobs to the Vietnam War and the shadow of nuclear holocaust. Neither the promise nor the threat is the cause by itself; but the two together have done it.

The promise comes first. We have all heard the promise: affluence, security, technology make possible a new life, a new permissiveness, a new freedom, a new expansion of human possibility. We have all heard it, but to persons born after World War II it means something very different. Older people learned how to live in a different world; it is really beyond them to imagine themselves living according to the new promises. The most basic limitations of life—the job, the working day, the part one can play in life, the limits of sex, love and relationships, the limits of knowledge and experience—all vanish, leaving open a life that can be lived without the guideposts of the past. In the world that now exists, a life of surfing *is* possible, not as an escape from work, a recreation or a phase, but as a *life*—if one chooses. The fact that this choice is actually available is the truth that the younger generation knows and the older generation cannot know.

The promise is made real to members of the younger generation by a sense of acceptance about themselves. To older generations, particularly Consciousness II people, great issues were presented by striving to reach some external standard of personal attractiveness, popularity, ability at sports, acceptance by the group. Many lives, including some outstanding careers, were lived under the shadow of such personal issues; even late in life, people are still profoundly influenced by them. Of course the new generation is not free of such concerns. But to an astonishing degree, whether it is due to new parental attitudes, a less tense, less inhibited childhood, or a different experience during school years, these are not the issues which plague the younger generation. If the hero of *Portnoy's Complaint* is the final and most complete example of the man dissatisfied with the self that he is, the new generation says, "Whatever I am, I am." He may have hang-ups of all sorts, insecurities, inadequacies, but he does not reject himself on that account. There may be as many difficulties about work, ability, relationships, and sex as in any other generation, but there is less guilt, less anxiety, less self-hatred. Consciousness III says, "I'm glad I'm me."

The new generation has also learned lessons from technology, by being born with it, that the older generation does not know even though it invented technology. It is one thing to know intellectually that there is a Xerox machine that can copy anything, a pill that can make sexual intercourse safe, or a light motorcycle that can take two people off camping with ten minutes' preparation, but it is quite another thing to live with these facts, make use of them, and thus learn to live *by* them.

These experiences and promises are shared to some extent by the youth of every industrial nation, and the new consciousness is, as we know, not limited to the United States. But Consciousness III, the specifically American form, is not based on promise alone. A key word in understanding its origin is *betrayal*.

Older people are inclined to think of work, injustice and war, and of the bitter frustrations of life, as the human condition. Their capacity for outrage is consequently dulled. But to those who have glimpsed the real possibilities of life, who have tasted liberation and love, who have seen the promised land, the prospect of a dreary corporate job, a ranch-house life, or a miserable death in war is utterly intolerable. Moreover, the human condition, if that is what it is, has been getting steadily worse in the Corporate State; more and more life-denying just as life should be opening up. And hovering over everything is the threat of annihilation, more real and more terrifying to the young than to anyone else. To them, the discrepancy between what could be and what is, is overwhelming; perhaps it is the greatest single fact of their existence. The promise of America, land of beauty and abundance, land of the free, somehow has been betrayed.

They feel the betrayal in excruciatingly personal terms. Between them and the rich possibilities of life there intervenes a piercing insecurity—not the personal insecurity their parents knew, but a cosmic insecurity. Will the nation be torn apart by riots or war? Will their lives be cut short by death or injury in Vietnam? Will the impersonal machinery of the state—schools, careers, institutions—overwhelm them? Above all, will they escape an atomic holocaust (they were, as many people have pointed out, the generation of the bomb). Insecurity sharpens their consciousness and draws them together.

Parents have unintentionally contributed to their children's condemnation of existing society. Not by their words, but by their actions, attitudes, and manner of living, they have conveyed to their children the message "Don't live the way we have, don't settle for the emptiness of our lives, don't be lured by the things we valued, don't neglect life and love as we have." With the unerring perceptiveness of the child, their children have read these messages from the lifeless lives of their "successful" parents, have seen marriages break up because there was nothing to hold them, have felt cynicism, alienation, and despair in the best-kept homes of America. And will have none of it.

Kenneth Keniston, in *Young Radicals*, found that one of the most telling forces in producing the political ideals of the new generation is the contrast between their parents' ideals (which they accept) and their parents' failure to live these same ideals. Keniston found that young radicals show a *continuity* of ideals from childhood on; they simply stayed with them while their parents failed to.

We might add to this that our society, with its dogmatic insistence on one way of seeing everything, its dominating false consciousness, and its ever-widening gap between fact and rhetoric, invites a sudden moment when the credibility gap becomes too much, and invites cataclysmic consequences to the consciousness of a young person when that occurs. For so vehemently does the society insist that its "truth" be accepted wholly and undeviatingly down the line, and so drastic are the discrepancies once seen, that a single breach in the dike may bring a young person's entire conversion. All that is needed is to participate in one peace demonstration and find *The New York Times'* report of it inexcusably false, and the whole edifice of "truth" collapses. Such "conversions" are constantly seen on campuses today; a freshman arrives, his political views are hometown-Consciousness I, and suddenly he is radicalized. The fabric of manufactured "truth," spread taut and thin, breaches, and one breach leaves it irrevocably in tatters.

If a history of Consciousness III were to be written, it would show a fascinating progression. The earliest sources were among those exceptional individuals who are found at any time in any society: the artistic, the highly sensitive, the tormented. Thoreau, James Joyce, and Wallace Stevens all speak directly to Consciousness III. Salinger's Holden Caulfield was a fictional version of the first young precursors of Consciousness III. Perhaps there was always a bit of Consciousness III in every teen-ager, but normally it quickly vanished. Holden sees through the established world: they are "phonies" and he is merciless in his honesty. But what was someone like Holden to do? A subculture of "beats" grew up, and a beatnik world flourished briefly, but for most people it represented only another dead end. Other Holdens might reject the legal profession and try teaching literature or writing instead, letting their hair grow a bit longer as well. But they remained separated individuals, usually ones from affluent but unhappy, tortured family backgrounds, and their differences with society were paid for by isolation.

Unquestionably the blacks made a substantial contribution to the origins of the new consciousness. They were left out of the Corporate State, and thus they had to have a culture and life-style in opposition to the State. Their music, with its "guts," contrasted with the insipid white music. Their way of life seemed more earthy, more sensual than that of whites. They were the first openly to scorn the Establishment and its values; as Eldridge Cleaver shows in *Soul on Ice*, and Malcolm X shows in his autobiography, they were radicalized by the realities of their situation. When their music began to be heard by white teen-agers through the medium of rock 'n' roll, and when their view of America became visible through the civil rights movement, it gave new impetus to the subterranean awareness of the beat generation and the Holden Caulfields.

The great change took place when Consciousness III began to appear among young people who had endured no special emotional conditions, but were simply bright, sensitive children of the affluent middle class. It is hard to be precise about the time when this happened. One chronology is based on the college class of 1969, which entered as freshmen in the fall of 1965. Another important date is the summer of 1967, when the full force of the cultural revolution was first visible. But even in the fall of 1967 the numbers involved were still very small. The new group drew heavily from those who had been exposed to the very best of liberal arts education—poetry, art, theatre, literature, philosophy, good conversation. Later, the group began to include "ordinary" middle-class students. In time there were college athletes as well as college intellectuals, and lovers of motorcycles and skiing as well as lovers of art and literature. But the core group was always white, well educated, and middle class.

Among today's youth, the phenomenon of "conversions" is increasingly common. It is surprising that so little has been written about these conversions, for they are a striking aspect of contemporary life. What happens is simply this: in a brief span of months, a student, seemingly conventional in every way, changes his haircut, his clothes, his habits, his interests, his political attitudes, his way of relating to other people, in short, his whole way of life. He has "converted" to a new consciousness. The contrast between well-groomed freshman pictures and the same individuals in person a year later tells the tale. The clean-cut, hardworking, model young man who despises radicals and hippies can become one himself with breathtaking suddenness. Over and over again, an individual for whom a conversion seemed impossible, a star athlete, an honor student, the small-town high school boy with the American Legion scholarship, transforms himself into a drug-using, long-haired, peace-loving "freak." Only when he puts on a headband and plays unexpectedly skillful touch football or basketball, or when a visitor to his old room back home catches sight of his honor society certificate, is his earlier life revealed.

As the new consciousness made youth more distinct, the younger generation began discovering itself as a generation. Always before, young people felt themselves tied more to their families, to their schools, and to their immediate situations than to "a generation." But now an entire culture, including music, clothes, and drugs, began to distinguish youth. As it did, the message of consciousness went with it. And the more the older generation rejected the culture, the more a fraternity of the young grew up, so that they recognized each other as brothers and sisters from coast to coast. That is its history up to this writing; let us now try to describe the content of Consciousness III.

A few warnings are needed. First, in attempting to describe Consciousness III systematically and analytically, we are engaging in an intellectual process which Consciousness III rejects; they have a deep skepticism of both "linear" and analytic thought. Second, we shall be talking about an idealized consciousness, and not about something that is to be seen in all aspects in any one person. The members of the new generation have their doubts, hang-ups and failings too, and Consciousness III may coexist with earlier patterns and values. Third, Consciousness III itself is just in an early stage of development, and probably the elements of it would have to be described differently in one or two years.

The foundation of Consciousness III is liberation. It comes into being the moment the individual frees himself from automatic acceptance of the imperatives of society and the false consciousness which society imposes. For example, the individual no longer accepts unthinkingly the personal goals proposed by society; a change of personal goals is one of the first and most basic elements of Consciousness III. The meaning of liberation is that the individual is free to build his own philosophy and values, his own life-style, and his own culture from a new beginning.

Consciousness III starts with self. In contrast to

Consciousness II, which accepts society, the public interest, and institutions as the primary reality, III declares that the individual self is the only true reality. Thus it returns to the earlier America: "Myself I sing." The first commandment is: thou shalt not do violence to thyself. It is a crime to allow oneself to become an instrumental being, a projectile designed to accomplish some extrinsic end, a part of an organization or a machine. It is a crime to be alienated from oneself, to be a divided or schizophrenic being, to defer meaning to the future. One must live completely at each moment, not with the frenzied "nowness" of advertising, but with the utter *wholeness* that Heidegger expresses. The commandment is: be true to oneself.

To start from self does not mean to be selfish. It means to start from premises based on human life and the rest of nature, rather than premises that are the artificial products of the Corporate State, such as power or status. It is not an "ego trip" but a radical subjectivity designed to find genuine values in a world whose official values are false and distorted. It is not egocentricity, but honesty, wholeness, genuineness in all things. It starts from self because human life is found as individual units, not as corporations and institutions; its intent is to start from life.

Consciousness III postulates the absolute worth of every human being—every self. Consciousness III does not believe in the antagonistic or competitive doctrine of life. Competition, within the limits of a sport like tennis or swimming, is accepted for its own pleasure, although even as athletes III's are far less competitive (and sometimes, but not always, poorer athletes as a result). But III's do not compete "in real life." They do not measure others, they do not see others as something to struggle against. People are brothers, the world is ample for all. In consequence, one never hears the disparagements, the snickers, the judgments that are so common among I's and II's. A boy who was odd in some way used to suffer derision all through his school days. Today there would be no persecution; one might even hear one boy speak, with affection, of "my freaky friend." Instead of insisting that everyone be measured by given standards, the new generation values what is unique and different in each self; there is no pressure that anyone be an athlete unless he wants to; a harpsichord player is accepted on equal terms. No one judges anyone else. This is a second commandment.

Consciousness III rejects the whole concept of excellence and comparative merit that is so central to Consciousness II. III refuses to evaluate people by general standards, it refuses to classify people, or analyze them. Each person has his own individuality, not to be compared to that of anyone else. Someone may be a brilliant thinker, but he is not "better" at thinking than anyone else, he simply possesses his own excellence. A person who thinks very poorly is still excellent in his own way. Therefore people are in no hurry to find out another person's background, schools, achievements, as a means of knowing him; they regard all of that as secondary, preferring to know him unadorned. Because there are no governing standards, no one is rejected. Everyone is entitled to pride in himself, and no one should act in a way that is servile, or feel inferior, or allow himself to be treated as if he were inferior.

It is upon these premises that the Consciousness III idea of community and of personal relationships rests. In place of the world seen as a jungle, with every man for himself (Consciousness I) or the world seen as a meritocracy leading to a great corporate hierarchy of rigidly drawn relations and manoeuvers for position (Consciousness II), the world is a community. People all belong to the same family, whether they have met each other or not. It is as simple as that. There are no "tough guys" among the youth of Consciousness III. Hitchhikers smile at approaching cars, people smile at each other on the street, the human race rediscovers its need for each other. "I felt lonesome, so I came looking for some people," a III will say. Something in the makeup and pride of a I or II will keep him from "confessing" that "weakness" in quite such an open way. But III does not want to stand head and shoulders above the crowd. III values, more than a judgeship or executive title, the warmth of the "circle of affection" in which men join hands. In personal relations, the keynote is honesty, and the absence of socially imposed duty. To be dishonest in love, to "use" another person, is a major crime. A third commandment is: be wholly honest with others, use no other person as a means. It is equally wrong to alter oneself for someone else's sake; by being one's true self one offers others the most; one offers them something honest, genuine, and, more important, something for them to respond to, to be evoked by. A work of art is not valued because it changes itself for each person who views it, it retains its own integrity and thus means something unique and marvelous to those who see it. Being true to oneself is, so Consciousness III says, the best and only way to relate to others. Consciousness III rejects most of what happens between people in our world: manipulation of others, forcing anyone to do anything against his wish, using others for one's own purposes, irony and sarcasm, defensive stand-offishness. III also rejects relationships of authority and subservience. It will neither give commands nor follow them; coercive relations between people are wholly unacceptable. And III also rejects any relationships based wholly on role, relationships limited along strictly impersonal and functional lines. There is no situation in which one is entitled to act impersonally, in a stereotyped fashion, with another human being; the relationship of businessman to clerk, passenger to conductor, student to janitor must not be impersonal.

But to observe duties toward others, after the feelings are gone, is no virtue and may even be a crime. Loyalty is valued but not artificial duty. Thus the new generation looks with suspicion on "obligations" and contractual relations between people, but it believes that honesty can produce far more genuine relationships than the sterile ones it observes among the older generation. To most people, there is something frightening about the notion that no oath, no law, no promise, no indebtedness holds people together when the feeling is gone. But for the new generation that is merely recognition of the truth about human beings. Moreover, getting rid of what is artificial is essential to make way for what is real, and Consciousness III considers genuine relationships with others, friendship, companionship, love, the human community, to be among the highest values of life.

The premise of self and of values based on human life leads directly to a radical critique of society. Many people are puzzled by the radicalism of Consciousness III—have they been infiltrated by communists, are they influenced by "a few left-wing agitators," have they been reading Marx? It does indeed seem astonishing that naïve young people, without political experience, should come up with a critique of society that seems to have escaped the most scholarly as well as the most astute and experienced of their elders. But there is no mystery, no conspiracy, and very little reading of Marx. Older people begin by assuming that much of the structure of the Corporate State is necessary and valid; starting there they never get very far. The young people start with entirely different premises, and all is revealed to them.

What Consciousness III sees, with an astounding clarity that no ideology could provide, is a society that is unjust to its poor and its minorities, is run for the benefit of a privileged few, is lacking in its proclaimed democracy and liberty, is ugly and artificial, that destroys environment and self, and is, like the wars it spawns, "unhealthy for children and other living things." It sees a society that is deeply untruthful and hypocritical; one of the gifts of the young is to see through phoniness and cant, and Consciousness III sees through the Establishment verities of our society with corrosive ease.

Consciousness III sees not merely a set of political and public wrongs, such as a liberal New Dealer might have seen, but also the deeper ills that Kafka or the German expressionists or Dickens would have seen: old people shunted into institutional homes, streets made hideous with neon and commercialism, servile conformity, the competitiveness and sterility of suburban living, the loneliness and anomie of cities, the ruin of nature by bulldozers and pollution, the stupid mindlessness of most high school education, the coarse materialism of most values, the lovelessness of many marriages, and, above all, the plastic, artificial quality of everything; plastic lives in plastic homes.

All of Consciousness III's criticisms of society were brought into sharpest focus by the Vietnam War. For the war seemed to sum up the evils of our society: destruction of people, destruction of environment, depersonalized use of technology, war by the rich and powerful against the poor and helpless, justification based on abstract rationality, hypocrisy and lies, and a demand that the individual, regardless of his conscience, values, or self, make himself into a part of the war machine, an impersonal projectile bringing death to other people. Those who said they could not go believed that compulsory service in a war they hated would be so total a destruction of their genuine values that even if they did return to the United States, they could never return to the ranks of the genuinely living.

The initial premise of self leads not only to a critique of society, it also leads, in many representatives of Consciousness III, to a deep personal commitment to the welfare of the community. This may sound contradictory to those who wrongly equate the premise of self with selfishness, and it may seem to contradict the premise that the individual, not society, is the reality. But there is no contradiction. It is quite true that the individual does not accept the goals or standards set by society. But of course he recognizes that society has a vast influence on the welfare of people everywhere, including his own desire to be an independent being. Mostly he sees this influence as bad, but he also sees how much better things could be. And therefore, for the sake of the welfare of individuals, he is committed to the improvement of society. It is the manner of commitment that differs from II.

There is one essential qualification to what we have said: dedication to the community is not to include means that do violence to the self. A Consciousness III person will not study law to help society, if law is not what he wants to do with his life, nor will he do harm to others in order to promote some good, nor will he deny himself the experiences of life for any cause. The political radical of Consciousness III is thus very different from the radical of the Old Left, the communist, socialist, or civil libertarian ready to dedicate himself and his life to the cause, puritanical, sour, righteous. To the new consciousness, to make himself an object to serve the cause would be to subvert the cause.

Subject to this qualification, the key to the Consciousness III commitment lies in the concept of full personal responsibility. In the case of Consciousness II, commitment to society means commitment to reform in the general direction already established by society (equality, better education), the notion of "reform" merely meaning that the "liberal" is somewhat ahead of where society is at. And the commitment has limits; the liberal enjoys his high status, his elegant house, his security, and comfort, and fights his battle from that position. Consciousness III feels that, if he is to be true to himself, he must respond *with* himself. He may take a job, such as teaching in a ghetto school, which offers neither prestige nor comfort, but offers the satisfaction of personal contact with ghetto children. He must live on a modest scale to retain the freedom that his commitment demands. He must take risks. And at the same time, he must be wholly himself in what he does. He knows that he is an agent of change, whether he plays music or works in a ghetto, so long as he affirms himself in his work, and so long as his work expresses the full responsibility of his feelings.

It is this notion of personal responsibility which makes the new generation, when it finds itself excluded from the decision-making process, demand a part in that process. For the liberal, it is sufficient to say, "I oppose air pollution, but in my job I have nothing to do with it, no responsibility in that direction, all I can do is try to influence those who do." That, to Consciousness III, is not being responsible; if one is not part of the decision-making process, responsibility requires that one gain such power.

It is this same personal responsibility that makes the young student feel himself to be an adult, not a person getting ready for life. By attempting to be fully alive *now*, young people grow more serious, more thoughtful, more concerned with what is happening in the world. Many adults of the older generation have smooth baby faces, the faces of men interested only in the Sunday ball game, the nearest skirt, or the bowling league, as if they were permanent juveniles, as if they never, not once in their lives, faced their world and took its concerns on themselves, or accepted the responsibilities of full consciousness. The faces of Consciousness III seem to have lived more, even in their short years. A look at a college classbook of today, compared with one of fifteen years ago, tells the difference. That is one reason why the people of Consciousness III have a sense of each other as a generation with something in common.

During the Columbia confrontation, a group of Columbia varsity athletes were invited to an alumni meeting to receive awards, then disinvited when they asked to make statements on the campus situation. The alumni didn't want to think of athletes having political views. The athletes, fencers who had won a national championship and basketball players who had won the Ivy League championship, then picketed the alumni meeting in a driving rain in their varsity C blazers, until the alumni finally let them in and let them speak (*The New York Times*, May 25, 1968). It wasn't the athletes' "job" to picket in the rain; they could have signed a letter if they wanted to express themselves.

At the Heptagonal Track Meet held at Yale in May of 1970, the athletes of eight of the participating schools insisted that before the meet could begin a statement of their views on public issues be read over the loudspeakers by a spokesman who was a member of one of the teams. The statement, expressing profound concern over the invasion of Cambodia, the persecution of Black Panthers, and other issues, also took the position, in explicit language, that athletics should not serve as an escape from public responsibility for the athletes themselves or for the fans; as an additional reminder, many of the athletes wore red or black ribbons on their sleeves or shorts during competition. No doubt many alumni and others in the stands were less than pleased with this intrusion of reality onto Yale's playing fields. When members of the Annapolis and West Point teams expressed dissatisfaction with the statement, they were offered an opportunity to express their own views; instead, they left without competing. But coaches, officials, and fans were forced to realize that the athletes who did compete were not the smooth-faced, ever-juvenile jocks of American expectations. They were serious adults. And they thought it essential, if they were to be *whole* as selves, to make a *personal* response, and thereby, as Sartre's Orestes did in *The Flies*, assume responsibility that "was not theirs," and thus achieve a full existence.

Because it accepts no imposed system, the basic stance of Consciousness III is one of openness to any and all experience. It is always in a state of becoming. It is just the opposite of Consciousness II, which tries to force all new experience into a pre-existing system, and to assimilate all new knowledge to principles already established. Although we can attempt to describe the specific content of Consciousness III at a given moment, its lasting essence is constant change, and constant growth of each individual.

These are the premises of Consciousness III and some of its resulting relationships with existing society. This is how it defines itself against the prevailing truths and values. But to see the affirmative scope of Consciousness III we must survey the life-style and culture it is in the process of creating. The culture is so expansive and varied that we must be selective; we shall deal with several major elements in some detail: clothes, career, music, community and consciousness. There are other elements, and it is all in a process of rapid change and development, but these will suggest the nature of what is being sought.

One quality unites all aspects of the Consciousness III way of life: energy. It is the energy of enthusiasm, of happiness, of hope. Some people assume that what they are seeing is merely the energy of youth, but it is greater than this; other generations never had such energy even in their youth. Consciousness III draws energy from new sources: from the group, the community, from eros, from the freedom of technology, from the uninhibited self.

A good place to begin is clothes, for the dress of the new generation expresses a number of the major themes of Consciousness III in a very vivid and immediate way. The first impression the clothes give is of uniformity and conformity—as if everyone felt obliged to adopt the same style. We shall try to show that this is an erroneous impression—that there is agreement on certain principles, but great individuality within those principles. Another first impression is of drabness—browns, greens, blue jeans. This is an accurate observation and for a reason. They are a deliberate rejection of the neon colors and plastic, artificial look of the affluent society. They are inexpensive to buy, inexpensive to maintain. They suggest that neither individuality nor distinction can be bought in a clothing store; clothes are primarily functional. The clothes are earthy and sensual. They express an affinity with nature; the browns, greens, and blues are nature's colors, earth's colors, not the colors of the machine, and the materials are rough and tactile. The clothes are like architecture that does not clash with its natural surroundings but blends in. And the clothes have a functional affinity with nature too; they don't show dirt, they are good for lying on the ground.

These clothes express freedom. Expensive clothes enforce social constraints; a grease spot on an expensive suit is a social error, so is a rip in a tailored ladies' coat, or a missing button. A man in an expensive suit must be careful of every move he makes, where he sits, what he leans against. A well-dressed woman is hardly able to walk or move. The new clothes give the wearer freedom to do anything he wants. He can work in them, read in them, roll down a hill in them, ride a bike in them, play touch football, dance, sit on the floor, go on a camping trip, sleep in them. Above all, they are comfortable.

The freedom of new clothes expresses a second

principle as well: a wholeness of self, as against the schizophrenia of Consciousness II. There is not one set of clothes for the office; another for social life, a third for play. The same clothes can be used for every imaginable activity, and so they say: it is the same person doing each of these things, not a set of different masks or dolls, but one many-sided, *whole* individual. We do not have another, secret life outside the office; as we are here, we are always. At the same time, these clothes say: a single individual may do many different things in the course of a day, he is not limited to a single role or a role-plus-recreation; each individual is truly protean, with unlimited possibilities including the possibility of whatever new and spontaneous thing may come along. Consciousness III is extremely reluctant to go to a restaurant or hotel where it is necessary to "dress up"—this would require a loss of wholeness and self; a dishonest constraint.

One reason the clothes are not "uniform," as people think, is that they are extremely expressive of the human body, and each body is different and unique. Men's suits really *are* uniform; they look the same on a man as they do on the rack in the clothing store; they hide the fact that one man may be muscular, another flabby, one soft, one bony, one hairy, another smooth. The pants give no hint of a man's legs, and when they wrinkle along body lines, they are quickly taken to the dry cleaners to be pressed back into straight lines. Jeans express the shape of legs, heavy or thin, straight or bowed. As jeans get more wrinkled, they adapt even more to the particular legs that are wearing them. Sitting across from a man in a business suit, it is as if he did not have a body at all, just a face and a voice. Jeans make one conscious of the body, not as something separate from the face but as part of the whole individual; Consciousness III believes that a person's body is one of the essential parts of his self, not something to be ignored while one carries on a conversation with his face and mind. Also the new clothes make the wearer conscious of his own body; a man's suit is at odds with his body all day long. The new clothes are a declaration of sensuality, not sensuality-for-display as in Madison Avenue style, but sensuality as a part of the natural in man. There is no masculinity or femininity hang-up. A boy does not feel he has to dress in a certain way or "he will not be a man"; he is not that anxious or concerned about his own masculinity.

If the individual wishes, he can add touches to his clothes that make them a costume, expressing whatever he feels at the moment. With the magic deftness of stage sorcery, a headband can produce an Indian, a black hat a cowboy badman. When a high fashion woman wears a costume, say a "matador" suit, it seems to have been imposed on her, mask-like, by her designer. She is an object that has been decorated. But the costumes of the young are not masks, they are expressions of an inner, perhaps momentary state of mind. The individual is free to be inventive, playful, humorous. A boy can wear a military dress jacket, all buttons and brass, and both mock the military establishment and at the same time express his small-boy's love of uniforms, and parade-ground pomp. Likewise with a Mexican peasant's blanket-shawl, or a David Copperfield hat, boots of all descriptions, gangster suits, phantom-of-the-opera cloaks. These costumes do not hide the real person as role-dress does, they show a state of mind and thus reveal him to us, and they add to the gaiety and humor of the world. Costumes raise existential questions for the person wearing them. For they confront a person, whenever he dresses, with questions that are never posed in our society—questions of identity and self. They allow experimentation and changes of mood that are characteristic of, and essential to youth. But they nudge the wearer with deep questions, because their very freedom reminds him that he does have choice.

Bell bottoms have to be worn to be understood. They express the body, as jeans do, but they say much more. They give the ankles a special freedom as if to invite dancing right on the street. They bring dance back into our sober lives. A touch football game, if the players are wearing bell bottoms, is like a folk dance or a ballet. Bell bottoms, on girls or boys, are happy and comic, rollicking. No one can take himself entirely seriously in bell bottoms. Imagine a Consciousness II university professor, or even a college athlete, in bell bottoms, and all of his pretensions become funny; he has to laugh at himself.

The new clothes demonstrate a significant new relationship between man and technology. Basically they are machine-made and there is no attempt to hide that fact, no shame attached to mass-produced goods, no social points lost for wearing something that sells at $4.99 from coast to coast and has its measurements printed on the outside for all to read. That is the freedom and economy of mass production, a thing to be valued, not despised or evaded, as seekers after "quality" do. Touches of the handmade, of the personal— beads, a hand-tooled belt, decorations sewed onto jeans—are then added to the mass-produced base. Imagine a Consciousness II intellectual buying a cheap unstylish suit and then adding a handmade tie! Consciousness II has to have a non-mass-produced, tailor-made suit from England. He is ashamed of, or "above," the mass production that is the foundation of his own society. Consciousness III starts from the machine, but is not imprisoned by it; he wears his own individuality on top of it.

The new clothes express profoundly democratic values. There are no distinctions of wealth or status, no elitism; people confront one another shorn of these distinctions. In places where status or money is important, clothes tell the story. On Wall Street, one can tell the banker or lawyer from the mere employee by the expensive, tasteful suit. On the campus, the faculty member is set off from the graduate student by tweed jacket and tie; law professors are distinguished from the unworldly humanities teachers by businesslike suits. And in former times, the prep school undergraduate could be recognized and distinguished from the public school boy. All of these differences spoke of competition, advantage, and disadvantage. The new clothes deny the importance of hierarchy, status, authority, position, and they reject competition.

In these many different ways, the new clothes make it possible for people to be as direct, honest, and natural with each other as possible, given other barriers. To the extent that clothes can do it, people have the opportunity to meet one another as real, total persons, mind, face, and body, not defended or walled off by any barriers or certifications. There is no automatic respect or deference, such as the executive expects when he walks into his club and receives obsequious bows from the steward, but people are more clearly visible to each other, and they can be respected just as people.

Finally, in a threatening time, the new clothes express a shared set of attitudes and values. They express the new unity of youth, and the reality of the new consciousness. It is not an exclusive society; the smiles are for anyone who will smile back. But the new generation feels beleaguered, and it finds strength in recognizing brothers and sisters. Two people who do not know each other at all, passing on a highway, might shoot V-signals at each other, and thus affirm the new and growing brotherhood.

To understand the Consciousness III attitude toward career, we must deal not so much with the style they have adopted (for it is still very preliminary and experimental), but with the style and values they reject. Here the change of goals that is so basic to Consciousness III assumes its full significance. The central point is easy to say but very hard for an older person really to grasp, so deeply does it go against the grain of Consciousness I and II. It is that the goals of status, a position in the hierarchy, security, money, possessions, power, respect, and honor are not merely wrong, they are *unreal*. A person whose life is one long ego trip or power trip has not merely chosen one kind of satisfaction in preference to others; he has chosen goals that have no real relationship to personal growth, satisfaction, or happiness.

When a Consciousness II person meets a federal judge, or the head of a giant corporation, or the holder of a distinguished professorship, he takes notice. The position itself makes the man worth meeting and the occasion memorable. A member of the new generation, on the other hand, might be completely, blankly unaware of the titles, positions, and reputations of persons he had met. Students a few years ago were keenly aware of whether they were being taught by an assistant professor or an associate professor. Students today have no idea at all of their teachers' rank. They do not see it because it is not there. It is a curious thing: the professor has put the best part of his life into acquiring a regalia of titles, degrees, publications, professional reputation, and the student *does not even see it*.

In terms of their own lives, Consciousness III people simply do not imagine a career along the old vertical, escalator lines. It is not especially important to get into a particular university, or to make a good record when there, or to get a good job afterwards. They are not planning to get anything "settled." They conceive of life as a whole series of goals and choices, and a career as something that will be constantly changing. Whether a young man goes to one college or another, or into one occupation or another, is not the all-important decision his parents think it is; all choices are the "right" choice (for all lead outward) and a career comprises the many different experiences, some planned, some fortuitous, that one might have. Instead of intense, ambitious concentration, one can relax and see what happens. The world is the way Arlo Guthrie described it in "Alice's Restaurant": illogical and improbable.

This world demands a different personality than the old world, which asked for aggressive, disciplined, competitive pursuit of definite goals. One prime attribute is that it is anti-competitive. The tough high school athlete, measuring and one-upping his opponents, catches a whiff of the elixir of Consciousness III and he plays varsity basketball with a happier sense of enjoyment, or he quits altogether in order to play his guitar. A young hiker of five years ago would tell you how many peaks he had climbed and how fast; the same hiker, touched by the elixir, would say, "I just go along and dig."

There are several different patterns by which these attitudes have been translated into life-styles. The closest to a "straight" career would be to pursue an ordinary career, such as teaching or law or medicine, but substituting for the usual goals the objective of having some worthwhile experiences and serving the community to the best of one's ability. A second choice combines the first with "going underground"—the individual is secretly at war with society, and aims to get the better of society whenever he can, like the Henry Miller of *Tropic of Capricorn,* who ran riot with his job at the Cosmodemonic Telegraph Company of North America. The third is a new line of work—as a rock musician or light show artist—that combines a remunerative "career" with a new life-style. The fourth is an "ordinary" job—such as working for the post office—combined with a new life-style the rest of the time. The fifth option is the drop-out—usually someone who quits school and lives on the border of things (the Berkeley street people are mostly this sort of drop-out). Finally, there is the full hippie life, an attempt to live as if the Corporate State did not exist and some new form of community were already here. Other choices are now being tried.

Unsympathetic observers of the new generation frequently say that one of its prime characteristics is an aversion to work. The observers are prevented, by their disapproving, puritanical outlook, from understanding the real significance of what they see. The attitude of Consciousness III toward career is indeed based on the belief that most work available in our society is meaningless, degrading, and inconsistent with self-realization. The new generation is not "lazy," and it is glad enough to put great effort into any work that is worthwhile, whether it is hours of practice on a musical instrument, or working on a communal farm, or helping to create People's Park in Berkeley. But they see industrialized work as one of the chief means by which the minds and feelings of people are dominated in the Corporate State. It is work, unrelenting, driven, consuming, that comes between the professor and his students, the lawyer and his family, the bank employee and the beauty of nature. Consciousness III regards freedom from such work, making possible the development of an individual's true potential as a human being, to be among the greatest and most vital forms of liberation.

When we turn to the music of Consciousness III, we come to the chief medium of expression, the chief means by which inner feelings are communicated. Consciousness III has not yet developed a widely accepted written poetry, literature, or theatre; the functions of all of these have so far been assumed by music and the lyrics that go with it. Music has become the deepest means of communication and expression for an entire culture. When someone puts a dime in the jukebox of a restaurant frequented by young people there is a moment of community. As the music starts, the people in the restaurant begin to *move*. Some nod heads, some drum fingers, others tap feet, others move their whole bodies. They glance with smiles of agreement toward the person who made the selection. If it is a song from the established canon, like Bob Dylan's "Mr. Tambourine Man," everyone knows the words, and many sing along to themselves. Even those just entering the restaurant join in.

The dominant means of communication in our society—words—has been so abused, distorted and preempted that at present it does not seem adequate for people of the new consciousness. Music, on the other hand, says all the things they want to say or feel. It tells of the discovery of soul by whites—a depth of feeling long denied to most Americans. It expresses raunchy, sweaty sex. It is a repository of fantastic energy—as anyone who has watched a rock band knows. It can tell of a tranquil and fresh closeness to nature— sea, mountains, wind, and clouds. It can express the staccato experience of modern American life. What other music than rock, played on the car radio, comes anywhere near being appropriate to the wonders and anxieties, the beauty and the tension and the excitement, of driving across one of the great bridges of San Francisco Bay? In another mood, the music tells of loneliness, the solitary self. It is a poetry of the wonder of being young and all aware ("I Am a Child," by Neil Young) and of love and heartbreak between the generations ("Teach Your Children," by Graham Nash). It can express the feelings of youth toward the good things of an older America ("Rockin' Chair" and "King Harvest," by J. R. Robertson), or the violence, fervor, and fury of revolution in the streets ("We Can Be Together," by Paul Kantner). It can express the terrors and transiency of youth in an alien society ("Four Days Gone," by Stephen Stills), the strangeness and mystery of the unpredictable new patterns of life ("St. Stephen," by the Grateful Dead), the happiness of discovering companions in the journey ("Stand," by Sylvester Stewart; "Look at You Look at Me," by Dave Mason and J. Capaldi), and yearnings that are profoundly spiritual and religious ("I Shall Be Released," by Bob Dylan). It brings out a poetry in people who, if confined to words, would be awkward and prosaic. It expresses, as the rock bands also show, a total way of life. In its supreme moments, it carries the listener into a new world ("Dark Star," by the Grateful Dead). Most of all, perhaps, it expresses freedom, not the technical state of freedom that we all possess by virtue of the law, but the living of freedom. For the new consciousness, this music is not a pastime, but a necessity, on a par with food and water.

Indeed, the new music has achieved a degree of integration of art into everyday life that is probably unique in modern societies; to find anything comparable one would have to look to the Middle Ages or primitive men. Like a medieval cathedral or the carvings in a tribal village, the art of rock is constantly present as a part of everyday life, not something to be admired in a museum or listened to over coffee, after dinner and the day's work are done. It is significant that nearly everyone who deeply feels the music also makes an attempt at playing an instrument and even at composing. For the lover of rock, as for men in earlier times, art is a daily companion to share, interpret, and transfigure every experience and emotion.

The new music was built out of materials already in existence: blues, rock 'n' roll, folk music. But although the forms remained, something wholly new and original was made out of these older elements—more original, perhaps, than even the new musicians themselves yet realize. The transformation took place in 1966–1967. Up to that time, the blues had been an essentially black medium. Rock 'n' roll, a blues derivative, was rhythmic, raunchy, teen-age dance music. Folk music, old and modern, was popular among college students. The three forms remained musically and culturally distinct, and even as late as 1965, none of them were expressing any radically new states of consciousness. Blues expressed black soul; rock, as made famous by Elvis Presley, was the beat of youthful sensuality; and folk music, with such singers as Joan Baez, expressed antiwar sentiments as well as the universal themes of love and disillusionment.

In 1966–1967 there was a spontaneous transformation. In the United States, it originated with youthful rock groups playing in San Francisco. In England, it was led by the Beatles, who were already established as an extremely fine and highly individual rock group. What happened, as well as it can be put into words, was this. First, the separate musical traditions were brought together. Bob Dylan and the Jefferson Airplane played folk rock, folk ideas with a rock beat. White rock groups began experimenting with the blues. Of course, white musicians had always played the blues, but essentially as imitators of the Negro style; now it began to be the white bands' own music. And all of the groups moved toward a broader eclecticism and synthesis. They freely took over elements from Indian ragas, from jazz, from American country music, and as time went on from even more diverse sources (one group seems recently to have been trying out Gregorian chants). What developed was a protean music, capable of an almost limitless range of expression.

The second thing that happened was that all the musical groups began using the full range of electric instruments and the technology of electronic amplifiers. The twangy electric guitar was an old country-western standby, but the new electronic effects were altogether different—so different that a new listener in 1967 might well feel that there had never been any sounds like that in the world before. The high, piercing, unearthly sounds of the guitar seemed to come from other realms. Electronics did, in fact, make possible sounds that no instrument up to that time could produce. And in studio recordings, multiple tracking, feedback, and other devices made possible effects that not even an electronic band could produce live. Electronic amplification also made possible a fantastic increase in volume, the music becoming as loud and penetrating as the human ear could stand, and thereby achieving a "total" effect, so that instead of an audience of passive listeners, there were now audiences of total participants, feeling the music in all of their senses and all of their bones.

Third, the music became a multimedia experience; a part of a total environment. In the Bay Area ballrooms, the Fillmore, the Avalon, or Pauley Ballroom at the University of California, the walls were covered with fantastic changing patterns of light, the beginning of the new art of the light show. And the audience did not sit, it danced. With records at home, listeners imitated these lighting effects as best they could, and heightened the whole experience by using drugs. Often music was played out of doors, where nature—the sea or tall redwoods—provided the environment.

Fourth, each band began to develop a personality; often they lived together as a commune, and their music expressed their group life. The names of the groups, while often chosen rather casually and for public effect, nevertheless expressed the anti-Establishment, "outsider" identity of the groups. One way to gauge this is to imagine congressmen from the House Internal Security Committee (formerly HUAC) trying to grasp the derivations and nuances of such names as Notes From Underground, Loading Zone, Steppenwolf, the Cleanliness and Godliness Skiffle Band. A name such as the Grateful Dead, with its implications of atomic holocaust, Hiroshima, bitter alienation from society, and playful, joking don't-give-a-damnness, would baffle the security investigators for a long time. The name may have been chosen for the band's own esoteric reasons. But it suggests the idea that in our society the living are really dead, and only the "dead" are really alive; this idea would probably escape the investigators altogether. In short, the bands, by achieving a high degree of individual identity, and being clearly "outsiders," members of the youth culture themselves, became groups with which young audiences could feel a great closeness and rapport. By contrast, Consciousness II people have little identification with band members or the musicians in a symphony orchestra.

Fifth, musician-listener rapport has been heightened by two other kinds of participation: an enormous number of the young listeners had instruments or even bands and played the new music themselves, and both bands and listeners considered drugs to be an integral part of the musical experience. Consciousness II people may love Mozart, or jazz, but comparatively few of them spend much time playing an instrument. The use of drugs, especially because they are illegal, establishes a blood-brotherhood before the musicians even begin to play. And drugs, as we shall point out later, add a whole new dimension to creativity and to experience.

Sixth, a pulsing new energy entered into all the forms of music. Not even the turbulent fury of Beethoven's Ninth Symphony can compete for sheer energy with the Rolling Stones. Earlier popular songs, jazz, and classical music all have their own greatness, but the driving, screaming, crying, bitter-happy-sad heights and depths and motion of the new music adds a dimension unknown in any earlier western music. The older music was essentially intellectual; it was located in the mind and in the feelings known to the mind; the new music rocks the whole body, and penetrates the soul.

Seventh, the new music, despite its apparently simple form and beat, gradually evolved a remarkably complex texture. It has a complexity unknown to classical music, even to symphonies written for full orchestra. Beethoven seems like a series of parallel lines, sometimes vertical, sometimes diagonal; Mozart a flow of rounded forms, but as few as three rock musicians, such as Cream, or Crosby, Stills & Nash can set up a texture of rhythms, timbres, kinds of sounds, emotions that create a world by contrast to which the classical composers seem to have lived in a world of simple verities, straightforward emotions, and established, reassuring conventions. It is no criticism of the eighteenth- or nineteenth-century geniuses to say that today's music has found a world they never knew.

Eighth, not only did many young people play the new music in one form or another, a great many, amateur and professional alike, began composing it. Nearly all of the successful rock groups of today write most of their own words and music. The distinction between composer and performer as professions has virtually disappeared. Thus songs are highly personal to the singer, not a mere "interpretation" of someone else's thought. Also, what is undeniably a mass culture is at the same time a genuine folk culture, because it is not imposed upon the people but written by them. And the writing is not limited to professional musicians; amateur and casual groups also compose some of their own material. And when one group does play another person's song, the group freely adds to it. There is no such thing, then, as the musician who tries in all things to be faithful to some remote composer, reserving for himself a display of skill and subtlety, spirit and nuance. The new music is a music of unrestrained creativity and self-expression.

Ninth, the new music has achieved a height of knowledge, understanding, insight, and truth concerning the world, and people's feelings, that is incredibly greater than what other media have been able to express. Journalists, writers for opinion journals, social scientists, novelists have all tried their hand at discussing the issues of the day. But almost without exception, they have been far more superficial than writers of rock poetry, and what is even more striking, several years behind the musicians. Compare a writer for *The New York Times*, or for *The New Republic*, talking about contemporary political and social ills, with Dylan's "It's All Right Ma (I'm only Bleeding)" or "Subterranean Homesick Blues." Compare a sociologist talking about alienation with the Beatles' "Eleanor Rigby" or "Strawberry Fields Forever." But more important than comparisons is the fact that rock music has been able to give critiques of society at a profound level ("Draft Morning," by the Byrds, "Tommy," by The Who) and at the same time express the longings and aspirations of the new generation ("Get Together," by Chet Powers, "Comin' Back to Me," by Marty Balin). The music has achieved a relevance, an ability to penetrate to the essence of what is wrong with society, a power to speak to man "in his condition" that is perhaps the deepest source of its power.

If we combine all of these aspects of the transformation we can begin to see how vastly different the new music is from the older forms that it seems superficially to resemble. The blues offers an example. The essence of blues is radical subjectivity; the singer follows a form, but he cannot help but express his own personality, his own life experiences, his own encounters with his world. When Janis Joplin, a white girl, sang "Ball and Chain" to a pulsing, communal audience of middle-class young white people, it was not the same as a black singer in the classic blues tradition. It was contemporary American white "soul," and it spoke of the bomb, and the war, drugs, and the cops as well as the intense sexuality of the blues and the yearnings and mysteries of black soul. A similar transformation takes place when the new groups play jazz, early rock, folk songs, or even classical music. Procol Harum's "Salty Dog" sounds like an ordinary folk song about a sea voyage when it is first heard. But when one listens more closely there is much more: classical music is blended into a folk style; the song has an almost unbearable tension; drums build up powerful climaxes; gulls' cries and a bosun's pipe give an eerie feeling; the words do not quite make sense; the captain is apparently mad; death is in the air; the ship goes to places unknown to man; the simple sea song has become an awesome, mysterious and frightening "trip" to some place beyond man's experience. Happy, sad, or spiritual, the new music transforms older forms into "trips" that enter a dimension which the original forms never reached.

What the new music has become is the first true example of a contemporary American culture that is originated by the people themselves, not by an elite or by the false consciousness machinery of corporate producers. Instead of an alienating false culture designed to rob us of self-knowledge, the new music has been, from the beginning, a source of that truth that is greater than mere facts, the kind of truth Ken Kesey meant when he said, "But it's the truth even if it didn't happen." Thus it is that America, the land of mass-produced ugliness, has finally created a music that is, beyond anything else, unbelievably *beautiful*. It is stirring, it is deeply moving, it is, like the greatest art, profoundly warming to the spirit and the soul. And so it touches and transforms each area of the new generation's experiences and feelings. The complex, frantic, disjointed machinelike experiences of modern urban existence were presented, with piercing notes of pain, and dark notes of anger, by Cream. The mystical transcendence of ordinary experience achieved by the hippies, the drug world, and the spiritual realm, soaring fantasy and brilliant patterns of rhythm and sound, are the domain of the San Francisco acid rock of the Jefferson Airplane, and the psychedelic meditations of the early music of Country Joe and the Fish. Irony, satire, mockery of the Establishment and of rational thought were the specialty of the Mothers of Invention. The open road is the realm of James Taylor in songs like "Fire and Rain" and "Country Road." A uniquely personal but universal view of the world has been achieved by the Beatles, gentle, unearthy, the world transformed. They are the supreme music makers of our time, and from "I Want to Hold Your Hand" to "With a Little Help from My Friends" to "Here Comes the Sun" they have been with us through the "long, cold, lonely winter," offering their help, inviting us to their magical land, reminding us, when we needed it most, that "it's alright." Another highly personal view of the world, but one close to the experiences of young listeners, is that of Bob Dylan. Dylan has gone through a whole cycle of experience, from folk music to social protest and commentary, next to folk rock, then to the extraordinary personal world of the ballad "Sad-Eyed Lady of the Lowlands," and finally to the serene, but achieved, innocence of the country music of the album "Nashville Skyline." Perhaps more than any other individual in the field of music, Dylan has been, from the very beginning, a true prophet of the new consciousness.

Among the most important forms of the new music is the blues, for it expresses what is common to all the individual types of music we have discussed—experience coming from the self, coming deeply, honestly, and searchingly from the self, expressing thoughts and feelings that most people conceal from their own view and from others. For the black man in the South, the blues expressed his identity, an identity oppressed, forbidden, and denied in other ways. So long as whites in America did not realize that their own identity was also oppressed and denied, so long as whites failed to search for their own selves, there could be no white "soul," no white blues to sing. The white man could be sentimental or romantic, but he had no knowledge of himself, and therefore no words of his own for the blues. The new generation, in its discovery of self, in its discovery of oppression, also discovered white "soul," and that is what its music is starting to tell about. The new music is uniquely and deeply personal, allowing individuals and groups to express their special vision of the world to all their brothers and sisters; it deals with the entire world as seen and felt by the new consciousness, and it takes listeners to places they have never been before.

But no single form of music can really claim preeminence. It is the richness and variety and continually changing quality of the new music that is its essence. It defies analysis and explication by critics because it never stands still to be analyzed; it ranges from the mystic expressiveness of Procol Harum, the emotional intensity of Jimi Hendrix, the heavy sounds of Led Zeppelin, to anywhere else the heads of the new generation have been. Its essence is the total scene: a huge and happy noontime crowd in Lower Sproul Plaza at Berkeley, some standing, some sitting, some dancing; every variety of clothes and costume, knapsacks and rolled-up sleeping bags; piled-up Afro hair and shoulder-length golden-blond hair; a sense of everyone's sharing the values and experience that the scene represents, music by the Crabs, a local group, mostly soaring, ecstatic, earthy rock that shakes the crowd, the buildings, and the heavens themselves with joy; and above the scene, presiding over it, those benevolent deities, the sungod, the ocean breeze, the brown-green Berkeley hills.

The Consciousness III idea of community among people is another basic aspect of the new culture. It rests on two integrated concepts: respect for the uniqueness of each individual, and the idea expressed by the word "together." We have already described the recognition of each individual as one of the initial premises of Consciousness III. Now we must attempt to explain the idea of "together." It does not mean what the suburbs speak of as "togetherness," an external conformity gained by doing things as a family unit, looking alike, adapting to one another. At the same time, "together" does not necessarily mean a relationship such as love, mutual dependence, or friendship, although it could accompany any of these. "Together" expresses the relationship among people who feel themselves to be members of the same species, who are related to each other and to all of nature by the underlying order of being. People are "together" when they experience the same thing in the same way. They need not be in love, they need not even be friends, and they need not give one another anything, materially or emotionally, to be together. A great throng can be together in a peace march or a rock festival; a small group can feel an intense sense of "together" listening to a record or watching a sunset or a storm. Many aspects of the new culture help produce this feeling, music perhaps most universally. The individuals preserve every bit of their individuality. They simply come together to share a feeling, a moment, or an experience, and thus feel united in a community based on having their heads in the same place at the same time.

Consciousness III is beginning to experiment with small communities of different sorts. Many of the communes that have sprung up in various parts of the country are based primarily on shared values, such as love of desert sunsets and use of drugs; the members get along with each other, but did not come together on the basis of personal affinity, as is the case with lifelong friendships. They are sharing a "trip." These "trip communities" are one aspect of the so-called hippie communes, with their unusual mixture of casual uncommitedness and intense communal feeling.

Consciousness III people are engaged in a constant search to discover forms and ways to be "together." They experiment with traveling together, with inventing games, with sensitivity groups, with political confrontations, building occupations, and demonstrations. Many of them believe that sharing creative work, such as playing in a band, composing music, making a film, writing a play, or studying poetry, will ultimately prove to be the most satisfying way to be "together"; they believe that where people are really "together," their motivation will be higher and their creativity multiplied far beyond the sum total of what they could produce as individuals.

Some students now in college are making plans to live with a group of friends as a community after graduation, pursuing different occupations but doing as much as possible as a community, perhaps including growing some of their own food. Such a commune might include married couples and children as well as single people. It would not be the more casual "trip commune" but a permanent living arrangement, an "extended family," perhaps with a number of different homes. In form it remains amorphous, but the idea clearly reflects the belief of many students that once one has experienced being "together" with people, conventional social relationships seem pointless and boring, and the prospect of life separated from one's friends seems too barren to be accepted any longer.

What the new generation has already achieved is a way of being with other people that is closer, warmer, more open, more sensitive, more capable of sharing, than prior generations have known. It is as if some unseen divider, a glass partition, a plastic coating, a separating curtain of conversation, had been removed, leaving people effortlessly closer. People of an earlier generation tried to get to know each other by asking questions that were searching or personal, by learning about each other's past lives, interests, and experiences, by striving for some almost psychoanalytic "truth." The new generation's knowledge of each other is more like the total perception of an artist. It is less intellectual, less translatable into words. They are all the closer to each other because their being together is not mediated or separated by words.

Of all of the characteristics man possesses, surely the one he must prize most highly is consciousness. We do not mean the special kinds of consciousness we have discussed in this book, but consciousness with a small "c," consciousness in the Henry James sense—awareness of all the phenomena of one's world. It is this consciousness that distinguishes the poet, the artist, the human being who is sensitive to others. Dostoevsky's underground man, in *Notes From Underground,* says, "Though I stated at the beginning that consciousness, in my opinion, is the greatest misfortune for man, yet I know man loves it and would not give it up for any satisfaction." Man shares many of his qualities with other forms of life; consciousness is what makes him distinctively human.

Of all the qualities of human beings that are injured, narrowed, or repressed in the Corporate State, it is consciousness, the most precious and the most fragile, that suffers the most. There is, as we have seen, a vast apparatus, working unceasingly to create a false consciousness in people. One aspect of this force seeks to manipulate our political consciousness, another to change our awareness of our own needs. But consciousness is also profoundly affected simply by the din and overstimulation of our society. It is pounded, battered, strained, exhausted, and inevitably, dulled. A traffic jam, buying a ticket at an airport, or a day in a busy office give consciousness such a merciless beating that it must develop an insensitive coating to survive. Encounters with people are so many, so brutish and impersonal, so fleeting and so harrowing that consciousness must be desensitized to reduce the pain. Television commercials, canned music in elevators, threatening notices in monthly bills assault us, and the only defense is to become less sensitive and less aware.

The terrible thing that happens to a person living in the Corporate State is that he suffers a substantial, and eventually permanent, impairment of consciousness. If the State impaired our eyesight, or our hearing, it would be bad enough, but permanent damage to consciousness is a worse loss. We lose all of our senses; we are unable to be adequately aware of people, or of the rest of the phenomena of the world. Man ought naturally to see his life as a steady growth of consciousness, which he cultivates with all his efforts; instead he must see it diminished, so that childhood and youth are the only times of life when man still has his consciousness. The faces in the subway are the faces of impaired consciousness, unmoving and unmoved.

One final aspect of the culture of Consciousness III is an effort to restore, protect, and foster human consciousness. It is most important because its aim is nothing less than to restore man's awareness of himself, of other people, of nature, of his own life. It seeks to make man, in everything that he does or experiences, more alive. To "blow one's mind" means to become more aware.

The aspects of culture we have already discussed, clothes, the nondirected career, music, and community, are all major components of the effort to increase consciousness. Here we shall mention several more. They divide themselves naturally into two categories: the effort to resist imposed consciousness and the effort to counteract dulling and blunting.

The search for consciousness begins with an effort to shake off the "false consciousness" imposed by society. One must counteract the influence of mass media, mass education, advertising, and all the other pressures on the mind. The devices for doing this are just in the experimental stage: underground newspapers, including high school underground newspapers, "free university" classes, and all kinds of discussion groups; personal participation in events, such as demonstrations, personal experience with law enforcement, personal work in areas such as ghettos, mental hospitals, or in the Peace Corps; extensive reading. One device is particularly important: an individual cannot hope to achieve an independent consciousness unless he cultivates, by whatever means are available, including clothes, speech mannerisms, illegal activities, and so forth, the feeling of being an *outsider*. Only the person who feels himself to be an outsider is genuinely free of the lures and temptations of the Corporate State. Only he can work in a bank or go to a cocktail party in "safety" because he will not be taken in. So the new generation struggles to feel itself as outsiders, and it identifies with the blacks, with the poor, with Bonnie and Clyde, and with the losers of this world, celebrated in folk songs such as Bob Dylan's album "John Wesley Harding." These suggest that only by an antisocial posture can people really be "alive" in a society that is essentially dead. Of course, every time the Establishment commits violence against the new generation, this increases their sense of being outsiders. But even more important is the creation of group identity among the outsiders. In one sense the whole "youth world" is an effort to achieve an independent consciousness.

Freedom from imposed consciousness requires freedom from the domination of technology. The new culture is built on the technology of the Corporate State, but not in the same way as the State's own culture is built: in the new culture, it is the technology that is dominated, not the people. The new generation's music makes use of modern electronics; its art (e.g., films) is technically sophisticated; its habits (reading) require affluence; its sexual mores require the pill. But the new generation does not use technology the way the older one does. Consciousness III does not use it for status or conspicuous consumption, nor for power over people, or competitive "success." They do not use it to further rationalize society, to make life less challenging, more passive; they do not use it as a substitute for experience. They do not ignore its aesthetic, environmental, and human consequences. In short, instead of letting the technology dictate to them, instead of being the frenetic, driven victims of its demands, they use it as intelligent men and women might, to further their own lives. A key illustration of this is the fact that technology is not allowed to rob them of experience.

Another effort is directed against the imposition of a role, and its ways of thinking. Escape from a role is painfully difficult for most people, which shows how important an effort it is. The high school athlete-leader, cool, competent, straight, finds it a tremendous effort to free himself from this role; he must learn to approach people instead of waiting to be sought after, make himself emotionally vulnerable, wear absurd clothes, spend time with people who are definitely not part of the accepted crowd. Fighting off a role makes for conflict with parents, school authorities, coaches; it is a prime source of misunderstanding, but it is essential to get rid of the imposed response.

One last aspect of trying to escape imposed consciousness is concerned with so-called rational thought. Consciousness III is deeply suspicious of logic, rationality, analysis, and of principles. Nothing so outrages the Consciousness II intellectual as this seeming rejection of reason itself. But Consciousness III has been exposed to some rather bad examples of reason, including the intellectual justifications of the Cold War and the Vietnam War. At any rate, Consciousness III believes it essential to get free of what is now accepted as rational thought. It believes that "reason" tends to leave out too many factors and values—especially those which cannot readily be put into words and categories. It believes that undue faith is put on "principle" when there are always other principles that have been neglected; if "free self-determination" is the principle behind the Vietnam War, what about that other principle, "Thou shalt not kill"? It believes that thought can be "non-linear," spontaneous, disconnected. It thinks rational conversation has been overdone as a means of communication between people, and it has invented a new term, "rapping," for communication when it does take the form of words. Above all, it wants new dimensions.

In its desire to escape any imposed system, Consciousness III declares experience to be the most precious of all commodities. All experience has value, all of it has something to teach, none of it is rejected because it fails to accord with some preexisting scheme of things. Of course this does not mean that the Consciousness III person will engage in actions that violate his basic values; he will never kill or rape to try the experience. But subject to these limits, he is open to trying new things; he does not judge or reject them in advance.

All of these are examples of means that are being used to escape patterns of thought imposed by the Corporate State—to liberate the mind. But what about the dulling of the mind? This is the problem of the man who has worked in a chemical plant so long that he has lost the sense of smell, or a man whose eyesight has dimmed. The most direct way to restore sensitivity is, of course, to begin a series of exposures to forgotten sensations. The Consciousness III person does a great deal of this. He burns incense in his home to restore the sense of smell. He attends a T-group or sensitivity group to restore awareness of other people; the experiments may range from telling personal feelings and experiences to touching other people's bodies (a necessary antidote, perhaps, to the desensitizing that inevitably takes place when people are forced to bump up against each other but "not feel it" in subways and buses). He takes "trips" out into nature; he might lie for two hours and simply stare up at the arching branches of a tree. He finds that motorcycling restores a sense of free motion. He might cultivate visual sensitivity, and the ability to meditate, by staring for hours at a globe lamp. He discovers Bach and Mozart. He seeks out art, literature, drama, for their value in raising consciousness.

One of the most important means for restoring dulled consciousness is psychedelic drugs. They combine with all the other means we have mentioned (for example, marijuana might be smoked while looking at the sea, or while listening to music) but they are important in themselves. Many people confuse the psychedelic drugs with the narcotic drugs and with liquor, and assume that oblivion, or a lowered awareness, or hallucinations, are the consequence of psychedelic drugs. The term "getting stoned" is confusing; it implies losing consciousness, rather than a higher awareness. But getting dulled has nothing to do with the psychedelic experience; using marijuana is more like what happens when a person with fuzzy vision puts on glasses. Listening to a familiar piece of music, such as a Bach orchestral suite, the mind is newly conscious of the bass line; listening to a conversation, the mind is more aware of the nuances of each voice. Music assumes shapes and comes out into the room, it is so vivid and so tangible. Grass is a subtle and delicate experience, an educated experience (one that has to be learned), and it is not too different from the heightened awareness that an unusually sensitive or artistic person has. Significantly, it is a sensitivity too delicate for the hassles of today's world; a truly sensitive person just could not stand to ride to New York on the Penn Central railroad. The other psychedelic drugs, such as mescaline and LSD, are much more powerful than marijuana, and may well be dangerous to some individuals. They make possible a higher range of experience, extending outward to deep self-knowledge, to the religious, and to vision. But the principle of increased awareness is the same.

Marijuana causes a concentration on what is immediately present: color, smells, sensory experiences, "nowness." The self is isolated, turns inward, feels loose, detached, soft, gentle. The hold of uptightness is relaxed, allowing all sorts of "illogical" relationships to seem perfectly natural; there are visual juxtapositions of sights that have no "rational" relationship, such as a huge box of Corn Flakes between two buildings on a city street, and the logic of the outside world is suspended; why not sit down on the sidewalk, if one feels tired; why not nuzzle the furry carpet of a formal, wall-to-wall living room, if one feels like nuzzling? In some less uptight society, marijuana would be just a toy, a harmless "high." But in a society that keeps its citizens within a closed system of thought, that depends so much on systematic indoctrination, and an imposed consciousness, marijuana is a maker of revolution, a truth-serum. Because it concentrates on "nowness" as reality, it takes people outside the enclosed system, releases them from domination of their thought, and makes *unreal* what society takes most seriously: time, schedules, rational connections, competition, anger, excellence, authority, private property, law, status, the primacy of the state, the standards imposed by other people and by society. It is a truth-serum that repeals false consciousness.

Used continually and to excess, drugs become a factor that dulls consciousness. They diminish awareness, cut off reality, and separate people from human contacts. Perhaps their greatest affirmative significance is to provide an initial breakthrough, a shattering of the euphoria and mythology of the Corporate State, a beginning of a new way of thinking. In the long run, they are not enough to support a new consciousness, and they may eventually become yet another bar to reality.

The effect of psychedelic drugs does not end when the drug itself wears off; it is lasting in the sense that the user finds his awareness and sensitivity has increased, whether he is using drugs at the time or not. In other words, something has been learned. In fact, there may come a time when a drug user feels that drugs are no longer necessary to him, or at least that they have become of lesser importance; he has achieved the increased awareness he wanted and it is part of him now.

All of the various efforts of the new generation to increase awareness combine to produce a remarkable phenomenon: the Consciousness III person, no matter how young and inexperienced he may be, seems to possess an extraordinary "new knowledge." Governor Rockefeller goes on an official trip to Latin America and returns "heartened" by his reception; the ordinary citizen, if he is not particularly sophisticated, may actually believe that the Governor was well received; the person with "new knowledge" sees right through the pretense and knows, without reading the newspapers carefully, that the Governor was practically run out of each country and survived only by virtue of forceful repression of protest by each regime. He does not "know" the facts, but he still "knows" the truth that seems hidden from others. The explanation for this political sophistication is primarily the repeal of pretense and absurdity. It is absurd to think that someone named Rockefeller, representing the United States from a limousine, will be "warmly" welcomed by a populace, just as it is absurd to think that high school students revere their principal or believe what is patriotically said at school assemblies. In a country as burdened as ours is with hypocrisy and myth, the mere repeal of untruth becomes a profound insight.

One of the ways to describe this "new knowledge" is to say that it is capable of ignoring categories. We are all limited in our thinking by artificially drawn lines; we cannot get beyond the idea that a university is "private property" or that prose is different from poetry. When the category-barriers are removed, "new" relationships are seen. But the "new knowledge" is more than this; it is as if everything, from political affairs to aesthetics, were seen with new eyes; the young people of Consciousness III see effortlessly what is phony or dishonest in politics, or what is ugly and meretricious in architecture and city planning, whereas an older person has to go through years of education to make himself equally aware. It might take a Consciousness II person twenty years of reading radical literature to "know" that law is a tool of oppression; the young drug user just plain "knows" it. Nothing is more difficult for an older person to believe in than this "new knowledge," but it is such a striking phenomenon, extending even to long-haired California teen-agers hitchhiking their way to the beach, whose experience with political thinking or newspaper reading is limited, that it must be taken seriously.

Much of what we have said is summed up by the phrase "where his head is at." The implication of the phrase is that we are dealing with some dimension utterly outside of the way most people in America have become accustomed to the world. One has only to look at the "Comix" of R. Crumb to realize what it means to have a head that is in some extraordinary place; the world of R. Crumb is not merely brilliant or satiric or grotesque, it is *in another place* than most people have been. It is a common observation among today's college students that freshmen, and even more so, high school students, have heads that are amazing even to the college students.

Perhaps the deepest source of consciousness is nature. Members of the new generation seek out the beach, the woods, and the mountains. They do not litter these places with beer cans, they do not shatter the silences with power boats or motorcycle noises. They do not go to nature as a holiday from what is real. They go to nature as a source. The salt water of the sea is the salt in their blood; the freedom of the sea is their freedom. The forest is where they came from, it is the place where they feel closest to themselves, it is renewal. They do not pay much attention to hiking equipment, or picnic gear for the beach, or swimming attire; they are likely to wade into the salt water with blue jeans still on. Nature is not some foreign element that requires equipment. Nature is them.

All of this search for increased consciousness culminates in an attitude that is the very antithesis of Consciousness II: a desire for innocence, for the ability to be in a state of wonder or awe. It is of the essence of the thinking of the new generation that man should be constantly open to new experience, constantly ready to have his old way of thinking changed, constantly hoping that he will be sensitive enough and receptive enough to let the wonders of nature and mankind come to him. Consciousness II regards it as a sign of weakness to be surprised or awed; III cultivates the experience. Consciousness III says "the full moon blew my mind" and is proud of it; II has seen the moon before and takes it in stride. For Consciousness III, camping, surfing, watching sunsets and stars, lying in the grass, humor and play, new forms of community, art, literature, knowledge and mystery are all freshly created. In *Why Are We in Vietnam?*, Norman Mailer's hero, D.J., rids himself of the machine consciousness and, in the vastness of Alaska's remote Brooks Range, rediscovers a childlike, breathless sense of wonder; this is the quality that Consciousness III supremely treasures, to which it gives its ultimate sign of reverence, vulnerability, and innocence, "Oh wow!"

X

BEYOND YOUTH: RECOVERY OF SELF

Consciousness III has up to now been almost entirely a youth movement—in fact, a movement limited to one segment of youth. As such, it can have little future. Its present adherents will grow older; they will lose the freedom of students and be required to live in the far more oppressive world outside the universities. A youth movement by itself cannot achieve much in the way of political or structural change. And the Consciousness III hope of community will be lost if workers and older people remain in bitter opposition. Instead, there will be a polarization that might produce violence, repression, or perhaps even a period of fascism. Consciousness III must reach beyond youth or fail.

The essence of Consciousness III is not something that is inherently limited to youth. That essence is recovery of self. Youth are in the process of recovering self from the world of their parents, from the pressures of school and from the looming demands of role, career, and the draft. But there is an even greater need on the part of workers and older people to recover self. They are the prisoners of the technological state, exploited by its economy, tied to its goals, regimented by its factories and offices, deprived of all those sides of life which find no functional utility in the industrial machine.

Up to now, the forces within the Corporate State that have produced a new consciousness in a segment of youth have had no similar impact upon workers or older people. Apparently some factor that decisively influenced the new generation is missing, or some factor not applicable to youth is holding the minds of the middle class in check. If we can bring these differences to light, we can uncover the route to a change of consciousness that would extend beyond the ranks of youth.

The basis for a change in consciousness exists today in the middle class as a whole. Their dissatisfactions are at least as great as those of their children; the middle class feels a sense of betrayal of the American dream, and a sense of personal claustrophobia, that is very much like the feelings of young people. What they do not feel as strongly is the promise—the promise that gives the new generation its optimism and joy, and its liberation. But the promise is there, waiting to be seen by everyone. The road taken by the new generation is open to all others.

Let us recall the teen-ager and the college student of the nineteen-forties and -fifties. These young people had all of the objective freedom that high school and college students enjoy today, yet everything from their political views to their life-style was oppressively conformist. Their dating habits, consumer preferences, competition for honor and prestige, style of dress, and the urgency with which they struggled for admission to college, to graduate school, and for the "best" jobs all revealed them as seeing reality in terms like that of the middle class and workers. The fact that the students were "free" to do otherwise mattered not at all.

How does an individual conversion take place, perhaps one of the sort that happens in college today? Before his conversion, the young person has built up a certain degree of doubt; too much affluence may have sated his appetite for material goals, or the unhappiness of his parents may have made him question their goal-choices, or the stupidity and hypocrisy of the school system may have made him wonder about "achievement." But older people have these doubts too; the doubts alone are not what counts, although a young person without doubts might be impervious to conversion. What does count, as we can see over and over again, is emulation of other young people and of the new youth culture. It is the group and their culture that makes the conversion possible; the youth looks around him, and likes what he sees. Perhaps his first reaction is strong disapproval. But it is probably also mixed with curiosity and envy; he would secretly like to try some of the new life-style himself. Youth today do not waste themselves for long on unsatisfied curiosity and frustrated envy.

Here we must note a crucial point. In the old days, in high school or college, there was plenty of curiosity and envy too: the scrawny freshman envied the big athlete or the accomplished ladies' man, or the "in group" of fraternity or club members. But only a few freshmen could succeed; success was haughty and exclusive and purposefully mysterious. In contrast, today those students who already are into the new culture welcome everyone else with warmth and affection; there is room for all, there are no secrets, there is no initiation, there is no competition. It is as if, in the old college days, the whole football team had come knocking at the scrawny freshman's door, saying "join us," "we're your friends," "come to our parties," "we'll teach you all about everything," "we think you're a great man, we respect you and love you."

Thus the key factor in conversions among the new generation is having a model to emulate. As we have recounted, Consciousness III began with people who were unhappy or maladjusted for personal reasons—artists, beatniks, Holden Caulfields. But the new consciousness spread rapidly only when youth who had no special personal problems found models to emulate. For the misfits and artists, a different way of life was an inevitability. For the new converts, it was a free choice, and they could make that choice only by seeing it demonstrated by others.

The vital importance of having a model to emulate is revealed by the influence of the black life-style and music in changing the consciousness of nineteen-fifties white teen-agers. It was black music, in the form of rock 'n' roll, which first offered teen-agers an alternative to their own sentimental and insipid music. And it was the hip black life-style, with its contempt for white middle-class values and its affirmation of the sensual, the earthy, and the rebellious elements in man, that gave high school and college students something to copy instead of the existing pattern; as early as the middle fifties, rebellious white teen-agers were copying black language styles.

What workers and the middle class lack, then, is a model to copy. They have not been able to identify with blacks or with youth, and they have no models of their own. Unmistakably, that is the missing factor. And we can be more precise: what is lacking is a model that demonstrates new goals, new values, a new definition of what constitutes being happy.

A vital aspect of any conversion to Consciousness III is a change of goals. A change of goals is not simply another form of words for a change in consciousness. A student undergoes a change of goals when, instead of wanting to be "popular," to be commended by his teachers, to be outstanding among his peers, he chooses his own more personal goals, such as to appreciate music, to have a small circle of close friendships, to develop his skill in recognizing birds. The same student undergoes a change in consciousness when, as a result of changing his goals, he begins to learn a radical view of politics and society, he starts to develop a sense of personal responsibility and commitment toward public issues, he develops values and standards that are not derived from technology, he begins actually to discover and experience what other people are like when seen without defenses and preconceptions, and, above all, when he begins what may be a lifelong search for self. A change of goals is a change in direction; a change of consciousness means traveling a distance in that direction, discovering what is there, beginning to make it part of one's way of life.

Why does a change of goals have this magical effect? The first thing that a change of goals accomplishes is a mental liberation. This takes place because a change of goals immediately puts one outside the existing system and thereby provides a new perspective on that system. The law student striving for a high ranking is hardly in a position to see the competitive grading system with any clarity or detachment; once he changes his goals, a very different viewpoint is obtained. Goals, moreover, carry their own reinforcement. We all know how much a man's point of view is influenced by his occupation or profession. The simple matter of time is important; someone largely preoccupied with getting good grades, or with another all-consuming activity such as competitive athletics, simply has not got the free time to think about the system he is in. Stepping outside the system thus produces the phenomenon of the conversion: a student comes to college with all of the attitudes of his parents and home town, and a year later he has totally rejected the whole of it. Envy, jealousy, and competition are no longer such significant motivations; with a broadening of goals, there is more of the world for everyone. Fear is lessened too; fear is mostly a consequence of having rigidly limited goals such as a particular promotion, which might be lost. When the promotion, and the job itself, no longer matter that much, courage to act independently increases. The individual is liberated, and the power of choice now is his.

We said that the older person or worker lacks an

affirmative vision of how life could be better. The affirmative vision comes as a consequence of this widening of choice. Suppose a person owns a house adjacent to an area of wilderness. Each year the campgrounds, trails and summits are more crowded, each year the woods are invaded by new "improvements," each year the lumberman cuts even closer; the sense of freedom and spaciousness diminishes and the person experiences a feeling of entrapment, and sees the future as bleak and hopeless. Suppose, however, that he can change his goals enough to develop a new appreciation of geology, botany, birds, and weather. He is no longer limited to much-used trails and summits; the wilderness begins to expand for him instead of contracting. People using the woods are no longer such a direct threat, and in time he may enjoy them too, especially if he can add to their appreciation of wilderness. Note that his change of goals has not represented a rejection of his basic values; he has not gone from enjoyment of trails to real estate development and sale of motor bikes for the trails. He has enlarged himself and thereby enlarged his world.

Indeed, a change of goals is really equivalent to having a new concept of oneself. Suddenly the individual can imagine himself doing entirely new kinds of work, having entirely new satisfactions. The new concept gives rise to a new freedom: with one idea of himself a man would feel ridiculously self-conscious wearing bell bottoms; he is a banker or lawyer making a fool of himself. But if he thought of himself as a person with a sense of humor he would feel at home in clothes with a lighter touch; he would have that new freedom. Thus the world is no longer bleak, because the individual has discovered that within his own creative ability lies the power to transform it; he can make a world, instead of remaining embittered at a world that seems hopeless. Wallace Stevens said this in all of his poetry: man has the power, not to substitute an imaginary world for the real one, but to find "A new knowledge of reality."

In summary, middle-class consciousness has remained unchanged because middle-class people have as yet no idea of self and have engaged in no search for self. They are the prisoners of goals set for them by the Corporate State. Among the new generation, and among blacks, a change of goals has provided liberation and a new vision. But the middle class lives without hope of a better life because its goals are tied to its present existence. The key to such a change of goals is the opportunity to identify with persons who have already changed and who serve as models to identify with and to join. Such models have been available to the younger generation and to blacks, but so far the middle class has found no way to identify with the forces of change.

It is widely and incorrectly assumed that the development of a new consciousness is dependent upon a process of radicalization: a growing dissatisfaction with one's own life and circumstances, plus an awareness that society is run on wrong or unjust principles. This assumption lies behind demonstrations and other efforts to "teach" people that the war is wrong, campaigns to expound such issues as the importance of conservation or the need to curb the defense-armament machine, and efforts by radicals to join workers on the job or on picket lines, and try to talk with them about imperialism, exploitation, and the goals of the New Left. If workers and the middle class have a consciousness different from youth, so the assumption runs, it is because they have not yet seen the light.

This theory simply does not fit the facts. In the first place, there is no lack of dissatisfaction in workers and the middle class; they share much of the anger and frustration expressed by youth. Blue-collar workers are bitter and dissatisfied with their work, with their homes, and with their status in society. Recent strikes have repeatedly shown the depth of worker disaffection, and the fact that it goes far beyond a mere question of wages. In even the most casual conversation, the blue-collar man is often openly bitter about his job or organization. He has no great hope of climbing a ladder of success. He occupies a low-status position, and therefore is a person whom society has judged to be of little merit. Every evidence suggests that he is angry with being inferior; a George Wallace can win his vote by telling him he is as good as any other man, as good as bosses and "pointy-headed intellectuals" and beautiful people.

Today the worker's complaints parallel the whole range of student dissatisfaction. He thinks the country is run by "the big boys" who have no interest in the ordinary man. The politician is only for himself. Inflation makes every raise in pay an illusion. Taxes are laid most heavily on the working man, while the rich escape lightly. Workers experience the deterioration of environment more directly than most people. They feel the increasing ugliness, pollution, crowding, and unfriendliness of the neighborhood where they live; the increasing difficulty of getting away to fresh air and sunshine. They have long felt their jobs to be a dead end, year after year of doing the same thing, for a company that is indifferent and for a product which is remote. And increasingly, they regard the moon venture, the space investment, and especially American spending and loss of life in war as senseless and wrong. In all of these areas and more, the complaints, considered alone, sound like the students'.

For the professional, an important area of doubt is the rat race of his career. So great is the competition of American life today at the levels of professional "success" that even the participants sense that it is debilitating them, leaving them without resources for anything else in life. Moreover, the job may seem, despite all of its prestige and possibilities of advancement, to be dull routine. The dentist feels he is just a plumber or mechanic; sometimes a surgeon does too. The young lawyer feels he has become a brief-writing machine, and the business executive finds a hollowness to his activities.

A second source of job dissatisfaction may arise from loss of autonomy, feeling oneself caught up in a vast system and a hierarchy which is oppressive even if one has more people below him than above him. And there are other dissatisfactions. A good education makes one want to do something "significant" or "socially useful" or "meaningful," and few professional jobs offer that. The professional is able to afford many of the luxurious rewards of society but he may be far too busy to enjoy them; he knows that when he retires he will be too old. And on top of these job dissatisfactions may come the acute personal misery of finding that his children are alienated from him, and perhaps his wife also, so that the joys of home life dissolve in bitterness and his work has become an end in itself.

Wives of middle-class professional men occupy a particularly questionable position; well educated and highly intelligent, they are forced into a position in which they cannot do any real work or assume any real independence. When their children grow up, they are left with empty lives, and often there are divorces and some rather sad middle-aged attempts to "begin a new life." But the wife feels a strong responsibility to her children and home, a strong sense of duty in her chosen role. And on the outside, should she seek a different life, there is no community waiting for her; the world is made up of married people, and there is no one to help her or affirm her new existence. So she doubts and wonders.

If we take white- and blue-collar people together, we can see how many of their dissatisfactions parallel those of the new generation. The majority of adults in this country *hate their work*. Whether it is a factory job, a white-collar job, or, with some exceptions, a professional job, or the role of being a housewife, they hate their work as much as young people rebel against the prospect of similar work; indeed, it is the parents' feelings that are a principal source of the children's feelings. The middle class also resents the authority that is imposed by work—the boss and the system— and they feel that they lack power over their own lives. If we turn to the world outside work, the resentments are there too: middle-class people are disappointed in democracy, feeling that "they" are all crooks; there is also resentment of society's priorities, the feeling that someone else is on the gravy train. Above all, the middle class feels the same claustrophobia as youth; dead-end jobs, routine lives, a society where the individual is powerless and that is indifferent to his welfare. If dissatisfaction were the only ingredient needed for revolt, a change of consciousness would have come long ago.

No matter what dissatisfactions the worker or older person feels, he is held back by the belief that "things have to be this way," that "no system is any better," that "you can't show me how any new system would improve things." The dissatisfactions are felt but they are accepted and acquiesced in; "reality" demands this acceptance. And no education short of a total overturning of an individual's picture of reality will alter his convictions.

We can see this clearly in the phenomenon of mistaken blame. Workers and the middle class consistently blame the wrong factors for the miseries they endure. They blame communists, atheists, hippies, blacks, people on welfare, and liberal reformers for the ailments of the country. In a more general sense, they blame a decline in morals and religion, lack of hard work, and other faults of character. And at present, they are likely to blame the very efforts of the student movement with which they ought to be finding common cause. This mistaken blame pays so little attention to the observable facts that it quite obviously derives, not from observation, but from an inner picture of reality which could accept no other explanation.

The importance of this picture of reality is also evident in the fact that workers and the middle class lack any affirmative vision of a better way of life. We said that the new generation is the product of two things: the threat that they feel and the promise they recognize. Older people do not believe in the promise. And without that, there can be no change of consciousness no matter what other awareness is present. Many well-educated liberals, for example, understand perfectly what are the real causes of the American crisis; they do not blame imaginary scapegoats. But they are still steadfastly Consciousness II because they do not believe in anything; the prospects of the world seem bleak and hopeless, they have little faith in improving "human nature," and they are left keeping on with the task at hand.

But the crucial piece of evidence that education alone does not lead to new consciousness is the fact that it is not by education that conversions to Consciousness III have occurred. There are two very different routes to a radical consciousness. One, which only a few people have taken, is a slow process of reading and studying, over many years. That is the route taken by some members of the Old Left, and even some members of the New Left. It requires an exceptional dedication to scholarship, and a scholar's willingness to pursue the truth wherever it may lead. It is no formula for rapid or mass conversions. But the transformation that takes place within the space of a year in college, or even earlier in high school, does not occur because of reading, political knowledge, understanding of economics, familiarity with the doctrines of the New Left, or any intellectual process at all. All of this seems to come, if at all, only *after* the conversion. If this is the sequence with young people, why should it be different with their parents? The solution to the problem of the middle class does not lie with an initial reliance on education.

In the paragraphs that follow, we will suggest how the new consciousness might come to the middle class. We will first discuss the affluent, professional group and then the blue-collar workers. There are important differences between the two groups. The former have considerable economic freedom; the latter are trapped in their jobs. The false consciousness of professionals centers on status and roles; the myths of workers focus more on symbols like patriotism and morality, which are not important in the thinking of professionals. But the professional, although less bound by myth, is more uptight in his way of life; he is further removed than the worker from his own self and feelings.

For the affluent white middle class, the route to change can be the same as that followed by white students. How can a young middle-class, Consciousness II couple, thirty years old with two small children and a rising status position, be encouraged to begin a search for self? The young couple must be aware of the widening gap that separates them from the culture of a generation just ten years younger. Consciousness II wants to be "with it," yet the young couple find they know nothing about the new music, poetry, art, literature, cinema or drama, nothing about new theories of politics and philosophy, nothing about the underground newspapers or "free university" classes, nothing about new forms of language and thinking, nothing about the drug experience, nothing about new styles of living and community. How can they help being uneasy and ready for something new?

This couple is profoundly vulnerable to the influence of the new generation. In fact, the opportunity for the new generation is so great, their position so powerful, that care must be taken in the process of raising questions so as not to shake the couple too violently. Indeed, the first reaction will be the couple's prickly defensiveness, a sure sign of vulnerability. Why is the young lawyer not working for the poor, or reading good literature, or finding time for his children? Why is the wife not a college teacher, why has she not finished the book of poems she once began to write? These are questions that the couple will find hard to answer. By example, by talking, by writing, by raising the issue in every way possible, the new generation has the power to make people of thirty wonder if they are a white version of Uncle Tom and the "Negro" with conked hair; whether they are not wearing themselves out in pursuit of a self that is not their own.

If we are correct that the middle-class consciousness remains unbreached by all the negative aspects of the Corporate State because of the lack of a *model of changed goals,* how can this missing factor possibly be supplied? The answer must lie in helping the middle class to understand that, behind the specific forms of youth culture with which older people are unable to identify, there are more general values that are meaningful to any age and condition of life. To date, the new life-styles have been developed primarily by and for youth. It is important to describe them in terms that are usable by older people as well; not skin-tight pants for those who cannot expect to regain the slimness of youth, but a meaningful and satisfying concept of adult culture and living.

The essence of the new culture does not lie in any of the existing manifestations of it. There is no need for an older person to become a fan of rock music, or to adopt any form of dress, or to attempt to become a surfer, or to start using drugs. All of these are simply concrete, contemporary examples of a deeper principle. The particular details are constantly changing, even for youth; styles in music and clothes are always in flux. Consciousness III can appreciate Vivaldi as well as the blues. It is the underlying principle that counts: a non-material set of values. For older people, a new consciousness could rest on growing a garden, reading literature, baking bread, playing Bach on a recorder, or developing a new sense of family, so long as it represents a true knowledge of self, rather than false consciousness.

If a young person wanted to introduce his parents to the beach life of the new generation, he would not necessarily try to get them to become surfers; surfing may be too physically demanding for them. But the essence of the beach life does not lie in surfing, but in something more spiritual: a renewal of self in the wildness, beauty, and freedom of the beach. Older people may have "enjoyed" the beach all their lives without feeling it in this way; if they can be turned on to this, there is no need for them to surf, and they will be able to watch the surfers without envy, and be a part of the surfers' world.

The problem of envy is central to this process of learning a new culture or life-style. A person who cannot acknowledge his own curiosity or envy will offer every form of resistance to change. But if he is shown how he, too, can participate in what he envies, the way to change is opened. Nothing makes us angrier than the fear that some pleasure is being enjoyed by others but forever denied to us. The pleasures of the new generation are, like their music, seemingly inaccessible, but actually open to all.

Each aspect of the Consciousness III way of life needs to be seen by the middle class in terms meaningful to them. Surfing or hiking represents the underlying value of a close relationship with nature. Rock music represents not any particular musical style, but the pleasure and happiness that results from immersion in music—"getting into it" as distinguished from casual listening. The clothes of the youth culture represent the value of personal expression in dress, and freedom from forced external standards. Peace march-ers and other demonstrations and protests represent, not any specific political viewpoint or form of protest, but the value of taking personal responsibility for what happens in one's community, and the value of fighting together against that which seems wrong. The concepts of career, of personal relations, of commu-nity, of self-discovery that are so crucial to the youth culture can also be seen in terms meaningful to older people.

The trap of the rat race can be modified along the same lines as those followed by the student in reassess-ing his own, obviously far lesser, responsibilities. Be-fore a change of goals the student "has no time," he "has obligations to his parents," he has commitments to teams or organizations, he is afraid of getting poor grades in school. His problem may seem microscopic compared to that of the man with a family to support, but for him it is an effective bar to change. By the same token, the liberal-intellectual, no matter how great his sophistication, may be trapped by the fact that he still keeps to such goals as excellence, approval of his colleagues, recognition and achievement. He has fewer myths or illusions, but his despairing view of life's possibilities bars his way to a new consciousness, and his dependence on goals involving outside ap-proval deprives him of courage to be himself.

A change of goals means a change from exclusively material goals to goals that include the non-material as well. The trap is, in part, the trap of exclusively mate-rial goals. Consciousness III embodies freedom to have non-material goals; liberation of man's faculties for dealing with non-material goals. A man who is "trapped" in a $25,000-a-year job gets free by realizing that the material things he thinks he must provide his family may well be replaced by non-material things, such as being a better father and husband.

Where members of the older generation have begun a search for self, the way is open to raise questions with them about the workings of the Corporate State. These issues should not be such classic left-wing rallying points as the profit system, or imperialism. It is important to emphasize issues that are immediately of concern to the people one is trying to reach: pollution, traffic jams, boredom on the job, inflation, decline of the spiritual and ethical element in life. These are not "trivial" issues in comparison to racism or imperialism; the point is that the Corporate State is a seamless web, that all issues lead to the same insights concerning what is wrong; that all issues are related; and that the place to start is where problems are visible and tangible.

Issues are everywhere; the real problem is how to discuss one in a meaningful way. It is not enough to show how bad polluted air is for the lungs, or how much the draft interferes with a person's individual freedom. That is like showing pictures of Vietnam atrocities; we all "know" the evils are there, but this knowledge leads us nowhere. To talk about an issue in such a way as to raise consciousness, at least two things are necessary. First, the issue must be discussed in relation to some more general value, and second, it must be explained in relation to the Corporate State. Suppose we are talking to a worker about excessive and "stupid" supervision of his work, or to a housewife about the prying questions on the new census form, or to a young doctor about the way he must conform to rigid standards in his relationships with his colleagues at the hospital, or to a welfare recipient about constant checking up by an agency. The value which is at stake in all of these examples is autonomy, privacy, or independence. It can be shown that the Corporate State is eroding this value in innumerable ways, and that its impact is being felt by people in many different kinds of work, professions, and activities. It can then be shown that the basic reason for this is that the inhabitants of the Corporate State have been induced to put a low relative value on autonomy, as compared with such values as technological improvement and efficiency. Once this is understood, the way is open for a shift in thinking on this particular issue, so that people might begin to say, "Wiretapping helps to catch criminals, but autonomy and privacy are values that we ought to consider as well as law enforcement." This represents a partial change of consciousness, and at the same time it means the introduction of values and controls into the machinery of the State.

The single value of autonomy can be pursued through a whole series of issues that deeply trouble different groups in society today. For the office worker: the question of vacations and the right to take time off; the question of unemployment insurance and old-age guarantees; and whether these benefits shall be administered so as to afford independence to the recipient. For the G.I., the right to free speech, assembly, and press while in the army, on political issues that concern him as a citizen. For the high school boy, the right to wear hair and clothing styles of his own choosing in school. For the doctor, the right not to belong to a highly political medical association. For the public employee or public school teacher, the right to take part in political activities like any other citizen, and to be free of any demeaning loyalty oath. For the lover of peace and quiet, the right not to have churches and banks play tape recordings of carillon music every hour on the hour. For the priest, the right to have his views respected in the church hierarchy. For all of us, the right not to be subject to sudden annihilation at the whim of certain "leaders."

In each of these examples, it would be meaningful to explain how one man's problem is related to all the other problems, so that people can see that their powerlessness is due to the fractured, divided nature of their vision—their inability to connect their own complaints to any more universal value; that if they ever united in favor of autonomy, the machine and the machine-tenders who pass as leaders would be compelled to recognize this value.

We can list other basic values that could unite other fractured issues: democracy and democratic participation in decision-making, freedom of expression, preservation of natural environment. Like autonomy, these values might bridge the gap between schoolteachers, G.I.'s, businessmen, housewives, day laborers, farmers, youth—groups who now see only "their own" issues. An example of this potential common ground is seen in the California grape strike, where careless use of pesticides is one of the strikers' complaints—a complaint they share with many conservationists. Like autonomy, each of the values we have mentioned, once introduced into the Corporate State, would begin the dismantling of the State as we know it. And if substantive education were combined with procedural education about the latent possibilities of existing democratic forms, the middle class might begin to feel its powers.

What about the blue-collar workers, those arch-opponents of the new consciousness? Can they, too, be induced to begin a search for self? Much of what we said about the middle-class couple applies to the worker as well. But there are fundamental differences. Workers really *are* trapped, caught between the rigid discipline of their jobs, the obligations to family, and the rising cost of everything. Freedom cannot come to them without a struggle; they must follow the route that the blacks have taken.

In America there has long existed a deep skepticism about the capacity of the average man for a higher life. From de Tocqueville on, the average man has been considered a threat to democracy, liberty, and all things aesthetic. The average man is the narrow-minded provincial of Main Street, the permanently crass and juvenile Babbitt, the boob who sits in his undershirt watching the ball game on television, the convention goer and shallow white-collar technician, the brainless voter who goes for Wallace or Huey Long or any other demagogue, the mass man who wants a new and more hideous car, lives in a plastic home, and leaves the countryside strewn with his beer cans. He is the man who hates the black race and the university graduate. He is despised and feared by intellectuals, and he despises himself. He is Dagwood, or some witless television father; he is the reason that democracy works so badly; he is "what is wrong with America."

This conclusion about the average man's incapacity ignores the whole contention that the average man was not born without higher capacities, but was systematically deprived of them by the industrial system. Marx, the great novelists of the nineteenth century, the sociologists of both centuries, and today's students of education, of personality, and many other disciplines all agree that industrial work deadens man's ability to enjoy nature, to love art, to relate to his fellow man. The average man has little appreciation of natural beauty, but his ancestors in Europe did; people in Europe still keep their land with care and an aesthetic sense. The average man is the descendant of men who loved music and singing, who were deeply spiritual, who could create the life and beauty of festivals, who felt themselves a part of nature just as today's youth feel they belong to the woods or the sea. And "human nature" was not necessarily always privatistic, grasping, competitive, materialistic. The "average man" is descended from people who had the capacity to put community ahead of their own immediate wants. The oldtime peasant had very real capacity for a non-material existence.

There is a crucial parallel between the contemporary condemnation of the average man and the prejudices that once were held against the "nigger." The black was once blamed for having all sorts of supposed deficiencies of character and intellect. But in the case of black people, the existence of centuries of deprivation and discrimination has gradually come to be seen in relation to these judgments, and with that insight has come a new recognition, by blacks and whites alike, of the black man's worth. But when we talk about the worker, we entirely fail to relate his present "nature" to the deprivation that he has undergone. We do not relate his "character" to the fact that he has been subjected to the enslavement of personality. Why have we refused to acknowledge that the white man has been systematically niggerized, that what we see as his shortcomings are the inevitable products of a systematic process of destruction?

In the most general terms, our refusal to see the white man as a victim goes back to the Consciousness I belief that human nature is "bad," that men have always been stupid and vicious, that nothing is to be expected of "popular taste" or mass man. Closely connected to this is the Consciousness I idea that all men are "free," and they are morally responsible for what they make of themselves or fail to make of themselves. The puritan doctrine of hard work enters in too; work is a virtue, and if men do not turn out well it is not because they work but in spite of the fact that they work. Consciousness II has most of these same attitudes; it would make a distinction for people who have been subjected to discrimination on the basis of race (and recently, for those who suffered extreme poverty), but it believes that the average man's place in the meritocracy, and his character and taste, are matters for which individual ability and personality are primarily responsible.

The history of the labor movement and the welfare state also helps to explain our blindness toward the causes of the average man's condition. From Marx to contemporary labor leaders and liberals, primary emphasis has been placed on the *material* condition of the worker, first on his material deprivations, and today on economic security and benefits. The labor movement and the welfare state virtually equate material gains with solution of all the worker's problems. Since material progress has indeed been made since the days of Marx, it is assumed that the worker has little to complain about; he is "the best-paid worker in the world," and the labor leader or liberal looks with scorn on those Marxists who still talk about capitalist exploitation. The fact that Marx himself was con-

cerned with human values as well as material ones
seems to have been long forgotten.

But these two explanations of our blindness, based
on beliefs and ideologies, cannot be the whole story.
Inability to see discrimination against blacks was due
not only to general philosophy, but to something much
more intense and immediate. In an Ivy League club in
midtown Manhattan, the sprucely dressed businessmen nod to the uniformed attendants (white), call
them by their first names, and get a deferential "Good
morning, sir" in return. In a popular restaurant at
lunchtime in San Francisco's financial district, the
waiter (white) is smiling, laughing and obsequious to
his regular customers, and a group of them (white), in
turn, are hovering obsequiously around a man of consequence who they constantly address as "Judge";
"how's your drink, Judge?" In a large office the people
(white) shuffle uneasily in the presence of the boss,
trying to say only what will please him. In a factory
authority is more blunt and obedience more sullen, the
forms are cruder, but the situation—the superior man
and the inferior man (white)—is just as clearcut.
Even among professionals—the younger doctor (white)
in a hospital, the younger lawyer (white) in a law
firm—a rigid caste system of superiority and servility is
observed by all. In all of these places, and among all
of these people, white men are acting the part of the
nigger, grinning and being humble and keeping their
mouths shut and stepping off the sidewalk quickly
when The Man walks by.

We do not see it because we cannot afford to—because the truth is too explosive. The superior man cannot afford to see what he is doing to his inferiors by
the way he treats them, he cannot afford to imagine

what they feel about him, he cannot afford the thought that his "excellence" rests on someone else's degradation. Even less can the white "nigger" afford to see that he is neither free nor white nor 21, that he is permanently kept a menial, that his job takes away not only his time but his manhood, that he who allows his pride and self to be degraded at work must be condemned to live that way at home too—enjoying pleasures that are harmless, juvenile and vicarious, never assuming the responsibility of a citizen, abandoning his claim to keep on growing and searching.

The orthodox left wing approach to the worker is to tell him that he is the victim of an unjust "system." But the worker may be unready to throw over the whole mythology of his society on grounds that seem like abstract theory. What George Wallace was successful in reaching was the worker's sense of self. But a search for self conducted exclusively in Wallace's terms would lead into a blind alley. The real question, for the worker just as for the black man, is "Who am I? What sort of culture should I have, what is my heritage, where should my pride be?"

Redemption might mean, among other things, a search for one's origins, background and uniqueness. One possible beginning might be a search for one's ethnic identity, the course pursued by the militant blacks. Most whites, when they came to this country, lost their ethnic identity in the melting pot. White youth, in searching for a culture of their own, have in large measure looked to black culture as a model; the whites started with none of their own. But white people have lost traditions too; folk music, arts and crafts, myths and legends, history, cooking. To rediscover this is to rediscover some of one's sources. But there is much more to recover—youthful pleasures like hiking or camping, forgotten talents such as music or art, the pleasure of reading, the pleasure of a renewed relationship with family, and personal relationships at a level not previously attempted. For older people, the great object of a new consciousness should be the recovery of self from the whole mass of duties, obligations, fears, external standards, necessities, and endless work; a recovery of the child's knowledge of how to be happy. The goals of a new consciousness are nothing less than the recapture of life itself.

Blacks were trapped at a level below that of white workers and the middle class. Realistically, their circumstances were far distant from affluent and well-educated middle-class youth. But it was the blacks, and not youth, who first developed a radical view of America and an alternative culture and life-style. Their culture was in part forced upon them by the fact that they had been kept isolated from the mainstream of American life. But in recent years it has become something highly affirmative: organizations for self-help, civil rights, and fighting for the black cause; a new attitude toward career, in which a "successful" individual might prefer returning to work in the ghetto to "making it" in middle-class terms; a sense of brotherhood and community; above all, a sense of pride which stands in contrast to the white worker's feelings about himself. At the same time, many blacks developed a militant radicalism which rejected the whole white middle-class view of reality, as shown in *The Autobiography of Malcolm X* and Eldridge Cleaver's *Soul on Ice*. Neither their culture nor their radicalism were identical with that of the new generation. But lack of self-knowledge was one of the most important issues for blacks. Cruse, in *The Crisis of the Negro Intellectual,* shows that even the most advanced and well-educated blacks lacked a sense of black identity and pursued a white identity and white goals. From Fanon to Cleaver, recent black writers have shown the same thing. How did blacks begin to encourage a search for identity among their ranks? One step was to raise questions about the existing "Negro identity," to show that it had an Uncle Tom quality, that it was humiliating and artificial, that it produced, under a black skin, an ersatz white man. At the same time, blacks were made conscious of their own African heritage, their own culture, their own pride. The story can be told in hair styles, from the "conking" that Malcolm X describes, an effort to make his hair look "white," to the nondescript short haircut, to the "natural" or "Afro" that is uniquely black. Today the black search for self is well under way.

When the black man began his search for self, he first became intensely aware of his status as a nigger. Eldridge Cleaver says, "Of course I'd always known that I was black, but I'd never really stopped to take stock of what I was involved in." It is even more true that the white worker has never seen what his true position is in American society. He too is a nigger, and the discrimination against him is as deliberate, as systematic, as devastating in its consequences as that practiced for so long against his black brother.

Our present system resembles a pyramid, with the elite of the meritocracy at the top, the white- and blue-collar working forces standing in the middle, and at the bottom the lowest skills, the marginally employed, and the unemployed. This meritocracy constitutes a class society, but not a class society in orthodox Marxist terms. It is not primarily a question of wages, surplus, and economic exploitation. It is a question of participation in society, of status, authority, and servility, and of the right to a full mental, creative, and emotional life. The pyramid of the meritocracy now allows only the elite at the top to live a reasonably full and varied life, while all others are condemned to a life of monotony and stultification. The great mistake of radicals has been to try to interest workers in a revolt based primarily on *material* injustice. The real deprivation has not been in terms of material goods but in terms of a deadened mind, a loss of feeling, a life that excludes all new experience. This is the true nature of contemporary servitude. For workers and the middle class, a Consciousness III revolution would express the need of all persons, old as well as young, no matter how employed, to keep on growing and learning throughout life, and therefore the need of the vast majority of the populace to overthrow the slavery of domination and of empty lives.

In conception, the meritocracy does not seem unjust. In place of the hereditary aristocracy of Europe, or the self-made aristocracy of nineteenth-century America, the first half of the twentieth century saw the coming of an elite supposed to be based upon ability and motivation. This elite was thought to be premised upon equal opportunity for all, recognized no "irrational" distinctions between people, and created a hierarchy that was functionally necessary to the requirements of an industrial society. To take only the "ablest" men into college or professional school seemed the only right way of doing things.

The meritocracy became a class system by degrees, and this process went unnoticed by the liberals who supported it most strongly. The least significant aspect of the class system was probably the purely economic discrimination. There were large and substantial differences in pay from the bottom to the top of the system, but these differences were probably narrower than they had been in the nineteenth century, and welfare-state programs were beginning to place a floor, however inadequate, at the bottom.

The first goal of a new consciousness might be to change the almost total exclusion from power of the lower echelons of the people. We have shown how the Corporate State moved steadily away from populist democracy toward "expert" and administrative decision-making. It needs to be underscored, however, that the low man in the meritocracy was *totally* excluded from *direct* participation. Are there any workers or clerical employees on our boards of trustees, boards of directors, presidential commissions, or government councils? The most that can be said is that occasionally they are "represented" by the head of some organization; a presidential commission might have a union leader among its members, but this man is personally one of the elite of the meritocracy. It is simply not part of the concept of meritocracy that "low achievers" should personally participate in decisions. Even where the decisions concern their own lives in an immediate sense—design of factory working-space and offices, actual working conditions, rules, promotions, hiring, and dismissals—there is at best only participation by an elite representative. The only remaining vestiges of populism are the jury system and some aspects of politics, and they are now frowned on as sources of continuing irrationality. It is quite true that technical "non-experts" might initially have little to contribute to decision-making. But the goal of change should be a growth of knowledge and responsibility in all.

An even more important goal might be to challenge the linking of job to authority and status. In the first place, there is no inevitable relationship between the division of labor and authority. There is no *logical* necessity for a man in a "higher" position to have that kind of authority over one in a lower position—a doctor over a nurse or intern, a lawyer over a secretary, a plant manager over a worker. Such working relationships might, at least in theory rest simply on acceptance of the division of labor by all parties, without coercion by anyone. A group might elect a chairman without conceding him authority beyond his function of coordination. In any event, his authority would not have to extend beyond his job. It is here that we encounter the far less defensible distinctions of status. One man might be a manager, another a manual worker, but why should each carry with him, when he leaves the job, a distinct status that separates the two in every phase of life? Why should the manager be deemed a higher form of life by society, the worker an inferior man? Status has extended outward from the job to permeate every aspect of life: housing, culture, clothes, social relations. One of the most striking things about America is its total failure to afford any means of recognition to work at any but the "highest" level. We do not even have medals for "heroes of labor," the clumsy Russian socialist effort in this direction. To be a manual laborer, a technician, a secretary, means to live wholly without the recognition that the higher statuses deem so essential to the health of their egos. "Lower" people simply do not exist, and their work does not exist. The meritocracy has fostered a class society by permitting its originally functional distinctions to become distinctions among the human beings themselves; a new consciousness could seek to restore all people to a level of equality as human beings.

Nowhere is the class system more crucial than in terms of educational differentials. The meritocracy does not believe it important that "lower" people be educated beyond what is functionally needed. A new consciousness could challenge this. Are not sabbaticals and long vacations needed for the renewal of all workers, not merely intellectuals? Why should workers not have a chance for continuing education in the humanities? Should we not have a concept of the white "educationally deprived," comparable to the emerging concept of black deprivation, and, on the basis of that, begin a program of preferential admission of the children of Appalachia and factory towns whose schools are little better than the black schools of today? The new consciousness could declare that everyone regardless of age, "aptitude," and job, has the right to a continuing growth of mind.

In *Soul on Ice*, Eldridge Cleaver describes, with passionate intensity, the black man's sense that he lives under a system in which he was deprived of mind, condemned to be the laboring body while the white man retained exclusive possession of the capacity for thought and domination:

Those who have been assigned the Brute Power Function we shall call the Supermasculine Menials. They are alienated from their minds. For them the mind counts only insofar as it enables them to receive, understand, and carry out the will of the Omnipotent Administrators.

The chip on the Supermasculine Menial's shoulder is the fact that he has been robbed of his mind. In an uncannily effective manner, the society in which he lives has assumed in its very structure that he, minus a mind, is the embodiment of Brute Power. The bias and reflex of the society are against the cultivation or even the functioning of his mind, and it is borne in upon him from all sides that the society is actually deaf, dumb, and blind to his mind . . . His thoughts count for nothing. He doesn't run, regulate, control, or administer anything. Indeed, he is himself regulated, manipulated, and controlled by the Omnipotent Administrators. . . .

When the white man discovers his servitude, we will see a real explosion in America. Black rage, black pride, black militancy, give us some idea what it will be like. But with whites, the self-deception has been greater, and perhaps that will make the truth all the more infuriating. Students are beginning to discover their servitude, and are angry, but objectively speaking the servitude of students is not very great; professors and college administrators are a timid lot, and students are quite free and easy. They talk about "the student as nigger" but their cringing is more a matter of form than of reality. Yet it is enough to provoke their anger. Workers are far behind the students and the blacks in awareness, but when that awareness finally comes, they will repossess their intellects, their selves, and their manhood.

What we have tried to show by the preceding discussion is that if Consciousness III is to spread beyond youth, it must do so by a process that is just the reverse of orthodox left-wing theories of radicalization. It will not work to educate first, and change individual lives later. A change of consciousness must precede a new and enlarged understanding of our society, just as it has in the case of our young people, who first "changed their heads," and then got new insight into the nature of the Corporate State. Radicalization comes only after a change of consciousness. The SDS strategy of showing the middle class the true oppressive nature of our society is thus mistaken—it begins where it should end. And radical New Left strategy is wrong for another reason. Confrontation, hostility, and guerrilla warfare cannot help to convert those against whom it is directed. The more people feel threatened, the more rigidly they adhere to their existing attitudes and patterns of life.

The task of the new generation is to be the teachers of their fellow men and women, so that the great liberating process of recovery of self, started by our youth, can become the means of liberation for all Americans; and so that the domination of self by false goals and false consciousness may be ended for all Americans. When self is recovered, the power of the Corporate State will be ended, as miraculously as a kiss breaks a witch's evil enchantment.

> Go take a sister, then, by the hand.
> Lead her away from this foreign land.
> Far away where we might laugh again.
> We are leaving, you don't need us.*
> From "Wooden Ships" by
> David Crosby and Stephen Stills

This task does not demand missionary aggressiveness, zeal, and self-sacrifice. Nothing could be further from the spirit of Consciousness III. The most important *means* of conversion is, and will continue to be, simply living one's own life according to one's own needs. Direct efforts at proselytizing, on the other hand, are all too likely to involve depersonalization and a loss of consciousness for both parties. But without going to that extreme, we have tried to suggest an attitude of openness for the new generation to replace what often has the appearance of hostility toward outsiders and rejection of them. Consciousness III will never convert anyone by abandoning its own life-style in order to become ideologists, pamphleteers and propagandists. But it can understand the possibilities of conversion in others, and it can live its own life in such a way as to help others to join.

To live in this way requires, before anything else, a rejection of hostility—even hostility toward those who are the outspoken opponents of change. Any efforts by the new generation to raise consciousness in others must be accompanied not by a hostile, threatening or rejecting stance, but by a demonstrated offer of acceptance and affection. We know that the greatest thing holding back most people is fear—fear and the lack of a significant group to join on the other side. If youth presents itself as a closed society, contemptuous of older, "straighter" or less well educated people, those who want to make a change will find that the most crucial encouragement of all is lacking—the promise of support and acceptance by those who have gone ahead. But when changes that affect their lives are sought for by the radicals of the new generation, there will be the potential for a growth of trust, understanding, appreciation and solidarity between the new generation and the middle class. For the new generation will be visibly helping the middle class, not threatening them. There is already evidence that when young people join hands in a cause that workers understand, they are welcomed.

The student radical of today is all too likely to call policemen "pigs," to be scornful of "straight" people and "uptight" people, to call right-wingers and George Wallace supporters "fascists," to be harshly critical of his own parents and their contemporaries. In doing this, students are reacting naturally to the anger and violence and lack of understanding directed at them, but they are nevertheless making the same mistake as those who are racial or religious bigots. Look again at a "fascist"—tight lipped, tense, crew cut, correctly dressed, church-going, an American flag on his car window, a hostile eye for communists, youth, and blacks. He has had very little of love, or poetry, or music, or nature, or joy. He has been dominated by fear. He has been condemned to narrow-minded prejudice, to a self-defeating materialism, to a lonely suspicion of his fellow men. He is angry, envious, bitter, self-hating. He ravages his own environment. He has fled all his life from consciousness and responsibility. He is turned against his own nature; in his agony he has recoiled upon himself. He is what the machine left after it had its way.

The task of the new generation is to see the humanity in all men, and to work for the renewal, the rebirth, the return to life, of all men. The new generation must bridge the gap that separates parents from children, and the still greater gaps that separate worker from student, white-collar professional from those who are young and liberated. They must realize that "youth" is not chronological age but the state of growing, learning, and changing, and that all people must be helped to regain the condition of youth. The new generation must make their revolution by the yeast theory; they must spread their life.

Those who have the good fortune to have attained Consciousness III must teach others where their true interests lie—not in getting a promotion, or in fighting communism, but in directions that will enrich their lives. The students may set an example simply by changing their own lives, or they may take jobs in the Establishment and educate from there, or they may fight for particular issues, or create culture; the means are unlimited, but the object must be to reach people. Consciousness III starts with an assumption of responsibility for oneself and one's community; now our young people must take another step and assume responsibility for their parents, their college teachers, their younger brothers and sisters, and on outward into society, to all those who seem to be enemies but are only the deceived, the broken, and the lost.

XI

REVOLUTION BY CONSCIOUSNESS

How can our society be changed? No matter how
many people join the ranks of Consciousness III, the
Corporate State seems likely to go on as before. There
is no convincing plan, no political strategy, for turning
new consciousness into something effective in structural terms. Quite the contrary: there is every reason
to fear that the State is growing ever more powerful,
more autonomous, more indifferent to its own inhabitants. But the liberals and radicals who despair because
there is no plan or strategy are simply looking for the
wrong thing. They would not recognize the key to
dismantling the Corporate State even if they saw it.
The Corporate State cannot be fought by the legal,

political, or power methods that are the only means ever used up to now by revolutionists or proponents of social change. We must no longer depend wholly upon political or legal activism, upon structural change, upon liberal or even radical assaults on existing power. Such methods, used exclusively, are certain to fail. The only plan that will succeed is one that will be greeted by most social activists with disbelief and disparagement, yet it is entirely realistic—the only means that is realistic, given the nature of the contemporary State: revolution by consciousness.

Any discussion of the means of change must start with a recognition that our present course, including nearly a century of liberal and radical struggles by orthodox means, has brought us to the brink of an authoritarian or police state. Liberals and radicals both assume that this proves only that more of such efforts are needed. Is it not possible that they are wrong? Despite all efforts at reform by legal and political means, for the past twenty years we have helplessly watched the coming of a closed society. One mark of it has been the institutionalization of war. The Cold War, Korea, the Dominican Republic, Vietnam, are wars without beginnings or endings. They fade into one another. Perhaps the Vietnam War will "end," but more likely it will drag on and slowly merge into a broader but less flagrant pattern involving semipermanent hostilities in Southeast Asia—one aspect of a worldwide defense system for Fortress America. Inside our borders, our country may be a fortress as well. The National Commission on the Causes and Prevention of Violence has predicted a pattern of urban life in which cities will become places of terror and widespread crime, work and public activities will be conducted

only under substantial police protection, and middle-
and upper-class people will live either in fortified
apartment buildings or suburbs, in either case protected by private guards, security devices, electronic
surveillance devices, and armed citizens in cars sup-
plementing the police.

One of the most clearly marked trends for over
twenty years has been the decline in civil liberties. The
condition of the Bill of Rights cannot accurately be
measured by Supreme Court decisions; the real situation depends upon surveillance and arrest procedures,
attitudes of public and private employers, the scope of
free discussion on television and in the press, and
other factors embedded deeply in the day-to-day
working of society. At this level, there has been a
steady increase in surveillance, wiretapping, spying,
police actions that are "political" in nature; there has
been a gradual acceptance of loyalty-security criteria
for more and more jobs. There has been a steady
monopolization of media of communication. The Bill
of Rights is less and less of a shield between the citizen
and the State.

An equally significant pattern is the growing aggressiveness of government toward its own citizens. The
politicization of police across the country is an index of
this; they have become a major political force, with an
interest in promoting "law and order." Police, led by the
FBI, seem to be independent of their civilian super-
visors. With the support of government, repression is
carried on in an ever more aggressive manner—with
technology used against the populace, random arrests
and clubbings, and politically motivated treatment in
prison. Government, notably the Nixon and Reagan
administrations, has become more partisanly militant,

aggressively taking sides against one portion of the population. It seems eager to promote a polarization of America—a division in which a majority will feel bound by loyalty and patriotism to support the State.

The trend is toward our becoming two nations. The two nations will be separated from each other by mutual fear, by differences in consciousness and culture so deep that even communication will be impossible. California seems to be two nations already—a nation of the old and a nation of the young. The young feel that government might as well represent a foreign country, they are so detached from it. This pattern of two nations is becoming a familiar one in the world— two Germanies, two Chinas, two Koreas, two Vietnams, a United Nations that does not include the largest nation in the world. Why not two nations here in America—the nation of the peace marchers and the nation of the headlights?

This is the point we have reached after more than three decades of the liberal welfare state, after all the hard-fought battles for civil liberties, for civil rights, for reforms in government administration, for a more just society based on law. This is where we are after the liberals, the radicals, the humanitarians have tried to make a better nation by making a better political structure and by dedicating their own lives to this greater public interest. The political activists have had their day and have been given their chance. They ask for still more activism, still more dedication, still more self-sacrifice, believing more of the same bad medicine is needed, saying their cure has not yet been tested. It is time to realize that this form of activism merely affirms the State. Must we wait for fascism before we realize that political activism has failed?

All orthodox liberal and radical thinking about social change or revolution concludes that there are two main approaches to translating consciousness into effective action. The first is favored by the liberal establishment: using the existing legal, administrative, and democratic procedures to advance change. These are the "lawful channels" through which students and radicals have been advised to work. The second approach is based upon power. At one end of the spectrum, it merges with politics such as the Gene McCarthy movement—elect people who will change the course of society. At the other end of the spectrum is the radical concept of revolution, street fighting, mobilization of the Left. Under this approach, the State must be changed by getting together more power—political or physical—than now is in the hands of the "Establishment" or the "ruling class."

The experience of new consciousness people with established procedures has made clear what should have long been obvious: these procedures are not designed for social change except within the terms of the existing system; for more radical change they are a dead end. There remained the alternative of power—the revolutionary tactics of the New Left. But how could power succeed against the State? Power, in the second half of the twentieth century, resides in organization, in technology, in the machine. Whether or not we postulate a "ruling class" in Marxist terms, power is a function of organization, not merely of economic position. How, then, can those who oppose organization and the machine expect to win a fight where the field of battle is power? It is a fight on the enemy's ground, a fight which the Corporate State is sure to win. It is the street fighters against the tank, the automatic rifle, the helicopter. It can only come to disaster and defeat.

Neither lawful procedures nor politics-and-power can succeed against the Corporate State. Neither can prevent the steady advance of authoritarian rule. If the new consciousness sticks to these tactics, it will throw itself away on an ideology that fails to take account of its real power. The power is not the power of manipulating procedures or the power of politics or street fighting, but the power of new values and a new way of life.

For the road to a new society is there nonetheless. Consciousness is capable of changing and of destroying the Corporate State, without violence, without seizure of political power, without overthrow of any existing group of people. The new generation, by experimenting with action at the level of consciousness, has shown the way to the one method of change that will work in today's post-industrial society: changing consciousness. It is only by change in individual lives that we can seize power from the State.

Can this really work? Have we not said that the Corporate State is subject to no controls whatever, even by a majority of the people? And isn't there evidence of this in the continuance into 1971 of the Vietnam War, which was already so unpopular years earlier that President Johnson was forced to retire, and both candidates promised peace? Moreover, almost all New Left theorists, from Marcuse on down, agree that no revolution is possible in the United States at the present time. And many people believe that if anything happens, it will be a right-wing reaction that will smash whatever there is of the New Left. In the light of all of this, what power can we expect a new consciousness to have? How, after all we have said about the invulnerable power of the Corporate State, could change possibly be so simple?

From the start of this book, we have argued that consciousness plays the key role in the shaping of society. The Corporate State is the creature of the capitalist economic system and the force of science and technology. This system and this force have been with us a long time, but they are nevertheless the choice and creation of man. In the Middle Ages, when a very different consciousness prevailed, neither technology nor the market was permitted to dominate other social values, no matter how great the "logic" of technology. The most efficient or economic way of doing something was often ignored for religious or social reasons. Thus, in a long-run sense, technology represents a choice (not an inevitability, as Ellul suggests), and we can make a new choice whenever we are ready to do so. We can end or modify the age of science and we can abandon the Protestant ethic. In this sense, it has been a long, long time since we made any real choices; since the end of the Middle Ages, technology and the market have made our choices for us. Perhaps the culture just now being developed by the new generation —the new emphasis on imagination, the senses, community, and the self—is the first real choice made by any Western people since the end of the Middle Ages.

The crucial fact to realize about all the powerful machinery of the Corporate State—its laws, structure, political system—is that it possesses no mind. All that is needed to bring about change is to capture its controls—and they are held by nobody. It is not a case for revolution. It is a case for filling a void, for supplying a mind where none exists. No political revolution is possible in the United States right now, but no such revolution is needed.

Revolution by consciousness is made possible by two basic conditions. First, a process of change of consciousness must be under way in the population—a process that promises to continue until it reaches a majority of the people. Second, the existing order must depend for its power on the earlier consciousness, and therefore be unable to survive a change of consciousness. Both of these conditions now exist in the United States.

We have shown that the Corporate State runs by means of a willing producer, who desires status, and a willing consumer, who desires what the State makes him want. Now all we have to do is close our eyes and imagine that everyone has become a Consciousness III: the Corporate State vanishes. It can no longer sell people things to satisfy any but real needs, which means that the consumer has regained power over what is produced. And it can no longer get anyone to work except for real satisfactions, which means that the status system is at an end, and people within organizations regain power over the organizations and structures of society. The Corporate State is succeeded by a state subject to human control.

The revolution must be cultural. For culture controls the economic and political machine, not vice versa. Consider production. Now the machinery turns out what it pleases and forces people to buy. But if the culture changes, the machine has no choice but to comply. For the willing buyer of whatever the machine produces is replaced by a buyer who buys only what he chooses. The machine is forced to obey, and the market power of buyers is restored. The machine has to turn out Beatles records, bell-bottom pants, or better hospitals. But to gain this power, the buyer must free himself from the power of advertising by developing a different consciousness. Once he does, the machine is his slave. Similarly, the employee liberates himself by turning his back on the institutional goals of advancement in the hierarchy, status, and security. He makes himself independent of the organization by a change of values, and the organization then loses the power over his individuality which it formerly had. Thus the machine can be mastered.

The essential point is that the political structure, the law, and the formal institutions of society are not the creative part of the Corporate State. They are merely its *administrative* department, and they administer whatever values there are to be administered. They do not have the power to change values; for one interested in basic change, law and political institutions are virtually irrelevant (except as theatres in which to stage exemplary battles of consciousness). Even a great political change, such as the New Deal, can accomplish nothing if there is no accompanying change of consciousness. On the other hand, the government of the Corporate State has proven unable to do anything whatever to stem the great cultural changes coming about with the appearance of Consciousness III. The case of marijuana illustrates the government's complete lack of power over culture, *once it loses the ability to create false consciousness.* Government, then, is mere management (it is significant that President Nixon has seen it in this light). Culture is the substantive part of society. Thus social change, instead of beginning at the palace, comes up from below. The law and the government are not the first things to be changed, they are the last. Should Consciousness III sweep the country, the federal government could simply be ignored until it became completely isolated from the people of the nation, and had no choice but to change. At that point, the President would have to don bell bottoms and a dirty T-shirt and go looking for his constituents.

The fact is that America still has, despite all we have said, a democratic form. Power is not exercised in this country by force of arms, as in some dictatorships. Power rests on control of consciousness. The state is not like tyrannies of the past that ruled by force; its unique strength, and, ultimately, its unique weakness, is its dependence on possessing the minds of those within it. If the people are freed from false consciousness, no power exists that could prevent them from taking the controls.

Our form of government may be antiquated in many ways, but it still has enough flexibility to permit a determined people to make the necessary changes. Elected officials show a remarkable ability to change when their constituencies change; New York's Senator Goodell, a backward-looking man when he represented an upstate constituency, grew sideburns and became a vocal liberal as he became the representative of the entire state; whether this was mere necessity, a genuine case of education, or privately held principles finally emerging, matters less than the fact of change. The machinery of government is also capable of change once political power has shifted. A change in *public opinion* is not enough to accomplish this at any but the superficial level of liberal reform. But a change of consciousness can strike deeper; it need not abolish the State; it can master it, and require it to submit to new values and a new vision.

The theory of revolution by consciousness appears to run squarely contrary to the teaching of Marx that the structure of society is maintained by the privileged or ruling classes for their own benefit, and hence cannot be changed except by a revolution which attacks the power of the rulers. Our theory might seem to be a weak type of revisionism, leaving out struggle and substituting persuasion—hardly a doctrine acceptable to any revolutionist. But we shall try to show that our theory is not inconsistent with Marx.

According to Marx, a capitalist society has a ruling class whose economic interests are consistent with maintenance of the status quo. The consciousness of the ruling class is determined by its material interest, and it will therefore not give up power without a struggle—only class struggle and revolution can bring about social change. It will be observed that the crucial premise in this thinking is the assumption, made by the theory of historical materialism, that consciousness is determined by material interests. Certainly all of the evidence available to Marx seemed to point that way. In the late 1960's, facts have developed that are not easy to explain by this theory. The new generation, who ardently desire social change, are largely members of America's affluent ruling class. And the greatest opponents of social change, the lower-middle-class workers, are members of the exploited class. These facts urge a reexamination of the theory.

We need not dispute the general thesis that consciousness is determined by a person's working conditions and basic interests. But the interests of a person should not be defined in narrowly economic terms;

they could, conceivably, include a person's needs beyond the economic, once the latter have been satisfied.
Throughout most, if not all, of the history with which
Marx was familiar, economic situation and "interest"
have perhaps been largely identical. But in an affluent
society, where everybody's economic interests are or
can be satisfied, other aspects of interest may become dominant in the formation of consciousness—
interests such as status or personal liberation. Marx
simply was limited by the evidence and the historical
situation of his times. It is by no means inconsistent
with Marx to suggest that new interests become dominant when, perhaps for the first time in history, the
economic ceases to be of primary concern in men's
lives.

Consciousness I seems to follow the classic Marxist
pattern: it rests on the individual material interests of
each individual. Consciousness II seems to rest on organizational interests—status, prestige, and power,
rather than on traditional economic interests. Consciousness III rests on those interests which the economic and organizational parts of society have failed
to supply. Today a member of the present American
ruling class might find that purely economic interests
dictated one consciousness, but that increasingly another consciousness was competing with the economic.
If the new consciousness began to prevail in this individual, that would mean that he would no longer have
a dominant interest in opposing social change. Of
course "conversions" could have taken place in the
nineteenth century (and a few did), but Marx would
have discounted these (his own was one, after all) as
sentimental or intellectual aberrations; most people's
true consciousness would remain with their true inter-

ests. Today there is a far more solid basis for a "conversion" to Consciousness III even by a member of the ruling class. Even a millionaire would in actual fact be "better off" if he chose liberation instead of the plastic world of material wealth. If he exchanged wealth, status and power for love, creativity, and liberation he would be far happier; he would "make a good bargain." The possibility of change of consciousness is therefore not the subject for cynicism it might have been in 1848. Today, in greatly varying degrees, we are all employees of the Corporate State and, what is more, exploited employees who sacrifice ourselves, our environment, and our community for the sake of irrational production. There is no class struggle; today there is only one class. In Marx's terms, we are all the proletariat, and there is no longer any ruling class except the machine itself.

Thus it is at least possible that social change can be accomplished without class struggle. The fact that the exploited blue-collar worker is a chief opponent of change is in a sense an optimistic sign, for his consciousness clearly does not rest on economic interest, and is therefore just as clearly subject to change. None of what we have said denies that today in America we have a privileged elite and an underprivileged and exploited many. In that sense, of course, we still have classes; of course there are still people getting fat on the labor of others; of course there are still mansions and slums—but that is a different struggle from the one we have made the subject of this book. Our theory, while recognizing the continuing urgency of that earlier battle, contends that in America, at least, the economic class struggle has been transcended by the interest of everyone in recapturing their humanity; this is the meaning of the rejection of class and economic interest by the children of privilege, the new generation.

If our theory of change can survive the objections of Marxist doctrine, what about the danger of cooptation, of blunting of radicalism by gradualist reform, of the new culture being taken over by the Corporate State and used to pacify people, as Marcuse described in *One-Dimensional Man?* It is quite true that the Establishment can take over the clothes, the music, the drugs of Consciousness III; in an age of technology the Establishment can even copy the hippies' leisure. (Bell bottoms fashioned by New York stylists do not have the revolutionary potential of Consciousness III culture.) But the heart of Consciousness III is not in the shape of its pants, but in its liberation, its change of goals, its search for self, its doctrines of honesty and responsibility. The Establishment cannot safely swallow those.

As for cooptation, the new generation shows us the answer: if buying off was really the danger it is supposed to be, surely no one would have been as effectively bought off as a pampered young person of today —they have far more of everything than the middle-class worker. Only those who have everything in our society have been able to transcend it. The new generation cannot be pacified or bought off, because it rejects false consciousness and false satisfactions, and the Corporate State is incapable of producing anything that will satisfy real needs. When the society does begin to satisfy real needs, that will not be pacification, it will be revolution.

The theory of consciousness changes our assumptions about cooptation and buying off revolution. Is not the real danger to social change not cooptation but the domination of consciousness? The middle-class America of Consciousness II suffers intolerable conditions of living, but it does not revolt because its mind is completely dominated by the consciousness-management of the Corporate State. As for the famous drive for security by the middle class, it is clearly based on fear—fear resulting from the atomization, anomie, and loneliness that is characteristic of Consciousness I and II. This security did not buy off their children of the new generation; it did not buy off anyone. The middle-class American of the Thirties, Forties, and Fifties failed to make a revolution because he lived without hope. It is fear and insecurity, not comfort and cooptation, that now hold the blue- and white-collar worker in thrall.

Even the civil rights movement, which is basically a battle against privilege—the older form of revolution —shows that pacification holds little power when there is strong hope for something better. The reforms to date—more legal rights and greater economic opportunity—raised hopes, and these hopes played a vital role in the militancy that followed. The reforms did not coopt the black man, they permitted him to see how bad his condition had been and how far he had yet to go.

What of the possibility, feared by so many liberal members of the older generation, that the students' revolt for consciousness will produce, not the changes they want, but an authoritarian reaction from the right, with accompanying repression of everyone's freedom? It would be foolish to deny the reality of this danger, for evidence that it is threatening can be found in every day's newspaper. Many of our most enlightened thinkers warn that the nation is not now ripe for revolution. And for many members of the new generation, the losing battles of 1969 have left a mood of discouragement, depression, and withdrawal. Nevertheless, we must ask whether such an attempted repression, if it came, could stop the trend toward a new consciousness. It is our belief that it could not. Repression of a revolt by the disadvantaged against those holding power certainly does work, up to a point. We question whether it could ultimately succeed against the very different type of change now becoming visible in our society.

It is our belief that repression cannot succeed against a change in consciousness. It is possible to repress economic demands, because a class exists with the interest to carry out the repression. But the elixir of consciousness can affect those who are doing the repressing. Here the repression would have to be against our affluent, well-educated young people—the true elite of this society, its taste-makers, and opinion-makers.

Moreover, a repression today would have to be by one age group against another. Is there any modern precedent to such a repression? Can families be expected to turn against their own children? We are beginning to get quite contrary evidence—that children sometimes radicalize their parents; that when the children of even conservative parents get in trouble with school or public authorities, or get beaten by the police, blood turns out to be thicker than ideology, and the parents often side with their children and turn against the authorities. Beyond this, it should not be forgotten that we are a country in which more than half the population is under twenty-five. Most power is in the hands of the older half, but could they maintain it in a struggle?

We have already described how change of consciousness is taking place in youth. The causes of this change can be expected to grow even stronger, and reach a greater proportion of youth, as time goes on. Since youth represents the future, the older consciousness cannot win a battle with youth. And the young have numbers on their side too; as one high school boy put it, "There are two parents and four kids in my family—two of them, four of us." The only way in which the old consciousness could survive as a repressive force would be if the young, when they become older, return to their parents' consciousness. But if consciousness is not a set of values or opinions, but a total understanding of reality, then there can be no return, for the experience is now part of the individual. Once an individual has experienced good relationships with others, relationships with openness, honesty, sharing and love, he will no longer be able to accept or tolerate relationships where nothing real is happening. Once a person has experienced a true sense of wonder in nature, a participation in the sea or the mountains, he will not go back to travel agent tours or mechanized camping. The new reality is just too much better.

For this same reason, more and more of the older generation will change allegiance from the forces of repression to the forces of change. Every new consciousness person becomes an evangelist seeking new converts. Many young people have already succeeded in converting one or both of their parents or older brothers and sisters, and a growing number of older people have experienced a change of consciousness on their own. The same forces that operate on youth operate on them as well; the madness of the Corporate State becomes more obvious, the breakdowns of its machinery multiply, its promise of happiness becomes more illusory. More and more daily events conspire to breach the unreal consciousness upon which the Corporate State depends. Subway collisions and fires, air inversions and power breakdowns, and the horrors of Vietnam all contribute. And repression is sometimes only another means of changing consciousness. In a typical example, when indiscriminate police violence occurred during a week of conflict at Isla Vista, the residential district adjoining the University of California at Santa Barbara, many faculty members were quoted as saying they had been "radicalized" (*San Francisco Chronicle*, June 11 and 12, 1970). But the greatest force against repression remains simply "the kids" themselves. After Powder Hill's "prohibited" festival, many of the local people of Middlefield, who had been waiting for the festival "like a Roman village facing an onslaught from the Visigoths," found the invaders irresistible (John Darnton, *The New York Times*, August 3, 1970). Mr. Darnton reported the first selectman, Arthur Mackley, as saying "the whole town has fallen in love with these kids." Mrs. Pat Devito, forty-two years old, welcomed some of the visitors at her bake shop. Beaming as she put her arms around two long haired young men, she said, according to the *Times*, "I'm not going to let these two leave." Mrs. Shirley Ness, a grandmotherly woman, said, "I don't think anybody here had ever spoken to kids like this before. But now we've taken them in, and, personally, I'm having a ball." The theorists who predict repression have overlooked a basic truth: people do love their own children, and, ultimately, they must accept their children's friends and world.

The above question brings us to another aspect of

the problem of repression: can a repression force people to do something against their will? A repression that prohibits behavior is one thing, but our society needs its young people, and particularly its best-educated young people, in its working force; it depends on the willing worker as much as on the willing consumer. Already bell bottoms and beads are being hired by the Post Office, perhaps because no other workers can be found; how long will it be before hippies man the FBI? Who will act as the force of repression? We are already witnessing the tiny beginnings of a revolt among G.I.'s against the war in Vietnam. Could army draftees be successfully induced to turn their weapons against other young people, members of their own youth culture, girls as well as boys, blacks as well as whites? The young men in uniform would have no personal stake in the success of the repression. They might have a considerable stake in its failure. As we have previously pointed out, our whole system of hierarchy, authority, and law depends upon a consciousness that accepts the system; it all collapses the moment people refuse to obey.

There is still another flaw awaiting any attempt at repression: Consciousness III is produced by the machine itself. It is the product of the machine's success, not its failure, and the machine cannot stop it without abandoning its own goals. It cannot repress and at the same time sell more products, more "freedom to consume." It cannot repress while all of its productive and advertising machinery is emphasizing a new and more liberated way of life—and needs to do so in order to sell its products. It cannot repress and maintain the willing consumer so essential to the machine's own life.

We have not intended, by the foregoing discussion of repression, to deny the very real hazard it presents, particularly when one finger on a button could destroy our entire society and the rest of the world as well. Certainly we must expect ugly and violent times ahead, with incidents such as People's Park in Berkeley, the Harvard bust, or the Chicago police riot steadily increasing in numbers and intensity; with more and more schools becoming armed camps like San Francisco State, with more repressive legislation, with helicopter or shotgun attacks upon our own population. An increase in all of these forms of conflict and violence will surely come, involving more and more of the population, causing increasing disruption of life, restriction of freedom, injuries, and deaths. Our point is that it will not succeed. The power of consciousness, that great discovery of the new generation, will not be stopped as readily as the demand for votes or bread.

In summary, we think that both the liberal and the SDS theories of how to bring about change in America are wrong. The liberals (the true liberals, that is, not the Establishment liberals) see change coming only after a massive effort at organizing: an effort directed at politics and law. We think that such an effort, even if it elected a President and a Congress, and appointed a majority of the Supreme Court, would end as the New Deal ended, with reforms that proved illusory. SDS and other believers in class struggle would engage in a hopeless head-on fight against a machine that could work for them instead, and against people who could be their allies instead of their seeming enemies.

The activist political radicals of the New Left are wrong in many ways. Their picture of the world is wrong; they explain America primarily in terms of the desire of the rich and powerful to keep what they have and to exploit the poor, at home and abroad. They fail to recognize that bureaucratic socialism or communism presents many of the same evils as America, and that in America capitalism is now only a subordinate aspect of the larger evil of the uncontrolled technological state. They make frontal assaults upon institutions which could be given changed values and a changed direction instead. They are basically believers in structural change *before* a change in consciousness; thus they make the same mistake the liberals made in the New Deal, and they ally themselves with Consciousness II in their belief in the primary reality of structure. They seek to create change by self-sacrifice, by going to endless dull ideological and organizational meetings, and doing endless unrewarding work, by getting arrested, suffering prison sentences, even by the terrible risks of fighting in the streets. Thus, despite their bravery, they fail to offer an example of an affirmative vision. Bob Dylan did what he wanted to do, lived his own life, and *incidentally* changed the world; that is the point that the radicals have missed. And finally, they frighten and make enemies of those who might otherwise be their allies, the workers and the middle class. The members of the New Left have made their own great contribution to consciousness; some of their tactics have had an extraordinary impact in radicalizing other people, and their life-style provides an inspiration of sorts, if not an altogether happy vision. But they must see that their real target is not a structural enemy, but consciousness. One does not fight a machine head-on, one pulls out the plug.

To bring the concept of revolution by consciousness

from the level of theory to the level of action, we must return to our analysis of how the Corporate State actually works. As we have said, its motive power is supplied by a willing producer and a willing consumer. Thus the motivating power of the machine is found *within each of us*. More specifically, the motivating power is that portion of each individual's life in which he acts as a machine-part, namely, where he acts as a motivated producer or consumer. Revolution by consciousness can be accomplished when enough individuals change that part of their lives.

Let us first consider a change in the "consumer" motive force. Here the crucial point is that a mere change of opinion is not enough, nor is a change at the level of politics. Suppose that, noting that the national environment is being steadily destroyed by the works of man, we decide that there should be more conservation. If at the same time we continue to believe in the basic values of economic and technological "progress" no program for conservation will be effective; conservation will always be "too expensive" or contrary to the public interest. The values of technology and progress, which remain unquestioned, are the real destroyers of the environment, rather than man's carelessness or wantonness. Suppose, on the other hand, we subordinate "progress" to the value of conservation, as is now just beginning to happen in this country. Genuine victories for conservation will follow. For there has been a genuine change in values, not merely a surface change.

Other illustrations suggest the same conclusion. If we want auto safety but continue to believe in auto profits, sales, styling, and annual obsolescence, there will be no serious accomplishments. The moment we put safety ahead of these other values, something will happen. If we want better municipal hospitals but are unwilling to disturb the level of spending for defense, for highways, for household appliances, hospital service will not improve. If we want peace but still believe that countries with differing ideologies are threats to one another, we will not get peace. What is confusing is that up to now, while we have wanted such things as conservation, auto safety, hospital care, and peace, we have tried wanting them without changing consciousness, that is, while continuing to accept those underlying values that stand in the way of what we want. The machine can be controlled at the "consumer" level only by people who change their whole value system, their whole world view, their whole way of life. One cannot favor saving our wildlife and wear a fur coat.

A report in the business section of *The New York Times* (November 22, 1970) foretells the future. Businessmen who hoped for a $45 billion "youth market" have discovered that they must alter their production and selling efforts in *response* to changes in the values of youth: nonmaterialism, concern for environment, a renewed interest in bicycles instead of expensive automobiles. "The 1960's illusion about the rich, recklessly spending and rapidly multiplying segment of the under-twenty-five population has given way to a fear of a turned-off generation that keeps its money in its faded jeans."

The "producer" motive force operates within organizations and institutions. To change it one must change the way in which one performs one's role. Those who act in such a way as to seek promotion, expansion of the organization, increasing monetary rewards, and professional success and recognition are causing the wheel to turn. The professional who fights for good causes outside his role, but dutifully performs his function during the working day, is defeating his own efforts. He may favor more money for hospitals, but as a member of a business organization, he helps make his organization grow, at the expense of hospitals if necessary. What he should do is take the position, in his official capacity, that further growth of his organization is undesirable because of competing social needs. If he is in a company that makes cars or jets, he should take the position that corporate growth cannot be justified if it contributes to air and noise pollution. He does not have to be at the top of the hierarchy for his views to be felt. Galbraith, in *The New Industrial State*, has shown that power is not at the top of organizations; decisions come up from below. In acting in this way, the organization man may not earn himself a promotion or a bonus, but he probably will not get fired either. And he will have helped significantly to rechannel the power of the Corporate State.

Today, for example, a steadily increasing number of the nation's most idealistic and forceful young college graduates are going into public school teaching rather than professions such as business or engineering. These young people will profoundly change the public school system despite every effort of the established school bureaucracy to prevent change. They will evade, defy, or overpower the school authorities *from within*, because, being a necessary part of the system they have the power to do so, just as the members of an athletic team, if they get together, can force the coach to accept long hair. The young teachers have this power because they are willing to accept the consequences of their resistance. They have not merely voiced opinions; they have put their opinions into their working lives. There are many such transformations in progress today. The largest and most conservative law firms are being forced to devote a portion of their time to kinds of "public interest" work they never before would countenance. The motivating power comes from the fact that young lawyers recruited out of law school do not merely ask for this change, but actually refuse to work for firms that will not spend time on public interest matters.

We are suggesting a vital distinction between attempts to change the State from "inside" and from "outside." By "inside" we refer to any action that affects the motive power of the State—"consumer" or "producer." By "outside" we refer to efforts to change the State without slowing down its motive power. A campaign to save the redwoods, to ban the SST, or to improve public welfare administration is an "outside" effort unless it either reaches people at the level of their way of life as consumers, or influences their way of life as producers, professionals, and members of organizations. Outside efforts have little effectiveness; the machine rolls on. Inside efforts—"consumer" or "producer"—*are* effective. The maxim is, act where you have power. When Americans refuse to buy what the State wants to sell—economically or politically— and refuse to produce by striving for the goals set by the State's organizations, the wheel will have no power to turn, and revolution by consciousness will have become a reality. A change in one's own way of life is an "inside" change.

The process of change by consciousness that we have described in theoretical terms has already been explored, although in very tentative fashion. That exploration has been the work of the student movement. They did not succeed in stopping the machine, although they had scattered victories. But their actions had a far greater, less immediate value. They provided a large-scale experiment in methods of social change, which tested all the theories, from that of the Establishment to that of the guerrillas. That experiment produced results. The student movement revealed, perhaps unknown to the students themselves, how the machine *can* be stopped. It provided the basis for a theory of how revolutionary change can take place in a post-industrial society such as the American Corporate State. For what the students discovered is that only tactics which reach people *at the level of consciousness* are effective. And so they began to develop forms of speech and action, new to America, which were designed to influence consciousness in others and in themselves. To see this, we must begin by retracing and analyzing the steps the young protesters followed.

What originally brought on the confrontations? The issues ranged on a continuum from the political to the cultural. If we look only at the political issues, it is striking to note that, instead of being radical and revolutionary, the issues around which the movement formed were drawn from the stated goals of our society, particularly the reformist goals of liberals. There has been conflict over admission of black students to universities and over the curriculum in relation to black culture. But both admissions policy and curriculum reflected injustices of the past, and one of the stated goals of our society is to erase those injustices. There have been encounters over student participation in decisions made by the university, but democracy and individual self-determination and independence are goals as old as the country itself. The ROTC issue involves the militarization of American life; prohibition of a standing army was one of the objectives of the founding fathers. In Chicago, the question involved representation in a national political convention. If we think over the whole list of issues, from university participation in urban redevelopment to free speech on university grounds, from using a street as a pedestrian walk to preserving a vacant lot as a public park, we will find little indeed that is not well within the range of moderate American liberalism and reform, and few objectives that have not been voiced by educators or by Presidents of the United States.

The issues at the cultural end of the spectrum were more radical: unrestricted use of drugs, an end of laws regulating private sexual behavior, the right to wear hair and clothing styles of one's own choosing, communal living arrangements. The issues were radical—but so far these cultural issues have not been the source of most of the significant conflicts that have taken place. There have been arrests, and a steady trend toward a more radical culture, but no visible political movement. The battles, then, have taken place over conventional issues. In short, what was unusual and unconventional, what caused so much anger and controversy, was not the students' objectives but their new forms of communication.

It is commonly believed that the confrontation resulted from "activism" and "militancy" by the students, who appeared to be following a pattern of making demands and then devising a strategy to get the demands met. But is this an accurate description of what was happening? Most of the Consciousness III people are notably unaggressive, nonviolent, uninterested in the political game, absorbed by their new culture and its possibilities, and mainly ask to be left alone. Music, nature, and drugs do not encourage political militancy. There is nothing worse than having to forego a beautiful outdoor day in order to attend a meeting. Who, then, was the aggressor?

In the case of draft resistance, clearly it was the State that was making the non-negotiable demands. To young men who asked nothing but to be left alone to pursue their own lives, the State brought the peremptory demand that they join the armed forces, subject themselves to a coercive discipline, training, and indoctrination, and then take part in a mass killing of the people of another race, for purposes they did not believe in. The students did not act, they were acted upon, and all that some of them did was to say no.

In other cases we might also find it was the State that had the aggressive role. First, as we have argued throughout this book, the State has been actively subverting American ideals and disrupting the American environment; it tears up neighborhoods for redevelopment, makes the university impersonal toward its students, or violates the privacy of its citizens. Josephine W. Johnson made this point beautifully in a newspaper column entitled "Who Is Really Uprooting This Country?" She asked, "Who is taking our country away from us before our eyes," and answered that it was not the black militants or the students, but the leaders of our society (*The New York Times,* May 10, 1969). If someone destroys a person's world, and he finally begins to resist, does that make him the aggressor? Beyond this, it should be recognized that it is the

State that sets the terms for education, the meritoc-racy, and work in the productive system, and it is the individual who is called upon to perform. The demand may not come in the form of a notice to report for induction. It may take shape as a rigid set of curricu-lum requirements or an antiquated grading system. And the State's aggression is marked by the use of violence. As the Jerome Skolnik report to the presi-dential commission on violence shows, it is the State that is the primary source of violence today. The State is the party that always accompanies its proposals by coercion, and backs them by force.

It is apparent, then, that the student movement was not the result of conventional activism. There were several factors. As we said before, Consciousness III feels a need for personal responsibility and involve-ment that is not satisfied by watching the accepted procedures grind to their usual dead end. And there existed a need, a profound psychological need, to get the system to respond. To young people, one of the most frustrating things about the system is that it does not even have to respond—and usually it gives no sign that it has even heard. Young people want to kick it—to at least force it to bestir itself. Anger is better than complacent indifference. But the crucial force behind the student movement was the fact that the State was making an aggressive assault upon the newly formed consciousness of the student generation. It was to preserve and advance their consciousness that the students embarked upon their own adventure in social change.

Having no leadership, no organization, a dislike of theory and a doctrine of "do your thing," the new generation, in the tradition of American inventiveness and ingenuity, began to experiment. They tried the sit-down strike tactics used by the labor movement in the 1930's, occupying administration buildings instead of factories. They tried the marches, songs, and sit-ins of the civil rights movement. They attacked draft files and the induction buses as temperance ladies had once attacked saloons. They interfered with bulldozers as tradition-minded citizens have sometimes done when a historic house or tree is threatened by the highway builders. They burned draft cards, signed pledges of resistance to the draft, and refused induction. They held teach-ins. They started underground newspapers. They demanded participation in all sorts of decision-making and administrative structures. They created a new poster art. They read Marcuse, Malcolm X, and Marx. They talked, endlessly, and held endless meetings. It was like their new music; they used old forms, but their style was protean, and they created something entirely new.

The first object of the students' tactics was to get attention. Their criticisms of society, their objections to war or domestic injustices, their outrage and their thinking were ignored by the mass media, the politicians, the authorities. They sought means that would compel somebody to notice their cause. An unusual action, likely to get into the newspapers, would accomplish this: a big march or burning a draft card. One of the most effective attention-getters is disruption, such as occupying a building. The essential thing was that the action be unconventional, that it be "news," because newspapers and television would not carry the real news.

The second object of the tactics was to explain the issues. Public and cultural issues are often complex, they cannot be readily summed up in the accepted television manner in order to preserve time for the commercials, and it takes even more time to show the relationship of a particular issue to the over-all structure of the Corporate State. A teach-in fulfills this explanatory function. So does a restaurant sit-in by blacks; it *shows* people that the restaurant discriminates, makes the issue personal and vivid; *enacts* rather than describes. An enactment is capable of presenting issues of great complexity. A sit-in against recruiting on a university campus by the Dow Chemical Company says: the United States uses napalm, a savage and horrible torture, against village families; Dow manufactured napalm and sold it for profit to be used in the manner described; Dow is recruiting students to use their minds and bodies, for money, to produce and develop this and other agencies of horror, and it tells them that they should not feel responsible for the way what they produce is used; the university cooperates in the whole system, from research to recruitment to the deadening of conscience; the views and participation of the students are not wanted in any of these decisions, they are only wanted as mindless parts of the process. The relation of university, corporation, and government appears if the police are called in; their repression serves all three and repeats the pattern of Vietnam. Of course, this entire message does not get across to everyone. But because of the unitary structure of the Corporate State, any issue at all has the potential to lead to insight into the State; it is a seamless web, and while it is hard to penetrate initially, any entry leads ultimately to the truth.

Indeed, almost any thinking at all will break credulity and raise the level of consciousness concerning the

Corporate State. Suppose that students demand that student representatives, including several blacks, sit on the university board of trustees. In the course of the controversy, they make the point that the trustees consist of the usual businessmen and lawyers, without a single minority person. If it becomes known that there has never been a single black on the trustees in all the years of the board's existence, the credulity of people will be severely strained or broken if they have always believed that the trustees fairly represent all the interests of the community, rather than a small management elite. Suppose that a "straight" college athlete, never interested in politics, tries marijuana. It will inevitably lead him to political and ideological concerns. Finding that the drug is comparatively harmless but nevertheless illegal, his credulity about laws will be strained. Realizing that far more harmful substances are legal, such as tobacco, alcohol, and various non-prescription drugs, he will begin to see that banning only marijuana presents an ideological rather than a scientific question. Seeing that alcohol and tobacco yield huge profits to industry and are pressed on people by high-pressure advertising that insists they are "good" for you, he may draw some general conclusions about profits, morality, and power in the Corporate State.

Another object of the tactics was to put messages in a language—visual, emotional, and symbolic—that would help it to be heard and understood. Poets and writers have long known the value of symbolism, that it is better to show, not tell, and that some ideas require emotional preparation before they can be taken in. So a group invades a Selective Service office and pours blood on draft files. They get attention—they force the mass media to take notice. They express themselves in symbolic terms that are readily understood from a single picture or headline—no need for a lengthy verbal discussion of the draft and the war. And by acting emotionally rather than setting forth their position in a detached intellectual manner, they prepare their audience emotionally for the idea that our nation, which always does "good," is actually requiring its young men to engage in bloody warfare against a small and distant nation. Burning draft cards is an effective and pointed commentary on the war. Sometimes parody and humor are used. A group of students at New York's City College appeared during an ROTC drill and proceeded to ape each exercise—crawling on the ground when the ROTC crawled, carrying each other on their shoulders when the ROTC did that. In Berkeley, students produced a "mill-in" in the administrative offices—a mass coming and going that disrupted work while implying the meaningless nature of bureaucratic busyness. A further development of this concept is revolutionary theatre in which, on the real-life stage, demonstrators act out their message. They might walk into a solemn and talky faculty meeting and loudly sell popcorn and hot dogs in an effort to break into the heavy flow of rationality and "freak out" their audience, saying, in effect, "You have been stuck in the same kind of thinking too long."

Usually the tactics are aimed at enlisting others. "Join us" is what marchers say. "Take sides" is what a building occupation says. When the tactics set in motion a whole process of official reaction and repression, others may simply be swept in. At San Francisco State College a student strike brought on faculty intervention, the faculty was subjected to adverse treatment by the administration, and a faculty strike occurred. A college underground newspaper induces high school students to start their own underground newspaper; they are disciplined for doing so and start their own campaign against the high school authorities. In both cases two significant processes have taken place. The first we might call a fission process, where action by A leads to the repression of B, and the heat of one dispute sets off new disputes. Many times actions by blacks have led to a general round of repression and consequent broadening of the original dispute. More important, perhaps, onlookers are led to the discovery of *their own servitude*. College teachers find that they, too, may be manhandled by the board of regents and the police. High school students find that they have fewer rights than the blacks whose demonstration they sympathized with. Professional people realize that they are subject to decrees as arbitrary as those enforced on students, including repressive limits on their personal lives.

One particular tactic may have all of the effects we have mentioned at the same time. This accounts for the great significance of marijuana. Simply by using marijuana in defiance of the law, young people: *1*) maintain their own community and radical consciousness; *2*) give a demonstration of the hypocrisy and irrationality of society; *3*) make this showing effective by forcing it on public notice through what is in effect civil disobedience; *4*) affirmatively demonstrate cultural liberation to the rest of the society; *5*) produce a repressive reaction that involves others and eventually makes these others realize their own lack of freedom.

All of the tactics we have described are as much

concerned with the demonstrators themselves as with their audience; they aim at solidarity and *maintaining consciousness*. They are usually group activities, and thus they create or maintain a sense of community among the participants. A great peace march creates a remarkable sense of common cause among the marchers, it becomes an unforgettable experience for them. Any group act of civil disobedience creates an intense feeling of togetherness. Students who lived in the occupied buildings at Columbia during the 1968 events reported that the communal experience was like nothing else they had known in their entire lives; they returned only with regret to more ordinary ways of living. But the tactics also do other things for the participants. They allow them to demonstrate in a way that is nonalienating to themselves, so that they are not required, like the old leftists, to make themselves into projectiles. It is vital not to lose one's own consciousness and self in the process of working toward some cause. The tactics all help demonstrators to learn about themselves and find out the strength and meaning of their convictions and feelings, and the demonstrators see, hear, and meet others with like convictions and feelings.

Where the students influenced only public opinion, no basic change resulted. This is illustrated by the campaign against the Vietnam War and the draft. President Johnson was ousted, peace was made a major issue in the 1968 election, negotiations began, a sizable part of the population became doves. On the other hand, students gained no political power whatever, failed to reform the draft, failed to influence the new administration, failed, as of this writing, to stop the war itself. The students succeeded in getting many people to change their opinion about the necessity of the war and the evils resulting from it. But no comparable change occurred in the thinking that took place within people's roles as "consumer" or "producer"; they continued to work for defense industries, the Pentagon, or as government strategists; a White House aide might plan the war while his wife hoped for peace. In consequence, a good many people began to want peace, but the war continued. Many people who have participated in peace marches come to feel that in a sense there is no "audience" at all; only silent buildings in Boston, New York, or Washington; the real audience is the demonstrators themselves. Their cause will win when they are the majority; the march perhaps only measures and reaffirms the numbers and strength of the converted.

The universities offer a series of instructive contrasts. The demand for "student power" has not produced much student representation on trustee, regents, or administrative boards. It has so far made few inroads on the powers of appointment, budget-making, and university government. But black studies courses and departments have suddenly come into being on campus after campus. Student ideas on curriculum have begun to get a response. A number of university presidents have been forced out. Columbia decided not to build its gym in the park. Some connections with the defense establishment have been severed. Far more important, the system by which the university is governed has changed. Whether or not their beliefs are manifested in action, more and more students accept the basic critique of the university as authoritarian, irrelevant, tied to the Establishment. And more and more faculty members and administrators, recognizing the realities of the new student presence, have *in fact* if not in any formal way begun to take student views into consideration when they reach decisions. From a lawyer's standpoint, university structure has not altered much; from a sociologist's point of view, many universities have undergone a transformation.

The students achieved these results primarily by the simple device of adding to the university system the students' own changed values. If a boy leaves his family for a year's visit to a foreign country, and returns having acquired a consuming interest in astronomy, the family, whether they approve or disapprove, have no choice but to change their thinking; they will be forced to deal with their son as he is now rather than as he was, no matter how hard they resist. It is a material fact, just as a rise of thirty degrees in the temperature is a fact, and the new fact cannot be avoided. When the students changed from individuals concerned primarily with courses, grades, careers, private lives, to individuals also concerned with the government of the university, the university had to take notice, and had to alter its thinking to take account of the new fact. It could respond by ordering more campus police or by setting up a new university council, but either modifies the university's existing structure. In short, the universities represent the case where students were part of an organization, and by changing their own role within the organization they had the power to alter the organization's structure, even if nobody's thinking changed but their own.

Where the students were able to influence a way of life directly, they had great success, even though they failed to have any effect at all on structure. This is true in the case of marijuana. Efforts to get criminal penalties repealed have made little headway and, in contrast, the actual use of marijuana has spread irresistibly. It is almost everywhere in some colleges, it has spread to many high schools, it is popular with many city dwellers, rich and poor, it is reportedly nearly universal among G.I.'s in the army, and it is frequently used by the sons and daughters of men prominently and publicly opposed to its use. All of this without a single line of advertising, and over the opposition not only of the law but also of the mass media.

In areas of culture not regulated by law, such as music, haircuts, clothes, and, to some extent, life-styles, the students have swept all before them. Long hair, for example, has crossed all barriers; no one has fought it successfully, not even athletic coaches trying to keep their teams "neat," or high school officials, or the managers of businesses. Can anyone doubt that it will reach all the men in our society within a few years? In the area of culture, youth is virtually autonomous.

One of the remarkable things about the students' tactics is that, although their success in achieving particular goals has been mixed, the *tactics themselves* have proved to be immensely contagious. Just as the new generation copies some of the tactics of the civil rights movement, so more and more groups have tried demonstrations, protest marches, sit-ins, etc., to achieve their own particular objectives. Conservationists block bulldozers with their own bodies. Taxi drivers circle city hall to get a pay raise. Dissident priests produce an unprecedented group statement. Even the police, the upholders of law and order, have increasingly used demonstrations, including overzealous traffic law enforcement, to put across a salary increase. The new generation has not sold the country on their objectives, but they have indeed sold a good many people on their tactics.

In the case of marijuana and long hair, students exerted an influence on the consumer thinking of the nation in matters of culture, but not on thinking about law and the structure of State institutions. The law remained the same, but culture and habits changed. In the case of their tactics, the students changed people's thinking as citizen-voters, with respect to how an individual can influence his government. The students did not change people's thinking about society as a whole, so that in consequence people tended to use the students' tactics when they were personally aggrieved, but to oppose these tactics if used by others.

From all that has been said so far, it must be apparent that the protean style of the student movement cannot be readily categorized under the old forms of tactics: economic pressure, coercion, violence, free speech, speech-plus-action, nonviolence, civil disobedience. The old categories have little meaning. What the students have done is to convert all of these forms into something else: tactics at the level of consciousness. They express consciousness, they demonstrate consciousness to others, they seek to raise consciousness in others, they preserve consciousness in the demonstrators. They are a physical embodiment, an intangible made into flesh and blood, a state of mind made real and visible. What the students did was to confront society with their whole values.

For the demonstrators, the tactics provide personal involvement, in contrast to the detachment with which liberal reformers risk nothing and opt out in their stylish private lives. The students interpose their own bodies—nothing less. And they give others a demonstration of "authentic existence" in the existential sense, by acts of dedication and moral courage, most notably risking imprisonment rather than being willing to fight in the Vietnam War. They have shown what it means to search for one's own culture and cultural identity. Every adult in the United States has the potential for a cultural identity too, made up of the past in "the old country," which can be rediscovered, plus his own searchings. The new life-styles challenge adults, and the effects are already visible. There is no question that some of the stirrings in professional men and women are caused by the examples that have been set.

What we have been observing, then, is the development of a new freedom—not freedom of speech, but freedom of consciousness. The object is always to influence consciousness: when the students succeed in doing this, they achieve their objectives; when they fall short, the tactics come to nothing. If freedom of speech is the right to reach other people at the level of rational discourse and to express oneself at that level, freedom of consciousness is the right to reach people at the level of consciousness and to express oneself at that level. Speech advocating a new form of government is part of freedom of speech; "revolutionary theatre" advocating the same thing is freedom of consciousness. Refusal to serve in the armed forces is also freedom of consciousness; so is wearing long hair to school or occupying a building. Those who criticize the students for going beyond mere speech are perfectly right; the students have exercised a greater freedom, one which the society has not yet accepted.

Once we recognize this, we begin to see what we have called student tactics in a larger perspective.

They are only the top of an iceberg, made visible by publicity, conflict with the police, and the fact that people expect unruly dissenters to use tactics of this sort. But underground newspapers, which have proliferated all over the country, are part of the tactics, too; they offer an increasingly effective answer to the closed society of newspapers which are virtually alike from one end of the country to the other. The tactics also include underground "comix," comic books with radical or absurdist themes that have hippies for heroes and Establishment figures as the goats, the recent developments in poster art, and political use of the arts. In a large sense, they include the whole culture of the new generation. Once we recognize that a sit-in or an antiwar march is merely a cousin to an underground newspaper or radical play, we can see even the most conventional political tactics in the new context of consciousness.

What, then, have the students shown? Structure, or established lawful procedures, comes to nothing without consciousness. By itself, the imposition of structure is useless. When social change does occur, consciousness proves to be the moving part of the engine of change. Structure is not irrelevant; it can influence thinking, as the First Amendment has influenced our thinking about free speech. But it is useless to seek changes in society without changes of consciousness. Consciousness is *prior* to structure. Thus, a student demonstration forces new factors into an existing situation, while the law-abiding liberal, who agrees to accept whatever decision is reached by the structure, has not changed his own consciousness and hence does not force the structure to take account of anything new. The liberal can be ignored because he will accept defeat without questioning the system; the student will fight the system and therefore cannot be ignored. Speech and appeals to rational procedures are adequate methods of change in a society where the state is controlled by the people and by reason; they are frequently inadequate in the uncontrolled and irrational Corporate State. Control of the Corporate State lies at the level of consciousness.

This same conclusion can be reached if we examine the existing "established procedures" of the Corporate State. The student movement did not turn away from "established procedures" without first attempting to use them. For one thing, they found there are a great many instances in which there simply are no established procedures by which protest could be made. The adoption of chemical Mace will serve as an example once again; no procedures known to the public were utilized in the decision to start using this chemical on people, and no procedures exist for challenging or changing the decision. Students also found instances where procedures existed but could not possibly result in a decision favorable to the individual. The draft is an example; there is a good deal of procedure, but selective conscientious objection to war is not recognized, and all the procedure simply runs into a stone wall. What about the cases where procedures did exist and a favorable result was at least theoretically possible? The procedures were often outrageously defective. Typical and very common defects are: failure to give notice of proposed action until it is under way, failure to provide access to needed information (such as the results of safety tests), absence of a hearing, failure to permit the complainants to make an argument to the authorities who hold the decision-making power.

The real problem in following administrative procedures was not any of those we have mentioned so far, but the fact that the decision-makers' frame of reference and values were too narrow and one-sided to make it possible for a change in policy to prevail. Suppose that a state highway department actually does have procedures for challenging the proposed location of roads, and suppose that some citizens make a presentation objecting to a road because it will destroy historic or scenic values. Who makes the decision after the "lawful procedures" have been completed? The state highway department. And the highway department, it is not unfair to suggest, thinks in terms of roads and dollars; it is understandably "highway minded." Can the department be expected to be a fairminded judge of the importance of preserving a forest or an old landmark? The procedures end with a decision by the very people who have a commitment in advance to the outcome. The decision has a momentum of its own, and there are vested interests behind it before the procedures are even started. And even where this is not so blatantly clear, the decision-makers bring a decisive viewpoint to the proceedings. The safety of atomic experiments is decided by the Atomic Energy Commission, whose membership's thinking starts with the premise that atomic development is good. A proposal to abolish competitive grading is brought to a vote before faculty members all of whom owe their positions to their success under the old grading system. At the deepest level, there are limitations of thinking. The decision-makers are asked to consider choices beyond the range of their logic, rationality and imagination. The State Department cannot even imagine that the communists are friends, not enemies; a faculty cannot even imagine a noncompetitive university.

Quite apart from the closed-mindedness of the procedures, students found the process itself undemocratic, impersonal, and demeaning. They did not have any opportunity to participate; the decisions were made by remote "authorities"; there was no opportunity for a discussion, dialogue, or interaction with the decision-makers. The students who offered a petition or made a submission were told it would "get every consideration" by somebody, and then, eventually, out came a result (usually bad). This was not the students' idea of government by the people.

The reason that "established procedures" presented these obstacles goes to the very essence of the liberal welfare state—what we have called the Corporate State. As we tried to show, the State rejects "conflict" in favor of administration; it defines only a small area as "political" and calls the outside area "deviance" that must be administered, controlled, treated, given therapy, cured, or if necessary, punished; but it cannot be recognized as "legitimate." Use of marijuana, occupation of "private" property for a public park, a sit-in in a university building, demand for non-faculty members as teachers, long hair, or the insistence on making an individual, nonreligious decision about the draft, were not issues that could find adequate expression within "established procedures." These procedures simply refused to recognize new consciousness attitudes or activities.

The political process was just as closed as "established procedures." The Vietnam War and the 1968 election furnish the best example, for it was not merely the younger generation, but a large segment of the country that wanted peace; but the political process produced opposing candidates who were equally unresponsive to this demand; the people never got a chance to vote for Gene McCarthy. An example that is even clearer, because more specific, is that of inequities in the draft laws; here a presidential commission of leading citizens made some very moderate proposals for reform to the Congress, proposals that surely could have won the support of a majority of the voters, but no action was taken. In short, even if the students could get "public opinion" on their side of a particular issue, it would make no substantial difference. What the students found was that America's political system, supposedly the sector of the State most subject to popular influence, is perhaps the most rigid and least "democratic" of all. It is far easier to get a change in a mass-produced product or a change in religious ceremonies than a change in government policy. They began to feel that the people were not sovereign after all, that there was a power structure that blocked off democracy; they began to be aware of their own subjugation.

But these same "established procedures," which seem so impassable, may become a route to change if they are accompanied by even a partial change of consciousness. Sometimes the liberals *have* succeeded by working through structure. One example is in conservation. For a long time, it appeared that no legal safeguards could accomplish much for conservation. The forces of "progress" were just too powerful; the "lawful procedures" bent with the prevailing forces. For example, the Federal Power Commission, with jurisdiction over hydroelectric projects on rivers, was supposed to protect conservation values, but normally ignored them. Thus, when Consolidated Edison of New York applied to the FPC for approval of its plans to construct a facility on the Hudson River near Storm King Mountain, the FPC approved the facility, ignoring the pleas of conservationists based on damage to aesthetic and historical values. The conservationists appealed to the courts; under established precedents they should have lost. Instead, the Court of Appeals reversed the FPC. It held that the agency should have given greater weight to conservation values. The structure of the Corporate State gave way to a degree, and an era of greater legal deference to conservation began.

We could cite a catalogue of similar changes through established procedure, from the school segregation decision of 1954, to cases involving the rights of welfare recipients, to the setting up of black studies departments in some universities without any prior demonstration or protest efforts. On the other hand, we could also cite many structural changes which have accomplished virtually nothing. The New Deal is full of examples; to some extent the school segregation decision is an example; we are all familiar with examples of new student governments that are powerless, new television regulations that are meaningless, codes of procedure that are ignored by the police. The liberals, then, produced all sorts of results: sometimes no change in structure, sometimes a change that had no meaning, sometimes a change that had profound meaning and signalled a major trend.

It should be clear by now that the controlling factor is consciousness. The liberals won when they influenced consciousness, or when consciousness was changing at the time of their victory. The Storm King case came at a time of changing consciousness regarding environmental values. In the United States Court of Appeals, the conservationists argued that environmental values should have been given more weight in the FPC's decision; they based this on their interpretation of the governing concept of "public interest." Thus their argument was explicitly an appeal for a change in consciousness with respect to "the public interest" and the relative weight of economic and environmental factors. To call it a "legal" argument merely means that it was addressed to a court, that it cited what Congress' original intention in passing the FPC Act must have been, that other court decisions were cited, and that it was claimed that the FPC failed to consider evidence put forward by the conservationists, all in an effort to show that environment was a factor that should be weighed.

The entire legal structure that we described as the backbone of the Corporate State is changeable once consciousness changes. Welfare administrators regarded unannounced midnight searches of recipients' homes as necessary to enforce the welfare laws; accordingly they deemed the searches reasonable and no violation of the constitutional prohibition against "unreasonable" searches. But arguments pointing out the importance of privacy and dignity to the individual welfare recipient succeeded in changing consciousness in this respect, and courts began to hold the midnight searches illegal. In the area of occupational licensing and other public benefits, the old theory was that denial or revocation required only the most abbreviated of procedures, because the license or benefit was a "gratuity." But after it was realized that such benefits were in fact extremely important and valuable, and that government actions such as revocation could be arbitrary and oppressive, the "law" began to change to require stricter hearing procedures, and more exacting substantive rules. In each of the above cases, it is possible to give a "legal" explanation of the change. But out point is that "legal" changes occur in precisely the same way as non-legal changes. The present concern and anxiety over domestically based nuclear missile systems is a marked change from previous acceptance of anything proposed by the military as "necessary" for the public interest. No courts and no laws are involved as of the present writing. But the process of argument is remarkable for its similarity to the Storm King case. The same process can be seen at work on the debate over money for domestic needs versus money for defense needs such as the missile system. The controlling concepts of "need" and "public interest" are given a new meaning as awareness and values change.

Changes in attitude with regard to conservation values, or privacy for welfare recipients, or defense spending, represent partial changes of consciousness, sometimes from Consciousness I to II, sometimes from Consciousness II to III. As such they give us valuable data, almost on a par with scientific experiments, on how particular changes of consciousness can affect structure. The changes are mostly small and ineffectual, but the process is revealed. When a federal judge holds that the draft laws cannot discriminate against non-religious conscientious objectors, when the Howard Hughes organization begins to question underground testing by the Atomic Energy Commission, when oil pollution is viewed as a possible ground for halting offshore drilling, when the necessity of the Vietnam War begins to be questioned, we can start to gauge the power of changes in consciousness.

To work within established procedures thus can succeed only when a change of consciousness is caused by or accompanies the work. This is the hard test that must be met by those who choose this method of seeking change, as distinguished from trying to change people's way of life by direct means. Self-deception is easy. To work within established procedures without changing consciousness merely affirms the existing system. Yet revolution by consciousness can take place in the court room, the administrative hearing chamber, the committee meeting, as well as in a private home or on the streets.

One of the most potent means of revolution during the 1970's is "subversion" through culture. There are two aspects of this "subversion," and both are already evident throughout the mass media. The first approach is the most obvious: those who create the mass culture simply start introducing radical ideas. Music, the theatre, and the plastic arts have become major avenues of ideas critical of our society, and there seems to be nothing the State can do to prevent this. At least in the case of pop music, the radicalism of Dylan, of the Rolling Stones, of the Jefferson Airplane reaches a vast audience in a meaningful way. Even television is vulnerable, if the creative people who write and edit television shows are becoming radical. News broadcasts begin suggesting that something is wrong with our foreign policy, dramas and advertising imply a radical life style, hip and "suggestive" language appears in dialogue. The television censors may successfully keep "controversial" political discussions off the air, but there is little they can do against a changing culture, which flows into every cell of any cultural medium, even the media which are the main purveyors of false culture.

The second aspect of cultural subversion follows the lead of Pop Art, and simply begins making new uses of existing mass culture. These new uses do not need to be obviously satirical. It is not necessary to make fun of comic strip heroes. All that is necessary is to stop taking them seriously, and begin enjoying them on a new level. To paint a Campbell's Soup can is to transcend that particular aspect of culture, to see it objectively rather than be dominated by it. That does not make the object "beautiful" but it does take away the object's power over man, and perhaps man may even learn something from it, or get a little enjoyment from it. One can watch television, the news, the ads, the commentators, the dramas, and just laugh and laugh and laugh; all the power of television turns impotent and absurd.

Thus each individual who wants to see change come about has a wide choice of personal means. He can concern himself only with his own life. He can try to influence the "consumer" way of life and values. He can take a job or profession and try to bring about change from there. Or, in a position such as that occupied by a lawyer, he may attempt the complex and subtle task of introducing new consciousness directly into existing structure. Each individual must choose and experiment. What is common to all the choices is this: none involve assaults on the machine from "outside." All depend upon changing consciousness. All require, as their one indispensable element, changing one's own life first.

In contrast to the efforts of radicals to attack and remake structure, up to now an almost total failure, stands the success of those who have simply changed their lives. These people have started to live in their own way without waiting for structure, politics, or ideology to "be right." And as they have done this, structure and politics have begun to seem utterly irrelevant and absurd. The newspapers make their front page news, day after day, out of the speeches and actions of a few men in Washington whose thoughts are ludicrous, predictable, stereotyped, banal, and above all, boring; who are utterly out of touch with American society; who deserve, beyond anything else, to be ignored. Those who simply change their lives feel a magnificent sense of detachment, a feeling in the poem "Stoned" from R. Crumb's *Head Comix:*

> Hey boparee stoned
> Omigod he stoned
> Whathehell is this stoned?
> Like nobody's bizness stoned
> Stone cold daid stoned
> Sick in the haid stoned
> He she it stoned!
> . . . .
> Woke up this morn stoned
> Just like bein' born stoned
> Around your neck a millstoned
> Hurt destroy kill stoned
> Dirty old man stoned
> Cute li'l Peter Pan stoned
> Ultra super cool stoned
> Jus' another fool stoned
> Shmuck from Keokuck stoned
> Ya wanna buy a duck stoned?
> Bored lethargic dull stoned
> Poundin' in my skull stoned

Nuclear holocaust stoned
All is not lost stoned
Look ma, the Pope stoned!
Most amazing dope stoned
Everything is now stoned
Macro-cosmic ever-flowing love-lite
Wow stoned.

"Stoned" refers to the drug experience, but it also expresses an attitude toward life, a way of life, that has found the immense power inherent in changing one's own life, the power that comes from laughter, looseness, and the refusal to take seriously that which is rigid and nonhuman—the power to "keep on truckin'." To fight the machine is to experience powerlessness. To change one's life is to recapture the truth that only individuals and individual lives are real.

To the sincere and dedicated liberal or radical, especially the one who has spent many years, perhaps his whole life, in battling for liberty and against the State, the idea that massive, authoritarian power can best be fought by changing one's own life must seem puny and absurd. It must seem like lying down in front of a tank, or, worse yet, the weak and watery moralism of some frightened, timid, sycophantic preacher who enjoins us to reform ourselves while, outside, rampant evil rages unchecked. It is difficult for anyone who believes in action and social responsibility not to feel this; but even the most courageous battle is senseless if it mistakes the source of evil. We must answer the doubters by saying that their methods have failed and failed and failed, and that only changing one's own life confronts the real enemy.

In Norman Mailer's great and moving novel of World War II in the Pacific, *The Naked and the Dead,* the unspoken question that broods over the whole book is what caused this senseless, meaningless, horrible war? In a series of flashbacks, Mailer takes us back into the lives of the men now engaged in battle. Without exception, those lives were bleak and barren, lives that had come to dead ends long before the war, lives that were starved for love, companionship, creativity, meaning, and all the other things that make for happiness. Even in the stress of the greatest adventure and the greatest horror of their lives, they could not relate to, love, or even trust each other; instead, each finds that he has gone all the way to Anopopei to find himself still absolutely alone. And so, Mailer shows us that the source of the war is in the barren, frustrated lives that are led in America: lives that lead men to aggression, force, and power; lives that are so repressed that they can yield only anger and bitterness and evil; lives that deny the very possibility of a human community. Marcuse saw the same thing in *Eros and Civilization* when he recognized that excess repression was the central fact of our society, and that it led inevitably to the state which must seek to dominate both those who live within it and those beyond its borders.

Twenty years after *The Naked and the Dead,* Mailer, like a haunted man, returned to that book's question once more. In *Why Are We in Vietnam?* Mailer took the reader on a businessmen's hunt for grizzly bear in Alaska, a hunt which turns into a paradigm of the Vietnam War. In this second book, Mailer retraces the steps of *The Naked and the Dead;* the old characters can be recognized in the new characters, the invasion has become a hunt, even the unforgettable landscape of Mount Anaka on Anopopei, which provides the setting for the climactic insights of

The Naked and the Dead, reappears as the remote, barren, and beautiful Brooks Range of Alaska, a secluded valley which becomes the end point of Mailer's second journey. Once again, the answer is the same: we are in Vietnam because of the way of life of the American inhabitant of technology-land, a way of life so regimented, repressed, and artificial that it has transmuted the brave and good qualities of Americans into forces of destruction. The difference between the two books is this: *The Naked and the Dead* ends without hope while *Why Are We in Vietnam?* has a new character, D.J., the youthful son of the businessman-hunter; D.J. may find a way to live differently and thus offer a chance for redemption and renewal.

In his poem "Sunday Morning," Wallace Stevens states the doctrine of the new generation, the doctrine of present happiness. The lady of the poem wonders if her Sunday coffee and oranges are enough, or whether she should seek some paradise, some "imperishable bliss." The speaker of the poem answers:

> Divinity must live within herself:
> Passions of rain, or moods in falling snow;
> Grievings in loneliness, or unsubdued
> Elations when the forest blooms; gusty
> Emotions on wet roads on autumn nights;
> All pleasures and all pains, remembering
> The bough of summer and the winter branch.

For, the speaker says, there is no paradise, no heaven of the future, no politics, no doctrine, no ideology, no structure, no system of government, which can offer the happiness and meaning that can be found only in one thing: life itself.

Like her remembrance of awakened birds,
Or her desire for June and evening, tipped
By the consummation of the swallow's wings.

If Stevens' voice is pensive and elegiac it is because he
was a man ahead of his time, a man alone. His vision
is the vision of today.

And so the way to destroy the power of the Corporate State is to live differently now. The plan, the program, the grand strategy, is this: resist the State, when
you must; avoid it, when you can; but listen to music,
dance, seek out nature, laugh, be happy, be beautiful,
help others whenever you can, work for them as best
you can, take them in, the old and the bitter as well as
the young, live fully in each moment, love and cherish
each other, love and cherish yourselves, stay together.

Dawn to dawn a lifetime
The birds sing and day's begun
The heavens shine from dawn to dusk
With golden rays of sun.
People on their way
Beginning a brand new day
All over hearing people say,
"It's a beautiful day today."

People in the streets
Rushing everywhere,
Moving fast, and now I know
They've got to get somewhere.
People on their way
Beginning a brand new day.
All over hearing people say,
"It's a beautiful day today."

Bob Mosley (Moby Grape)

Perhaps there are bad times ahead. Change will follow an up-and-down course. There may be periods of

apathy, cynicism and despair, episodes of violent repression, times when hope is difficult to maintain. Perhaps it will be necessary to seek shelter, to avoid
unnecessary exposure, to struggle, to form small communes and communities away from the worst pressures, or to take jobs within the Establishment and try
to preserve one's freedom nevertheless. But the whole
Corporate State rests upon nothing but consciousness.
When consciousness changes, its soldiers will refuse to
fight, its police will rebel, its bureaucrats will stop
their work, its jailers will open the bars. Nothing can
stop the power of consciousness.

To the realists, the liberals and radicals and activists
who are looking for a program and a plan, we say: this
is the program and the plan. When enough people
have decided to live differently, the political results
will follow naturally and easily, and the old political
forms will simply be swept away like immovable logs
when the river rises. And so, although we seem to be
living in the worst of times, we can already visualize
the unfolding of the revolution. The new consciousness
will bloom, and whatever it gives life to, a university, a
public school, a factory, a city, and finally the courts,
the Congress and the Presidency, will become respon-
sive to human needs.

To those who would like to believe in the possibility
of change, but are held back by fear of the repressive,
all-powerful State, we say: the State's own instruments
are human, and they are turning against it. Report
after report from Vietnam shows that G.I.'s, sent out
to search and destroy those whom the State considers
"enemies," simply seek the safety of some foliage and
peacefully smoke marijuana, rap, and sleep. Fred
Gardner writes (*The New York Times,* November 21,

1970): "President Nixon may claim credit for phasing down the war; Congress may debate a timetable for pulling out; but the fact is that rank-and-file G.I.'s are ending the fighting on their own."

There is a great discovery awaiting those who choose a new set of values—a discovery comparable to the revelation that the Wizard of Oz was just a humbug. The discovery is simply this: there is nobody whatever on the other side. Nobody wants inadequate housing and medical care—only the machine. Nobody wants war except the machine. And even businessmen, once liberated, would like to roll in the grass and lie in the sun. There is no need, then, to fight any group of people in America. They are all fellow sufferers. There is no reason to fight the machine. It can be made the servant of man. Consciousness III can make a new society.

XII

THE GREENING OF AMERICA

Today we are witnesses to a great moment in history: a turn from the pessimism that has closed in on modern industrial society; the rebirth of a future; the rebirth of people in a sterile land. If that process had to be summed up in a single word, that word would be freedom. Freedom from outmoded economic and political doctrines, freedom from oppressive institutions, freedom from the San Quentin consciousness by which we lock the doors of our minds. Freedom that is expressed in every metaphor of the new consciousness, long hair, a new way of walking, the ocean and the open road. But freedom is incredibly complex in a complex society. And our discussion of Consciousness

III has not yet approached the most important questions concerning it. How permanent is it? Where does it fit into the larger perspective of history and philosophy? Can its way of life actually do the necessary work of the world? What ideas does it have for a new social order?

We are only beginning to realize the incredible vastness of the changes that are coming. Most views of what is happening are woefully inadequate. Liberals can only imagine another stage of reform, a rearranging of priorities, a revitalization of the bill of rights. Many blacks, and many spokesmen for the poor, cannot see much beyond the issues of social justice and the end of domination by one culture. The New Left is still playing out the battle against capitalism and imperialism. Even Marcuse speaks primarily in terms of an end to surplus repression and a liberation of the instincts. But if we think of all that is now challenged —the nature of education, the very validity of institutionalism and the legal system, the nature and purposes of work, the course of man's dealing with environment, the relationship of self to technology and society—we can see that the present transformation goes beyond anything in modern history. Beside it, a mere revolution, such as the French or the Russian, seems inconsequential—a shift in the base of power. Moreover, almost none of the views we have mentioned recognizes the crucial importance of *choosing a new life-style*. This has been passed over as if it were no more than an indulgent product of affluence, a more tolerant form of "administered happiness." But choice of a life style is not peripheral, it is the heart of the new awakening. What is coming is nothing less than a new way of life and a new man—a man with renewed energies and imagination—a man who is part of the living world.

To begin to locate Consciousness III in a proper perspective, we must review our history. What happened to the American people? In a word, powerlessness. We lost the ability to control our lives or our society because we had placed ourselves excessively under the domination of the market and technology. Finally we totally abandoned ourselves to the Corporate State, cutting ourselves off from our sources and our consciousness to such an extent that we were threatened with destruction as a species. This history makes clear that the great and urgent need of these times is transcendence. To survive, to regain power over our own lives, we must transcend the machine. We must recapture the ultimate sovereign right to choose values for ourselves. Many philosophers and poets over the last century have called for a return to non-machine values. But by seeming to preach a regression to the past they have caused us to miss the real point. Reality is not served by trying to ignore the machine. Our history shows that what we must do is assert domination over the machine, to guide it so that it works for the values of our choice. The last two hundred years have fundamentally and irrevocably altered the terms of man's existence. The price of survival is an appropriate consciousness and social order to go along with the revolution of science and technology that has already occurred. The chaos we are now experiencing is the inevitable and predictable consequence of our failure to rise to this necessity. Consciousness I and Consciousness II have proven inadequate to guide our society any longer. What is called for is a higher logic and a higher reason. The creation of a new consciousness is the most urgent of America's real needs.

Once we recognize this need, we can see what is evolving in the form we have called Consciousness III. Consciousness III is an attempt to gain transcendence. This becomes apparent when we compare Consciousness III to Consciousness I and II. I and II are more alike than they are different. They both represent the underlying form of consciousness appropriate to the age of industrial development and the market economy, beginning in the eighteenth century. Both subordinate man's nature to his role in the economic system; Consciousness I on the basis of economic individualism, II on the basis of participation in organization. Both approve the domination of environment by technology. Both subordinate man to the state, Consciousness I by the theory of the unseen hand, II by the doctrine of the public interest. Both see man as basically antagonistic to his fellow man; neither has any theory of a human community except in terms of consent to law, government, and force. Both deny the individual's responsibility for the actions of society. Both define man's existence in material terms, and define progress similarly. Both define thought in terms of the premises of science. Consciousness II differs from I mainly in that II is adjusted to the realities of a larger scale of organization, economic planning, and a greater degree of political administration.

The new consciousness is utterly different. It seeks restoration of the non-material elements of man's existence, the elements like the natural environment and the spiritual that were passed by in the rush of material development. It seeks to transcend science and technology, to restore them to their proper place as tools of man rather than as the determinants of man's existence. It is by no means anti-technological, it does not want to break machines, but it does not want machines to run men. It makes the wholly rational assertion that machines should do the bidding of man, of man who knows and respects his own nature and the natural order of which he is a part. The new consciousness seeks new ways to live in light of what technology has made both possible and desirable. Since machines can produce enough food and shelter for all, why should not man end the antagonism derived from scarcity and base his society on love for his fellow man? If machines can take care of our material wants, why should not man develop the aesthetic and spiritual side of his nature? Prophets and philosophers have proposed these ways of life before, but only today's technology has made them possible. *Consciousness III could only have come into existence given today's technology. And only Consciousness III can make possible the continued survival of man as a species in this age of technology.*

Each of the characteristics of Consciousness III that we have described is a specific illustration of an underlying logic. The logic is obscure if we do not see the assumptions upon which it is based, and these assumptions are rarely articulated. But when the assumptions are recognized the seemingly irrational disappears and a realistic logic appears instead. Reasoning that starts from self is necessary because the prior consciousness forgot self in an obsessive fixation upon organizations and the state. The self and its sources in nature are real; machines alone cannot create real values. The preservation of the self against the state is not "antisocial," it is of great and vital importance to the human community. Protection of nature and man from the machine is logical because of the power of the machine to dominate nature. (It is no surprise to the new generation that we can land on the moon.) A personal moral code that transcends law is necessary where law has ceased to express a balanced set of values. A flexible and personal approach to career is necessary because technology itself is rapidly changing and because technology will dictate to man unless he preserves the power to choose his own work. Participatory democracy is necessary because the comprehensive planning that technology requires is incapable of taking into account all significant factors unless many people participate in the process. A powerful new music is necessary to help lift people's minds out of the seductive logic of machinery so that they can have vision beyond the machine and thus escape its domination. Adaptable clothes are necessary because man's rigid compartmentalization into roles has prevented him from enjoying the freedom that technology makes possible. It is perfectly possible to work in an office for a few hours and then ride out on the road on a motorcycle, but formal clothes deny the individual's adaptability. Authority and hierarchy are rejected because they represent the subjection of human values to the requirements of organization. An intense feeling of community is necessary because technology has rendered all men interdependent. Competition, rivalry or personal flights of ego and power have become socially destructive. Given an abundance of material goods, the possibilities of a human community are finally made real, for it is now possible to believe in the goodness of man.

In light of what we have said, we can now see the

true significance of the central fact about Consciousness III—its assertion of the power to *choose* a way of life. The people who came to this country chose a lifestyle; it was for that freedom of choice that they left their native countries. But when the machine took over, men lost the power of choice, and their lives were molded to fit the domination of the machine. The machine slavery, extending upward to the white collar and professional ranks, became the key reality of twentieth-century existence. The power of choice, the power to transcend, is exactly what has been missing in America for so long. That is why a new life-style is capable of dismantling the Corporate State, when both liberal reform and radical tactics are powerless. The elements of that life may vary and change; the supreme act is the act of choice. For the choice of a life-style is an act of transcendence of the machine, an act of independence, a declaration of independence. We are entering a new age of man.

In preindustrial times, man's life was integrated with his community and with nature. God dwelt in each man, in growing things and in the sky. Communal life was governed by tribal authority and by tradition. Existence was harsh, dull, limited, and virtually static from generation to generation. Religion and ethics expressed the realities man knew.

The industrial age represented man's enormously successful attempt to raise his level of existence by dominating life through reason and science. Man drove himself to ever higher achievements by isolating each individual and forcing him into the competitive struggle. Work and culture were uprooted from the communal setting and required to serve the industrial machine. Life was regulated by a political system designed to control and regulate man's war against his fellow man. Economic power was heavily concentrated, although Marx and others began a movement toward equality and social ownership of the means of production. Religion, divorced from the realities of life, offered an ethical system to minimize the harm of the competitive and functional basis of existence, but without actually challenging that basis. Man harnessed himself to the machine.

Beyond the industrial era lies a new age of man. The essence of that age must be the end of the subjugation of man, the end of his subordination to the machine, and the beginning of the subjugation of the machine—the use of technology to create a still higher level of life, but one based upon values beyond the machine. The politics of controlling man become unimportant, the politics of controlling machines and organizations become the new concern of government. Economic equality and social ownership of the means of production are assumed, but they are now only a means to an end beyond. Man's religion and ethics will once again express the true realities of his way of life: solidarity with his fellow man, a genuine community representing a balanced moral-aesthetic order, and a continuing expansion of man's inner capacities.

Surely this new age is not a repudiation of, but a fulfillment of, the American dream. What were the machines for, unless to give man a new freedom to choose how he would live? What were they for, unless to expand individual freedom, and the range of human possibility? What is the central idea of America, unless each man's ability to create his own life? The dream was deferred for many generations in order to create a technology that could raise life to a higher level. It need be, it can be, delayed no longer.

What Consciousness III represents, in the long range terms of human evolution, is the beginning of the development of new capacities in man—capacities essential to living in the present age. The historical, organic nature of the change is felt by many people. David Crosby, the rock musician, in an interview in *Rolling Stone* (July 23, 1970), described Graham Nash, a friend and co-musician, as "one of the most highly evolved people on the planet." Consciousness III is developing, in place of the childish immaturity of so many American adults, a new independence and personal responsibility. It is seeking to replace the infantile and destructive self-seeking that we laud as "competition" by a new capacity for working and living together. It is creating a system of ethics—ecological and human—to accompany the amoral know-how of science. There have been many warnings that man must change himself or be annihilated by his own technology, but most of these warnings conclude by calling for a return to the moral simplicities of an earlier day. Consciousness III says that man cannot turn back, he must grow. In Consciousness III we can see, not a superficial moralistic improvement, but a growth of understanding, sensibility and the capacity for love that for the first time offers hope that man will be able to control and turn to good uses the machines he has built.

If we are correct so far, then we can respond to the question of whether Consciousness III is practical and realistic, whether its way of life can really work. That question should, in the first instance, be addressed to our present way of life. It is our present society that does not work. It is the machine-dominated world that represents a fantastic distortion of reality. In seeing our present society without the distortions of false consciousness, in declaring that the choice of values is our greatest need, Consciousness III is more realistic than anything we have known in America for a century. Nor is it bent upon destroying anything that is realistically essential to our life. It does not propose to abolish work, or excellence, it proposes to abolish irrational and involuntary servitude. It does not propose to abolish law, organization, or government, it asks instead that they serve rational, human ends. Consciousness III is neither lazy, defenseless, nor incompetent. It does not reject technique, it rejects domination by technique. Consciousness III is practical in the most profound sense, because the historic time for man's transcendence over the machine has come.

What social order does Consciousness III propose? To ask this question is to fail to see the basic thing that is wrong with the Corporate State. The great error of our times has been the belief in structural or institutional solutions. The enemy is within each of us; so long as that is true, one structure is as bad as another. Consciousness I and II believed that, to design or describe a society adequately, it was only necessary to refer to its structures and institutions. Consciousness III says, for the present, *all that is necessary to describe the new society is to describe a new way of life*. When we have outlined a different way of life, we have said all that we can meaningfully say about the future. This is not avoiding the hard questions. The hard questions—if by that is meant political and economic organization—are insignificant, even irrelevant. Once a new way of life is established, structural and institutional questions may again become worthy of discussion. The form of society will once again influence how men live. But existing forms have become so irrational and irrelevant that all that is needed to begin a new way of life can happen without reference to them. We repeat: to describe a new way of life is to describe fully the society that is coming. For the locus of that society is not in politics or economics, but in how and for what ends we live.

If this is true, then it is also true that a new way of life does not have to wait for a new world, it can be built out of the elements now available. Pop art illustrates this process. The artifacts of modern life, such as neon signs, juke boxes, Campbell's Soup cans, present dominating images of sterility, forming man's life in a sterile pattern. But the pop artist regains power over his environment by using these elements in his own creations, thereby taking responsibility for their ultimate form. He has selected and chosen what he wants, and thereby transcended the artifacts. Likewise the new music chooses from many elements of earlier music, and from many forms of technology, to produce the form it wants.

Tom Wolfe recognized this process in his preface to *The Kandy-Kolored Tangerine-Flake Streamline Baby* (1965). He was writing about subcultures such as stock car racing or surfing. He came to see that affluence had made it possible for various groups to "build monuments" to their own life-styles. By implication, this meant that various groups were getting to a position where they could choose a way of life. The life-styles they chose, which Wolfe described, were not very meaningful, and they were still closely tied to the machine. But the element of creativity, of artistry, was unmistakably there. Using such artifacts of the Corporate State as the 1955 Chevrolet, the hamburger drive-in, the technology of neon, groups were able to create something of their own. To do this with a job, to do it with an institution, to do it under all the pressure and burdens of the present society will take much more. It will require imagination, strategy, cunning. But it will be the cunning of art, for it is art when we make something of our own out of the elements of the existing world. It only requires that we not lose sight of what we are doing: creating a way of life that is better for human beings.

The first major theme of this new way of life must be education—education not in the limited sense of training in school, but in its largest and most humanistic meaning. The central American problem might be defined as a failure of education. We have vastly underestimated the amount of education and consciousness that is required to meet the demands of organization and technology. Most of our "education" has taught us how to *operate* the technology; how to function as a human component of an organization. What we need is education that will enable us to make use of technology, control it and give it direction, cause it to serve values which we have chosen.

We have already shown, in discussing the industrialization of America and the New Deal, that Americans never faced the question of how much education and understanding would be necessary if mass democracy were really to be effective in a technological society. Even before technology, de Tocqueville and others expressed well justified skepticism about self-government by poorly educated masses. The New Deal tried to rely on experts and specialists, but quite aside from their own failings, they could not govern an electorate that did not understand. Our failure in democracy has now been surpassed by our failure in control of the things we have made, and our even greater failure to realize the affirmative possibilities of technology. We know how to drive a car, but we do not know how to keep cars from destroying our environment, or how to use a car to make cities and countryside more beautiful and more of a community, and to make man's life more creative and liberated. Henry James was acutely aware of this incapacity; he believed that time, tradition, and sensibility were needed to "civilize" manufactured innovation. We can give his ideas a contemporary meaning by saying that today education and consciousness are needed to humanize all the new forms of work, things, and experiences that are thrust upon us.

We are prone to think of the capacity to make affirmative use of innovations as a moral quality, an aspect of "character." A man who drives to the country for a picnic, drowns out the sounds of nature with a transistor radio, and leaves beer cans strewn around when he departs is said to lack "character." This is the same fallacy of the human heart that has made us see so many issues of government and technology as moral questions. Capacity to appreciate nature, to benefit from it, and to be enhanced by it is a matter of education. The beauty and fascination of nature is not available to the uneducated eye, any more than the beauty of painting or poetry. But it is not just a question of specific education, it is a question of a more general consciousness, a readiness to receive new experiences in a certain way.

We have also greatly underestimated the amount

and kind of education needed to make any given individual able to adapt to change. The individual whose education stops at eighteen or twenty-one is a pathetic sight in our society. Increasingly he is obsolete in his work; he is kept on because of his long service, and would be unable to find a new job if he lost his existing one. He is unable to understand his society, unable to vote in a responsible way, unable to communicate with his own children, or to understand their culture. He is allowed to become human wreckage, because his mind stopped growing while all the elements around him moved on ahead.

Our present ideas of education are absurdly narrow and primitive for the kinds of tasks men face; education now is little more than training for the industrial army. What is needed is just the opposite of what we now have. A person should question what he is told and what he reads. He should demand the basis upon which experts or authorities have reached a conclusion. He should doubt his own teachers. He should believe that his own subjective feelings are of value. He should make connections and see relationships where the attempt has been made to keep them separate. He should appreciate the diversity of things and ideas rather than be told that one particular way is the "right" way. He should be exposed and re-exposed to as wide a variety of experience and contrasts as possible. Above all, he should learn to search for and develop his own potential, his own individuality, his own uniqueness. That is what the word "educate" literally means. What we urgently need is not training but education, not indoctrination but the expansion of each individual—a process continuing throughout life; in a word, education for consciousness.

Such education cannot stop at the age of twenty-one. We now "educate" most of our people through high school, a minority through college, and virtually nobody thereafter. When a difficult choice comes along, such as whether the noise of the SST is worth its additional speed in crossing the country, the thinking of most of the population over thirty turns out to have frozen as of the time their education ceased, so that they think that our greatest need is "advances" in technology. Thus, even if "education" itself were adequate, a majority of the people would no longer be learning or thinking. Dr. Kenneth Keniston has said that youth is emerging as a new and separate stage of life—a time for gaining experience and learning, for acquiring consciousness, we might say. Dr. Keniston seems to be correct in this, but the stage of life that he calls "youth" is better described as the stage of education. "Youth" in this sense must now of necessity continue all through life.

In the light of these needs, we can place much of the culture and attitudes of the new generation in perspective; we can see that the new generation has been attempting to develop its own form of education along the lines we have described. Much of what seems to outsiders to be aimless or self-indulgent turns out, when reexamined, to fit precisely the true requirements for education today. Activities which seem irrational all make perfect sense as part of a higher reason; they are good for the individual and good for society.

The new generation insists upon being open to all experience. It will experiment with anything, even though the new "trip" does not fit into any preconceived notion of the individual's personality. If a Consciousness II person, old or young, is asked whether he wants to see a far-out film, try a new drug, or spend a week living in a nature-food commune, he feels uncomfortable and refuses; the experiment is out of keeping with his already established character. The new consciousness is always flexible, curious, and ready to add something new to his "character." At the same time, the new generation constantly tries to break away from the older, established forms which, in a changing society, must forever be obsolete. Authority, schedules, time, accepted customs, are all forms which must be questioned. Accepted patterns of thought must be broken; what is considered "rational thought" must be opposed by "nonrational thought"— drug-thought, mysticism, impulses. Of course the latter kinds of thought are not really "nonrational" at all; they merely introduce new elements into the sterile, rigid, outworn "rationality" that prevails today.

Young people today insist upon prolonging the period of youth, education, and growth. They stay uncommitted; they refuse to decide on a formal career, they do not give themselves fixed future goals to pursue. Their emphasis on the present makes possible an openness toward the future; the person who focusses on the future freezes that future in its present image. Personal relationships are entered into without commitment to the future; a marriage legally binding for the life of the couple is inconsistent with the likelihood of growth and change; if the couple grows naturally together that is fine, but change, not an unchanging love, is the rule of life.

Seeking an education for an unknowable future, the new generation rejects the idea that a school or college is the only possible institution to supply it.

The new consciousness uses many other "institutions" for its education. It founds "free schools" as alternatives to high schools or colleges. It seeks job-experiences such as work in a ghetto school, or migrant labor, or the Peace Corps. It takes part in political activism and radical politics with education in mind. It uses underground newspapers, work in theatre or film, summers in the wilderness, or a rock festival as institutions of education. Just as an earlier school of hard knocks gave the frontiersman his practicality and adaptability, so today's efforts to transcend the terms of society make possible an open consciousness for a frontier far more unknown than that of the pioneers.

In a very real sense, it is misleading to give a name to the new consciousness, such as "Consciousness III," for almost by definition the new consciousness will always be growing and changing. If it is static, it will suffer the same obsolescence as Consciousness I and II, and even more speedily. So we must look forward to Consciousness IV, V, VI, and so forth; or if we say that change is inherent in the definition of III then new degrees of Consciousness III. Education forms the avenue for this constant and life-giving change.

A fundamental object of the education we have described is transcendence, or personal liberation. It is a liberation that is both personal and communal, an escape from the limits fixed by custom and society, in pursuit of something better and higher. It is epitomized in the concept of "choosing a life-style"; the idea that an individual need not accept the pattern that society has formed for him, but may make his own choice. It is seen visually in the growth of the student-gypsy world, a new geography of hitchhikers, knapsacks, sleeping bags, and the open road: not a summer vacation or a journey from one fixed point to another, but a new sense of existence in the immediate present, without fixed points. It can be heard in the song from the rock opera "Tommy" by the Who, "I'm Free."

To talk about transcendence in a less metaphorical way, we might consider the thinking behind the creation of People's Park in Berkeley. There was a large, muddy lot near the campus in Berkeley. It was the property of the University of California, which expected to make use of it for university purposes in due time. But a group of people, "street people" and students, thought it should be used for a park. They saw it in terms of the human and ecological situation of the city. They utterly failed or refused to see it in legal terms, as "private property." In placing human needs and ecology (as they saw them) ahead of "law," they proposed nothing less than a new social order. They proposed a society in which aesthetics, ecology, and human requirements would be paramount, and in which decisions concerning these matters would be made not by the persons designated by law in our society, but by self-constituted local groups whose legitimacy came only from their proximity and concern. To call this "anarchy" is to miss the point. It was not anarchy but a wholly different form of society, with different priorities, different sources of authority, a different process of decision-making. Perhaps the new form was not a viable or desirable one. But by their actions, the makers of People's Park hoped to further our liberation from the current forms of society, so that we might be free to choose among new forms of social order, just as individuals might be free to choose among life-styles. Social forms, the creators of People's

Park might say, are not absolutes, they are mere machinery. Like any other machinery, it cannot supply man with a view of what life should be. It cannot take from him the responsibility for answering that question. Reason does not begin or end with any form of government. Liberation means freedom to search for the highest form of man's existence.

The creative, imaginative, life-giving power of transcendence can be seen whenever Consciousness III people are found. They transform a city rooftop in Berkeley into a theatre for watching the sunset and the lighting of the darkened city. They transform the impersonal toll booth plazas of the Massachusetts Turnpike and the New York Thruway into something interesting, comical, and filled with possibilities for meeting new people. They make the sidewalk into a place for sitting, and the night a time for staying up. They place a sculpture of a giant lipstick in the middle of a pompous plaza, and bring sterility back to life. They are the genii of change and transmutation, and thus they fulfill the ultimate biological need to change, to adapt, to grow, to die, and to be reborn.

The concept of education we have used up to now, although far broader than formal "education," is still not adequate to our meaning. For we are really speaking of the continuing growth of awareness and consciousness, the search for new dimensions of experience. It is this undertaking that Ken Kesey pursued as Tom Wolfe describes it in *The Electric Kool-Aid Acid Test*—not a frolic, but a purposeful undertaking using drugs, costumes, day-glo paint, a cross-country trip in a psychedelic bus, the founding of a Pranksters' community in California, a series of "fantasies" played out with the Hell's Angels, the Unitarians, the Acid Tests, and finally the Acid Test graduation—an undertaking that represented a serious search for awareness and new knowledge. It is the same search for awareness that might make one drive 100 miles and then turn around and come home, or travel to the beach or mountains, or look upon any experience—a laundromat on Telegraph Avenue in Berkeley, a lunch at a businessman's seafood restaurant in downtown San Francisco, a lawyer's conference in Washington, D.C., a visit to an ice cream parlor in Seattle—as a "trip" to some new dimension. The attitude of Kesey, like that of Henry James or Wallace Stevens, placed a supreme value on the development of consciousness, sensitivity, experience, knowledge. No trouble, no expense, no disruption, no uprooting, could stand in the way of the continuing growth of one's mind.

For it is of the essence of this search for awareness that it must provide the guidance for how to live in our society. Is Consciousness III unthinking and spontaneous? Sometimes it appears so, but in a deeper sense it knows that living in this world requires the ultimate in strategy and highest in art, and so it thinks and knows before it acts. Consciousness III searches itself before it undertakes work or play, and it constantly reevaluates what it is doing; it lives in a never ending state of tentativeness and uprooting. Consider the sequence of events in Ken Kesey's life. Kesey first diagnosed the world and planned a strategy for it in his novels, *One Flew Over the Cuckoo's Nest* and *Sometimes a Great Notion*. It was not until several years later that he tried actually to live the Randall McMurphy role that he had designed. This is living not by unconsciousness, but by consciousness. If life itself, work, culture, community, are to be lived as something creative, as a work of art, the power to do this must be found in a never ending activity of education.

If we turn from education to a second major theme, the nature of work, we can see a similar movement toward a higher rationality. Contrary to what many people think, the new generation does not regard work as an evil. What they reject is the present employment relationship. They refuse to be subject to arbitrary authority over their work; they will not be servile; they will not be a "nigger" while on the job. They refuse to play a role while at work that forces them into a different personality than is actually theirs. They deny the relationship that society creates between work and status, a relationship that arbitrarily categorizes some jobs as low, some as high, in a scale of status. They insist upon responsibility for what they do and what they produce, and are unwilling to be the unthinking servants of "the public interest" or some institution. Above all, they refuse to be driven and disciplined, imprisoned and impoverished by work; they will not be robot-tenders of the machine, but human beings whose work is always subordinate to this humanity. Up to now, the new consciousness has been concentrated in youth, and new patterns of work have not yet been formed; we can, however, try to suggest how these patterns might develop.

Most Consciousness III people are now at the stage of liberation. They are trying to throw off society's demand for alienated labor. Therefore many Consciousness III people seem, to others and to themselves, to be in a state of uncertainty and drift, in which they have no concept of serious work, no standards of craftsmanship and excellence, no ability to develop a high degree of skill and discipline, no promise of being able to do the work that a complex society will need. They seem to yearn only for a simple and undemanding life; they do not seem willing or able to do such things as design a transportation system, do medical research, or study the biology of the oceans. But this is only a transitional stage.

When the Consciousness III person has achieved liberation from alienated labor he will want and need to function. And he will want to function in a manner that engages his full capacities in a socially meaningful way. Work and function are basic to man. They fulfill him, they establish his identity, they give him his place in the human community. Life without function is the nightmare of Kurt Vonnegut's *Player Piano*, not the dream of a more humanistic existence. The next stage after liberation from labor must be "getting into something," and it is already visible on today's campuses.

What is beginning to evolve is the concept of a "noncareer" or "vocation." The old way of choosing a career was to find what one was "best fitted for." That is, the individual reviewed the list of all the functions that society wanted filled and was prepared to pay for, then tested his own abilities, and finally fitted the two together as best he could. Finding a noncareer requires a better knowledge of self to start off with; a decision, necessarily tentative, about what one would find most satisfying and fulfilling. This decision is not, of course, made with total indifference to the needs of the community, for one vital aspect of satisfaction is the sense of helping other people. But the starting point is the question of what would affirm the self, and this offers its own answer to how the individual can best contribute to his fellow men.

With a vocation discovered, the concept of a non-career requires that the individual ignore the question of whether or not his choice is one that has been defined and accepted by society; whether it represents an established occupation. Even if it does, the established outline of that occupation will probably be too rigid and general to suit a personal vocation. So the individual must define his own career and his own terms. He must continually remake his definition as he learns more about himself and about his world. That does not mean, however, that a personal definition will not include careful training for competence and excellence. Indeed, the personal standard of excellence should be far higher when a person chooses his own work than when he passively follows a route that society has defined.

It is then necessary to find ways and means to pursue this noncareer within the existing society. Hopefully society will grow ever more flexible, more willing to support individual vocations, and more receptive to work individually defined. But the Consciousness III person cannot wait for society to reform. He must create his noncareer out of whatever elements are available, even the oppressive structures of today. A higher consciousness concerning one's work provides unexpected freedom. The worst of today's institutions are not so inflexible as they appear if the individual is determined to make his own vocation.

The first step in the transformation of work we might call de-institutionalization. If a person is working within an institution but does not share the institution's goals, and does not desire to rise in the hierarchy, if his interest is not in the affairs of the institution itself but in his own work, he unexpectedly has a great deal of freedom. Many of the controls that an institution has over its employees derive from the individual's desire to please and to get ahead, not from precise supervision. For example, a high school teacher, despite all the imposed curricular requirements, reports, and other rigidities of the system, cannot be prevented from opening the minds of his students if he wants to. If he is required to use a certain textbook, he can nevertheless raise questions about its accuracy. If he is required to teach about the evils of communism, he can nevertheless point to the parallels between socialist bureaucracy and forms of bureaucracy that are closer at hand. The individual who is free of the conventional goals can make an amazing amount of independence for himself within any organization, simply because organizations are so cumbersome, inefficient, and unable to meet the demands upon them. They are confounded by anyone who takes initiatives. In any organization, the advantage is all with whoever acts, because the means for stopping action are ill-developed. The organization, as we have said before, "has no ideas" and while changing the organization itself is very difficult, doing something new within the organization is certainly possible so long as one does not expect rewards such as promotion or official approval. Thus it becomes possible to work for the betterment or transformation of society through almost any job, even though the job is located right within the Establishment.

The second step we can call de-alienation: making the work meaningful and satisfying to the worker himself. Even if work genuinely helps others and thus serves a real social purpose, it will still be alienating to the worker if it does not add to his development and represent a satisfying expression of his abilities. A job running an elevator in the world's finest hospital, or in a building where a new and better society is being planned, is still repetitive, mechanical, and destructive of the worker's personality. Can only the creative artist find happiness in his work? Or can "ordinary" jobs take on new qualities? Consciousness can regard any job as a potential opportunity for self-expression, for play, for creativity, for the furtherance of social objectives, and it can arrange the factors in the job so that they form a means of self-expression. The nose and throat doctor can define his job as an opportunity to learn about human nature, or to learn how to help people to cope with and think about the perennial miseries of mankind. In doing this, he transcends the specialized professional task, and makes his work his own. Of all of the new things that can be done within an organization, one of the most important, and the one that the organization is least able to hinder, is a return to the true objectives of the work at hand. The high school teacher begins to make his main work not discipline, administration, indoctrination, or self-promotion, but teaching. When he does this, the alienation between him and his students starts to disappear, and so does his own alienation from his work.

On a camping trip, it is fun to wash the dishes after dinner. For an employee in a busy restaurant, it may not be so much fun. One is play, the other is not. The difference does not lie in the physical act of washing dishes. It lies in how much one can set one's own pace; how communal and social the activity is, how voluntary, how much respect or lack of respect one feels for oneself, whether one works to exhaustion, whether there are moments of leisure and distraction, whether the work is a part of one's whole personality. The question is whether one can turn the task, whatever it is, into play, art, feeling; whether one can make it a teacher and not merely a taskmaster. It is not true that all work must be "creative" to be satisfying. People who do intellectual work know how good it feels to wash a car, clean the house, paint a boat, or chop wood. They also know that the most "creative" and "intellectual" work can be drudgery if pushed too hard and too fast, if done without interruptions, if pursued to the exclusion of everything else. In *Eros and Civilization* Marcuse suggests that work of many kinds can be made an erotic experience, or a play experience.

How does work become an erotic experience? We shall not urge that this is possible for every kind of work; with Marcuse we agree that many machinelike jobs can and should be taken over by machines. But for other kinds of jobs, the first requirement would appear to be a degree of individual control over working conditions, enough so that personality is not entirely regimented. Let us consider the lawyer's day. Does he stop to read the newspaper or a magazine from time to time? Does he exchange sociable conversation with the other people who work in the office, lawyers and non-lawyers, and with his clients? Does he take an occasional walk around the block? Does he have a relaxing, non-business lunch? Does he put on an occasional classical or popular record while he is working? Does he take off his shoes? Does he relieve the eternal seriousness of his profession with moments of humor? Does he once in a while refuse to work at all, and go to sleep on the couch, or depart for woods or fields? Does he tell an occasional client to take his business elsewhere? Does he have power over the hours he works, the amount of work in a day, a month, a year? Does he express himself when he is angry or happy? Does he keep, as a good athlete does, that looseness, that essential distance from what he does, that enables one to walk in and out of an activity at will? Does he, also like a good athlete (and like Sherlock Holmes) make his work a performance for an audience, in the manner of a player on a stage? He can then find pleasure and satisfaction where alienation once reigned.

A third step might be called de-specialization. We have said enough to suggest how a particular job or occupation might become a source of satisfaction, but this still leaves us with the problem of the specialization that jobs necessarily entail, and the resulting limitation on the personality of the individual. For we assume that for most people there is more than one kind of ability, more than one field of interest, and that a man may possess both the qualities of a chef and of a musician, and perhaps of an actor as well. Despite dealienation, jobs will still take considerable training and development of skills, and thus will force limitations upon even the most independent consciousness.

The answer to this is that each person should pursue several careers, either simultaneously or successively during his life. This is not only feasible today, it is necessary and essential. It is necessary so that individuals do not become technologically obsolete, with skills that are no longer needed. Constant change in technology means that a varied and changing career is mandated for all, even if they would prefer to remain in just one occupation and just one institution. There are today many instances of individuals having more than one career, either at the same time or in sequence; indeed, large corporations sometimes make it a policy to move their men from one job to another. This is the protean man of the future, living several different lives and having a variety of work-experiences. But there is a great difference between him and the role-playing man of today whose several roles are schizophrenically separated from each other and from the self within, like masks that a player puts on and takes off at will. What consciousness must do is help the new protean man to integrate his many experiences into a whole: a single, meaningful life.

Suppose that a young man finds in himself the interests and the abilities to be a swimming coach, a physician, and a student of literature. Pursued separately, these careers may add little to each other, producing a divided individual. But leisure, continuing education, and reflection will allow a person to find a way to integrate what he does. Perhaps literature will broaden his interest in, and understanding of, his patients; perhaps it will give him a subject of conversation with his patients. Medicine will obviously be useful in coaching; coaching, by its understanding of the psychology of health and bodily achievement, will also be valuable in medicine. And should he ever try his hand at teaching medicine or literature, coaching will give him a good deal of insight into teaching. The result will be diversity and wholeness; in which the different sides of a person's life all converse with each other. This is one side of de-specialization, but there is a second aspect: sharing the specialty with others. On the earliest experimental trips of the Penn Central turbo train between New York and New Haven, the trainmen mingled with the fascinated passengers, explaining details of the trip, and the passengers took turns watching the engineer, clearly visible through a glass panel. Thus the train employees assumed a teaching relationship, a despecialization process in which they shared their specialties with others and thereby enhanced the meaning of these specialties for themselves. Every teacher can testify to this effect. And it is through teaching that relationships infused with feeling come into existence. Can ordinary, non-glamorous activities become subjects for teaching? Machinery and technology are now put out of sight but if they were exposed it would be interesting; many people would enjoy hearing about flying from a jet pilot, or being a policeman, fireman, or automobile mechanic. This is the stuff of literature, so why should it not be interesting in real life, if the barriers are once cut down that prevent people in jobs from talking to, and teaching, those they serve.

What we have said so far describes work as it approaches being a free, satisfying, independent, and educational life-activity. But in our description it still lacks a crucial dimension. One of the great complaints of Americans today is that there are no longer any man-sized jobs, no challenges, no occasions that will cause an individual to extend himself, to grow to his utmost powers. There is "nothing to do." Work can be pleasant, satisfying, and free, without making man feel that he has done anything worthwhile with his life—that he has lived greatly. And so the ultimate question concerning work is this: how can it be heroic? What does it mean to be heroic, and how can this be translated into contemporary terms?

Traditionally, heroism is valor in battle, courage in any form of struggle, perseverance in a great cause, some major contribution to humanity, or integrity and devotion to principle. Does this mean that without battles, danger, or great causes there can be no heroism? This assumption, which is commonly made today, rests on an unduly narrow understanding of the heroic life. Homer, Vergil, and Milton knew better what heroism really is. The kind of life they showed in their epics is still available today; indeed it is available far more widely than ever before. In the *Odyssey*, in the *Iliad*, and in the *Aeneid*, the essence of the epic lies in the development of the hero; his growth in experience and wisdom. If epics are stories of a quest, the quest is for adventure in the growth of self, for transformation sometimes, but always for some form of education or change. Valor and courage are elements of the heroic only if the hero gains wisdom through them. In our terms, the heroic life is a quest for consciousness.

If we can conceive of work in this fashion, then there is no need to fear that in a new society there will be no one who is competent, no one who knows how to think, no one to perform surgery, pilot a jet, or manage a factory. These jobs will be done better than they are now, because they will have meaning, and because they will be an expression of freedom instead of domination. In *Sometimes a Great Notion* Ken Kesey shows us work as it ought to be: integrated with nature and with life, satisfying and adventurous, a full expression of man's being.

The next aspect of Consciousness III philosophy concerns culture—the way in which men live. We have already made clear that the new culture will not be a return to a primitive age but will be based on existing technology. Consciousness III must create a culture that knows how and when to use technology, a culture that is not plastic or artificial but guides and uses technology in pursuit of values that are derived from human sources.

The fact that we now have inexpensive mass-produced bread does not mean one has to become a slave to it. There are pleasures, satisfactions, and relaxation in baking and eating homemade bread. The wisdom of the new generation is simply this: buy bread at the store when you want to spend your time in some way other than baking; bake your own bread when you feel the need to get back to basic things like dough and yeast. The hippie agricultural communes are not a rejection of technology, they are a choice, by people who have had too much plastic in their lives, to live close to the soil for a while. They are free to return to technology when they wish, and there is no inconsistency, any more than a man is inconsistent who uses electric heat at home but likes a log fire too. Consciousness I and II have embraced technology so eagerly that they have all but forgotten the fire.

Transcendence of technology also means a culture that rejects the substitution phenomenon we described earlier, wherein artificiality replaces the natural. Culture does not need to impoverish man, it can enhance his world. Supermarkets can provide TV dinners but they can also provide new varieties for meals that are imaginatively cooked and ceremoniously eaten. Freeze-dried foods and light, down sleeping bags can provide an enhanced pleasure for wilderness hikers who find a new freedom in lightened packs. It is the difference between adding to something we enjoy doing, and substituting another thing for it.

The difference between the false culture that goes with false consciousness and a true culture that uses technology when it sees fit is a difference that depends largely on the attitude which we have described. In discussing the Corporate State, we referred to skiing as an example of false culture. How could skiing be turned into a part of real culture? The first requirement would be that the individual choose freely to try the activity, without the pressure of salesmanship, social prestige, and image-fulfilling. He would choose skiing the way a person today chooses snowshoeing; from an inner affinity. Having chosen to try skiing, he would then set about "making it his own." There are many ways of doing this, and he would of course not try all of them. He might begin by learning the technique of skiing, including the needed physical conditioning. Unlike today's lessons, where the object is "instant" skill, he would learn slowly enough and well enough to develop a personal style, a way of skiing that expressed his own self and abilities.

Perhaps he might become interested in the history of skiing; its origins and the way in which people first used skiing as part of their own culture and the needs of a natural setting. He might be interested in the way skiing has played a part in travel and exploration, in hunting, in mountaineering. Then there would be the history of competitive skiing, with the achievements and personalities of the past, with all their excitement. The growth of skiing in the United States would be yet another part of that history.

The skier is to some extent dependent upon weather, and he might develop his knowledge of, and consciousness of, weather. He could learn about winds, air masses, fronts, the inner workings of storms, and while he was out skiing he could learn to observe these processes, to read the signs for himself, to watch the constant changes hour by hour as only a person who is outdoors all day can. At the same time, he might learn to cope with and appreciate skiing in all sorts of different weather conditions. The skier who waits for the "right" weather is a consumer of weather; the skier should find how to make each kind of weather an additional experience.

Then there is the study of nature in winter, an infinitely fascinating world that is uniquely on display to the skier. There are animal signs, there are all the shapes and patterns of snow and ice, there are the almost invisible seasonal life patterns in trees and vegetation. The study of natural history easily merges into an artistic appreciation of the aesthetics of winter, its colors, shades, smells, and feelings. And today's skier has the privilege of intimacy with mountains in winter, a privilege to know them at their grandest and most splendid.

Geography and travel are another aspect of skiing. The skier goes to many parts of the world. In each he can take an interest in all the things, from food to architecture, that the traveler sees. But the skier's geography is a special one, for he particularly sees small, northern, rural places, winter ways of life in many parts of the world. Skiing ends at dusk, and the hours afterwards are partly for enjoying all that is unique about some corner of the world only visited on these special occasions.

We have said all of this without even mentioning other people and their role in skiing. Clearly skiing affords opportunities for a companionship that is unlike any other, based on the unique combination of place, weather, physical exertion, and a variety of experiences possible to each skier, which can be shared, sometimes during the day, sometimes afterwards. Like surfing companionship, and camping companionship, skiing friendship can be a nonverbal thing in a world that is terribly limited to verbal communication. Out of skiing there might also be formed groupings of people unlike the groupings that could exist in any other setting.

These are some of the ways in which an activity which is now an example of false culture and the consumer ethic might take on genuine meaning. There would be less in the way of production and sales, for there would be a greater proportion of human activity to purchase of commodities; a slow building-up of relationships between things and people, such as the relationship between a hiker and his old and comfortable boots. Fewer sales, but more use. Man must learn to use each part of the technology that he comes in contact with, and this process is far slower, more difficult, and more challenging than the hucksters of today's technology would have us believe. All of us know that buying a pair of boots is easy, but developing a relationship with them takes pain, patience, skill, thought, and knowledge, plus a lot of time and care. But how many of us have any idea of what would be involved in developing the same relationship to jet travel? The experience we all now have when we travel by jet is false culture, a machine-made experience that does violence to the traveler in every way. What would we have to develop in the way of skills and habits, experience and information, to make something of our own out of a jet trip? The drive to the airport, the uncertain time waiting at the airport, the problems of baggage and airport restaurants, the proper reading material, conversation in airplanes, understanding the geography of the earth from 35,000 feet—these are some of the skills which even the most frequent travelers do not possess.

Many people in our society deplore its neon culture. But in truth the possibilities for a real culture are greater today than they have ever been before. There are so many more materials to work with. Music has a whole electronic dimension. Art has so many new media, including motion pictures, light, metal, steel, and moving sculptures. The old art of cooking can benefit from the greatest variety of ingredients ever known, and the heritage of many nations to choose from. Motorcycles, all-night restaurants, supermarkets, swimming pools, skin diving sets, can be made a part of a real culture if we have the time and knowledge to do it, and just as long as we realize the high proportion of thought which we must add to the inanimate product. Is a neon-lit, glass-enclosed, all-night restaurant a hideous example of false culture? It can be something else. It can be a haven for nocturnal writers and nocturnal walkers, a setting for conversations, a place to think and observe, a place where night-consciousness is welcomed and given a chance to grow and flourish. The art to be taught by the new generation is how to use and transcend that machine. To travel at rush hour, fight crowds in restaurants and theatres, suffer terrible anxieties when a plane or train is late, is to live by the machine's standards. But if one is free of too much machine organization, one can travel at off hours, allow some extra time for planes and trains to be late, eat in restaurants at 3:00 P.M., and go to motels only when one wants a super-laundromat—clean sheets, clean towels, gleaming bathrooms, air conditioning, and mindless entertainment on television. After a day on the road, an overnight hike in the woods, too many museums, or even too much intellectual labor, stopping at a super-laundromat can be good for body and spirit.

One of the most important means employed by the new generation in seeking to transcend technology is to pay attention to the great nonmachine elements that are always with us—to respect and obey the body, to pay heed to the instincts, to obey the rhythms and music of nature, to be guided by the irrational, by folklore, and the spiritual, and by the imagination. That is one reason that young people today seek out "sources" such as the sea or the forest; they understand the vital need to keep in touch with sources that are close to man's own nature. A person who harkens to these voices some of the time will be able to use the machine or not as he chooses; he can, when his body tells him, turn off the telephone and just stay in bed.

A truly successful culture must be one in which education, work, and living are integrated. A man's recreations should be part of his work, and vice versa, as it was before the days of industrialism, just as art and work were not separated in the making of a spear, a canoe, or a stained-glass window. For a teacher to watch his students play basketball is education, profession, and recreation all at once; for a lawyer to read literature is to gain new perspectives on the "human nature" that is his daily business. Those who are alienated from their training and labor naturally want their recreations to be an escape; those whose work expresses their selves find that integration of the different sides of life leads to a recovery of meaning.

One of the most fundamental themes of the new

consciousness has to do with the nature of the community that our technological society makes possible. On the one hand, Consciousness III rejects many of the laws, forms of authority, and assumptions that underlie our present political State. On the other hand, it posits a community of a very different sort, based upon love and trust. Both of these beliefs are a further working out of a higher rationality. They make good sense in terms of the changes wrought over the last fifty years.

The crucial point is that technology has made possible that "change in human nature" which has been sought so long but could not come into existence while scarcity stood in the way. It is just this simple: when there is enough food and shelter for all, man no longer needs to base his society on the assumption that all men are antagonistic to one other. That which we called "human nature" was the work of necessity—the necessity of scarcity and the market system. The new human nature—love and respect—also obeys the law of necessity. It is necessary because only together can we reap the fruits of the technological age. And it is necessary because only love and human solidarity can give us the strength of consciousness to withstand the overwhelming seductions and demands of the machine.

Our present system of government is based on the assumption that "man is a wolf to man" and that "only the law makes us free." It assumes that all men have an unlimited will for power over other men, and therefore it has elaborate constitutional checks and balances to keep power divided and limited. It assumes that all men are primarily motivated by their own material self-interest, and therefore it provides a system of pluralism to balance and compromise these conflicting interests. It assumes that men will infringe each other's rights unless restrained, and therefore it puts the law above all men. It assumes that men care only about themselves, and therefore it establishes as a state religion the worship of the *machinery* of government—the democratic forms—rather than the worship of the *substance* of a good society. Perhaps democracy, law, and constitutional rights will still be wanted in a new society, but they cannot be based or justified any longer on assumptions such as these.

The view of human nature we have held to so long is based on materialism. It is not "man" we knew, but "economic man." "Self-interest" was defined in *material* terms. It is "economic man" who is aggressive, competitive, eager to win in sports or in life, eager for status and power, jealous and envious, unwilling to share his private property, intensely privatistic about his family, relating to all others primarily in ways defined by his "interests." Even psychiatry has adopted this narrow definition of human nature as valid. But everything is different once a society turns from purely materialistic goals.

In the new society, the existence of technology means that man's great goal must be consciousness, for all the reasons we have already given. And consciousness is a very different thing than material goods or their equivalents, honor and status. These are by their nature in short supply. But consciousness, or, to use an old expression, wisdom, is not a substance that is subject to upward limit. In seeking wisdom, men's interests are not antagonistic. No person's gain in wisdom is diminished by anyone else's gain. Wisdom is the one commodity that is unlimited in supply.

Indeed, each man, his experiences, his personality, his uniqueness, becomes an asset to other men when their object is to gain in wisdom. Each person, by practicing his own skills, pursuing his own interests, and having his own experiences becomes of increasing value to others. In a society that pursues honor and status as goals, each person's deviation from the "norm" is likely to be mocked and subject to group disapproval. But where people seek wisdom, the "deviance" and "absurdity" of others is respected, for each person is like a novelist, seeking knowledge of all the varieties of life, and, like a pilgrim, reverencing all that he sees. The more unique each person is, the more he contributes to the wisdom of others. Such a community makes possible and fosters that ultimate quest for wisdom—the search for self. Each person is respected for his own absolute human worth. No such luxury was possible during most of man's history. It is wealth and technology that have now made community and self possible.

In a community devoted to the search for wisdom, the true relationship between people is that all are students and all are teachers. Teaching in this sense consists of helping each person with his own personal search for experience and his own goals. Although the goals are individual, it is apparent that the search for self cannot take place in isolation, that self must be realized in a community, and therefore the community enhances each person no matter what his particular endeavor.

Consciousness III therefore rejects the idea that man's relation to man is to be governed primarily by law or politics, and instead posits an extended family in the spirit of the Woodstock Festival, without individual "ego trips" or "power trips." But it is a complete misconception to suppose that this community is not governed by law, or that it tolerates no individuality and instead demands submergence in a group. On the contrary, the community of Consciousness III has a far more genuine concept of law than exists in the Corporate State, and an infinitely greater respect for individuality.

The basis of a Consciousness III community must be agreement on major values. The oppressiveness of the Corporate State is due in large part to the lack of such values; destruction of environment, inequality, exploitation of individuals, even mass killing are permitted if they "serve the public interest," i.e., the interest of the State. Life is a struggle for power and advantage because no agreement exists to respect any value or any person. That is not the way of Consciousness III. The V-signal, the recognition of strangers as friends, the intense feeling of community, all bespeak shared values. They all bespeak a community that does have law, in the sense of standards that are universally respected.

We have already described those basic laws upon which the Consciousness III community rests. Respect for each individual, for his uniqueness, and for his privacy. Abstention from coercion or violence against any individual, abstention from killing or war. Respect for the natural environment. Respect for beauty in all its forms. Honesty in all personal relations. Equality of status between all individuals, so that no one is "superior" or "inferior." Genuine democracy in the making of decisions, freedom of expression, and conscience. If this is not a community of law, what is? This is law in the true sense, not in the perverted sense of mere coercion that we know today. This is a community bound together by moral-aesthetic standards such as prevailed before the Industrial Revolution. At the Woodstock festival hundreds of thousands of people were crowded together without violence or disorder of any kind. That was a community of law, in the sense we mean here; it could only have happened among people who shared a basic set of values.

The values we describe must be accepted democratically by a whole people, as our Bill of Rights was once accepted, and they may of course be changed from time to time. What matters is the concept: the Corporate State tramples all values and ignores all laws, as is recorded indelibly in Vietnam; a true human community is based upon a balanced order that includes land, self, equality, beauty, and openness to change, and thus makes freedom possible.

Individuality is protected because the Consciousness III community is based on organic principles, not on identity. Nature is an organic community; its different elements and inhabitants do not resemble each other, they carry out very different functions and they rarely communicate, yet they all contribute to each other and depend upon each other; the squirrel needs the acorn and the acorn needs the squirrel. And each needs the other in all its uncompromising individuality; nature does not ask the squirrel to be like an oak, or an oak like a squirrel. In an organic community, the craftsman, the engineer, the artist are related whether or not they speak to each other, whether or not they are alike in any way.

The Consciousness III community is also based upon a sense of species solidarity, a feeling that is expressed by the word "together." Love is not given by

419

one person to another as a sovereign act; love is discovered, it is generated, it is in the community, and not merely the product of each individual's will. People gain strength and warmth and energy from the species community; it multiplies whatever is inside of each of them. It shares a common task—the task of creating lives that are composed of the kind of education, work, and culture that we have described, the task of transcending and using technology, the task of creating a life that is philosophic, artistic, and heroic.

Ultimately, as the film *Alice's Restaurant* clearly shows, intimate communities will have to be based on something more than love or a common "trip." The most successful communes today seem to be the rock groups that live and work together. When liberated individuals are able to achieve excellence in work of their own choosing, it is possible that such common interests will form a more solid basis for the "extended family." And at that point, these "families" will not necessarily want to live in places far removed from the rest of society, but rather in the heart of it, where their work lies, retaining a link to farm or seashore. Eventually they should be able to bring back with them into society the ways of life cultivated in the earlier communes located in remote areas. Such integration promises more than the Brook Farm experiment that failed even in Hawthorne's day. In the long run, a communal family will surely need shared interests, shared conversation, shared standards and aspirations.

It seems likely that the Consciousness III community, and particularly the concept of "together," represent an effort to recover one of man's deepest needs and experiences. Man may not be a herd animal, but he is a gregarious, tribal animal and before the Industrial Revolution he usually lived within the "circle of affection" of an extended family, and his work in the fields or at a trade was shared and done side by side. The peasants of a medieval manor, or the anonymous craftsmen who worked on a great cathedral, must have had a feeling akin to "together." It seems doubtful that they felt a need for our society's individual egocentric recognition and separation of individual work from that of the group. Art and workmanship came out of a cultural tradition, not an act of "individual genius." The Consciousness III community transcends the technological state by restoring some of the wordless security and sharing of tribal man, the ineffable meaning of experience that is shared. It is no accident that marijuana joints are always passed around from hand to hand and mouth to mouth, and never smoked separately when people are in the same room; or that a single pizza or a single Coke is passed from person to person in the same room; the group is sharing its bread and wine.

The spirit inherent in the Consciousness III idea of community, combining the feeling of together, an organic relationship, a shared set of laws or values, and a shared quest for experience and wisdom, is just now beginning to be visible. One of the few places to observe man partially free of the forces of competition and antagonism that are the norms of our social system is in a college dining hall where many of the students are Consciousness III people. A college dining hall has always been a happy spot, because of youth, high spirits, lack of care, and, of course, the all-important presence of food. It is a far different place from a restaurant, where people are stiff and formal, carefully playing out roles, or the cafeteria of some large organization, where shirtsleeved employees sit, reduced to pettiness and docility, or a Consciousness II dinner party with everyone untouchably separated from everyone else. A college dining hall has a music of its own, the buzz of different conversations, some professorial and serious, some joking, some intensely intellectual. But in a college dining hall of today there is something more: unguarded smiles, uncalculated gestures of openness, an atmosphere whose dominant mood is affection. It is the atmosphere of breaking bread together; of communion. In dining halls of earlier years the smiles were given cautiously, measured after some thought, after assurances that they would be received and returned; people were afraid of being vulnerable. But with some of that fear gone, with much of the sense of competition gone, with many individuals no longer thinking of their places in some outside hierarchy, students show the naturalness of caring for each other.

In the summer of 1967, when Consciousness III was just beginning and the forces of repression had not yet moved in to create an atmosphere of tension and hatred, one could see the new community in the streets and shops of Berkeley, near the University of California. For just a few months at the very beginning of Consciousness III, there was a flowering of music, hippie clothes, hand-painted vehicles, and sheer joy to match nature itself. It seemed to be everywhere, but perhaps one could see it best of all in a vast, modern coop supermarket in Berkeley, open late at night, almost a community center with a self-service laundry, a snack bar with sweet fresh doughnuts, a highly intellectual selection of books, and a community bulletin board. It possessed an amazing variety of goods—Polynesian frozen foods, San Francisco sour rye, local underground newspapers and guides to the Sierras, dry Italian sausage, the glories of California vegetable farming, frozen Chinese snow peas—a veritable one world of foods—and genuine, old-fashioned, unhomogenized peanut butter, the very symbol of the world that has enjoyed technology and transcended it. If the foods gave the supermarket its sense of gleaming opulence and richness, the people gave it the sense of community. There were hippies looking like Indians, with headbands and proud, striking features; ordinary middle-class families doing their shopping late at night. Hell's Angels of California, in their black leather jackets; frat men with block letters; very young couples in some stage of transitory housekeeping; threesomes, foursomes, fivesomes, all possible varieties of housekeeping, in fact; people going on camping trips and returning from trips; and the checkout clerks, very much a part of it all, joining with smiles in the general scene. For the atmosphere was one of mutual respect and affection—visibly and, even more, felt in the vibrations that a casual visitor received. Somehow, all these people were together. The checkout lines, with beards, old ladies, mothers with perambulators, and hippies whose purchase was a single carrot or turnip, resembled nothing so much as a peace march where all kinds of people are joined by a common cause. The scene as a whole, though, was not a march but a kingdom—the peaceable kingdom of those old American paintings that show all manner of beasts lying down together in harmony and love.

What we have said about education, work, culture, and community shows how technology may provide a new basis for generating and guiding the energies of man. Instead of summoning man's energies by the lash of hunger, competition, and perpetual dissatisfaction, man can find his sources of energy in the variety, stimulation, and hope that technology can provide. Satisfaction can be a greater stimulant than deprivation. Technology need not sap our energy; it can augment it, amplify it, multiply it, as it has done already with music. And the community that technology makes possible can be a still greater source of energy —the energy of group effort and of Eros. When man is reunited with self and with the larger community of nature, all of the cosmos will add to his own sources.

Thus the new age of man can take the best from the ages which preceded it. From the pre-industrial age it can take the integration and balance of life, the sense of God in everything. From the industrial era it can take technology and the steady rise to a higher level of life. From its own age it can take the control and use of technology, and the way of life of satisfaction, community, and love, a way of life that aspires higher and higher, without forgetting its human source. In *Eros and Civilization* Marcuse spoke of releasing man's instincts, but the new age will do more; it will not only release but augment and inspire, and make that the chief end of society. And it will do so within a society that makes the Judeo-Christian ethic not merely an ignored command, but a realistic way of life.

This, then, is the plan for a new society, a workable way of life, a realistic approach to the nineteen seventies and beyond. Many will deny that it is a plan at all, but they are looking for a plan where it can no longer be found. Others will say that it rejects reason. But we have shown that it is our present system that is irrational. Or it may be called utopian, in the sense that it hopes for what never can be. But man that could build the machines of today, and could learn to live *for* them, can also learn to live *with* them. If "human nature" can teach itself to serve a lifetime in a factory or office, then it can also teach itself the far more rewarding service of self and community that we have described. Some may say we are unduly optimistic—the only answer we can give is that the new way of life is better for man—has been found better by those who have tried it, and will be found better by those who try it hereafter.

What we have said concerning consciousness, technology, the search for wisdom, and community—about the dining halls and the supermarket—is that man must create his own fictions and live by them. Consciousness takes the elements it finds and arranges them to make a life and a society that reflect man's needs and hopes. In Kesey's *Sometimes a Great Notion,* in Vonnegut's *Cat's Cradle,* in Wallace Stevens' poetry, in psychedelic music, man seeks to create for himself an order by which he can live. As Vonnegut says, "Live by the *foma* [harmless untruths] that make you brave and kind and healthy and happy."

To call this order "fiction" is just a way of saying that the only reality man has is the one he makes. The Corporate State cuts man off from his inner sources of meaning and attempts to impose on him an order derived from the State or from the abstract, rational universe. But this imposed order is a fiction too, and it is one that is bad for man. The dining hall and the supermarket, the concept of work as play and of life as a search for wisdom are fictions that are good for man.

For underlying the higher reason of Consciousness III, its search for meaning, for community, for liberation, is an exalted vision of man. Man, it says, is not part of a machine, not a robot, not a being meant to starve, or be killed in war, or driven like a beast, not an enemy to his own kind and to all other kinds, not a creature to be controlled, regulated, administered, trained, clipped, coated, anesthetized. His true nature is expressed in loving and trusting his own kind, being a part of nature and his own nature, developing, growing, living as fully as he can, using to the full his unique gift, perhaps unique in the universe, of conscious life.

Of all the many ways of life known to history, Consciousness III seems the closest to valuing life for its own sake. Almost always, men have lived subject to rigid custom, to religion, to an economic theory or political ideology. Consciousness III seeks freedom from all of these. It declares that *life* is prior to all of them. It does not try to reduce or simplify man's complexity, or the complexity of nature. It values the present, not the past, the future, or some abstract doctrine of mythical heaven. It says that what is meaningful, what endures, is no more nor less than the total experience of life.

It is little more than twenty years since the first members of the new generation were born. And it is only that long since, in Holden Caulfield, the hero of J. D. Salinger's *The Catcher in the Rye*, we heard their first voice. Today Holden Caulfield's dream seems, to most people, further away than ever. A movement exists, a new generation and a new culture have come into being, but repression has grown harsher and the Corporate State has won most of the battles, from

People's Park to Harvard. The movement is divided, confused, and deeply depressed, and the forces of death are everywhere. Increasingly, rigid administrators, police, national guard troops, penal laws, prisons, and technological weapons are the dominant realities of today.

But this is a view without perspective. Only a few years ago, during the stifling 1950's and the cynical 1960's, the only appropriate way to feel about America was complete despair; an account of our country would rationally have been called "The Coming of the Closed Society." How long ago was it that we first heard of hippies? That we first heard the sounds of acid rock? That we saw the first student demonstration, the first peace march? By the standards of history, the transformation of America has been incredibly, unbelievably swift. And the change to Consciousness III is not, so far as we know, reversible. Once a person reaches Consciousness III, there is no returning to a lower consciousness. And the change of generations is not reversible either. Every evidence we have is that youngsters in high school are potentially more radical, more committed to a new way of life, than their elders in college.

From the perspective of history, change is coming with astonishing speed to the rest of the population as well. The daily newspaper is full of it. More and more people are dissatisfied, are actively protesting something, are drawn into controversies with the State concerning freeways, urban renewal, transportation, or missile systems. More and more groups are resorting to militancy, experiencing repressions, and becoming radical in turn. If young people are in conflict with the State, parents are not immune. Draft refusers have parents. Young people beaten by the police have parents; so do those arrested for possessing drugs. And there are more and more stories of kids turning their parents on—sharing their life-style with them, and gradually, their politics as well. Many of the G.I.'s in Vietnam have been exposed to the new consciousness, and a great many are bringing it home with them. (It is almost equally prevalent in domestic army camps.) Perhaps we can look forward to having a million or more young men, army veterans, having a life-style in common with the students and with the new crop of high school students just coming along. The new life-style is no longer just on a few campuses, it is to be found in every region of the country; it is even invading the countryside. And wherever it goes, underground newspapers, free schools, rock music, clashes with the law, rejection of the machine go too. Before long, the sideburns, beards, and long hair will mean votes as well.

Nineteen sixty-eight was the year of Chicago. Nineteen sixty-nine was the year of Woodstock. That speaks of the distance we have come, and the speed with which we are traveling. The new consciousness is sweeping the high schools, it is seen in smiles on the streets. It has begun to transform and humanize the landscape. All of these signs might mean little if change had to be produced by the efforts of a minority, working against the power of the State. But the State itself is producing these changes, and its self-destruction has only begun. The people of the Movement may grow tired and discouraged, but time and the force of the machine are on their side. And there is nothing on the other side. There are no enemies. There are no people who would not be better off, none who do not, in the depth of their beings, want what Consciousness III wants. If it be said that the new consciousness is not yet realistic truth, but rather a vision, the answer is: the vision is there, if we want it.

We have all known the loneliness, the emptiness, the isolation of contemporary America. Our forebears came thousands of miles for the promise of a better life. Now there is a new promise. Shall we not seize it? Shall we not be pioneers once more? The breakdown of the Corporate State and the growth of radicalism would still lead nowhere, would still justify only despair, if there were not a new vision. It is the power of the vision that can turn hope into reality.

The extraordinary thing about this new consciousness is that it has emerged out of the wasteland of the Corporate State, like flowers pushing up through the concrete pavement. Whatever it touches it beautifies and renews: a freeway entrance is festooned with happy hitchhikers, the sidewalk is decorated with street people, the humorless steps of an official building are given warmth by a group of musicians. And every barrier falls before it. We have been dulled and blinded to the injustice and ugliness of slums, but it sees them as just that—injustice and ugliness—as if they had been there to see all along. We have all been persuaded that giant organizations are necessary, but it sees that they are absurd, as if the absurdity had always been obvious and apparent. We have all been induced to give up our dreams of adventure and romance in favor of the escalator of success, but it says that the escalator is a sham and the dream is real. And these things, buried, hidden, and disowned in so many of us, are shouted out loud, believed in, affirmed by a growing multitude of young people who seem too healthy, intelligent, and alive to be wholly insane, who appear, in their collective strength, capable of making it happen. For one almost convinced that it was necessary to accept ugliness and evil, that it was necessary to be a miser of dreams, it is an invitation to cry or laugh. For one who thought the world was irretrievably encased in metal and plastic and sterile stone, it seems a veritable greening of America.

ACKNOWLEDGMENTS

This book owes so much to so many written sources that it is only meaningful to mention a few of the most important. They are: Karl Marx, *The Economic and Philosophic Manuscripts of 1844* (New York: International Publishers, 1964); Herbert Marcuse, *Eros and Civilization* (1955), *One-Dimensional Man* (1964), *An Essay on Liberation* (1969), all published in Boston by Beacon Press; Karl Polanyi, *The Great Transformation* (Boston: Beacon Press, 1957); Jacques Ellul, *The Technological Society* (New York: Alfred A. Knopf, 1964); Kenneth Keniston, *The Uncommitted* (1965) and *Young Radicals* (1968), both published in New York by Harcourt, Brace & World; John Kenneth Galbraith, *The New Industrial State* (Boston: Houghton Mifflin, 1967); E. J. Mishan, *The Costs of Economic Growth* (New York: Frederick A. Praeger, 1967); R. W. B. Lewis, *The American Adam* (Chicago, Ill.: University of Chicago Press, 1955); Stan-

Acknowledgments

ley M. Elkins, *Slavery* (Chicago, Ill.: University of Chicago Press, 1959); Friedrich A. Hayek, *The Road to Serfdom* (Chicago, Ill.: University of Chicago Press, 1944); Arthur J. Vidich and Joseph Bensman, *Small Town in Mass Society* (Princeton, N.J.: Princeton University Press, 1958); Peter Laslett, *The World We Have Lost* (New York: Chas. Scribner's Sons, 1965); *The Autobiography of Malcolm X* (New York: Grove Press, 1965); Eldridge Cleaver, *Soul on Ice* (New York: McGraw-Hill, 1968); Norman Mailer, *Why Are We in Vietnam?* (New York: G. P. Putnam's Sons, 1967); Ken Kesey, *One Flew over the Cuckoo's Nest* (1962) and *Sometimes a Great Notion* (1964) (both published in New York by Viking Press); Tom Wolfe, *The Kandy-Kolored Tangerine-Flake Streamline Baby* (1965), *The Electric Kool-Aid Acid Test* (1968) (both published in New York by Farrar, Straus & Giroux). Of all of the many books now available, Ken Kesey's *Sometimes a Great Notion* probably comes closest to being in the fullest sense a work of the new consciousness.

The typing of the manuscript was done primarily by Mrs. Susan Bruce, with assistance organized by Mrs. Isabel Malone, and with further help from Mrs. Dorothy Egan.

My greatest individual debt, extending over twenty years, is to Thomas I. Emerson.

The late Mike Entin was the first person I knew who believed in the consciousness of the new generation, and his irrepressible enthusiasm and hospitality in Berkeley were crucial to the book.

The book owes much to long talks with the following good and generous friends: Hugo L. Black, James E. Brogan, Fred Buell, William O. Douglas, Joan Emerson, Karl Pavlovic, Dan Peters, Robert P. Sedgwick, Philip Turner.

Among many other friends who influenced the book are: James Amoss, Robert Bingham, Toni Burbank, Doug Carroll, Michael C. Davidson, Richard Ekfelt, Michael Gecan, Chuck Goettsche, John Griffiths, Brian Heaney,

Acknowledgments

Derek U. Huntington, Hugh Jenkins, Friedrich Kessler, William Kiernan, Chris Legg, Eugene Linden, Mark Luoto, Isabelle Lynn, Alice Mayhew, Bill McGovern, Peter Munks, James R. Newman, Jeff Pollock, William Shawn, John J. Simon, Alice Stewart, Jim Stokely, Mike Wollan, and Jean Pohoryles.

I have three special debts: to Leon Ferber, to Donald D. Matson, and to Richard Sewall.

Much of the book was written in the Stiles-Morse dining halls at Yale, and the encouragement, the coffee, the warmth of all the people of the dining hall, are a part of it.

I do not feel that this is my book so much as it is a community book, the product of many people. I have tried to speak for the feelings, ideas and hopes of my friends among the students at Yale. It has the faults and limitations of its individual author, but in the truest sense it is their book.

CHARLES A. REICH
Washington, D.C., 1960
Berkeley, June–July, 1967
New Haven, 1970

ABOUT THE AUTHOR

CHARLES A. REICH teaches law at Yale University Law School. He was born in 1928 in New York. His articles have appeared in the YALE REVIEW, THE PUBLIC INTEREST, THE NEW REPUBLIC, THE NATION, the YALE LAW JOURNAL, HARVARD LAW REVIEW, and other popular and scholarly journals.